Intellectual Trespassing as a Way of Life

The Worldly Philosophy: Studies at the Intersection of Philosophy and Economics

General Editor: Philip Mirowski, University of Notre Dame

Testing, Rationality, and Progress: Essays on the Popperian Tradition in Economic Methodology
by D. Wade Hands

Edgeworth on Chance, Economic Hazard, and Statistics
edited by Philip Mirowski

Intellectual Trespassing as a Way of Life: Essays in Philosophy, Economics, and Mathematics
by David P. Ellerman

Intellectual Trespassing as a Way of Life

Essays in Philosophy, Economics, and Mathematics

David P. Ellerman

ROWMAN & LITTLEFIELD PUBLISHERS, INC.
Lanham • Boulder • New York • Toronto • Plymouth, UK

ROWMAN & LITTLEFIELD PUBLISHERS, INC.

Published in the United States of America
by Rowman & Littlefield Publishers, Inc.
A wholly owned subsidiary of The Rowman & Littlefield Publishing Group, Inc.
4501 Forbes Boulevard, Suite 200, Lanham, Maryland 20706
www.rowmanlittlefield.com

3 Henrietta Street
London WC2E 8LU, England

Chapter 2 is reprinted with minor changes from *Journal of Post-Keynesian Economics* 13, no. 4 (Summer 1991): 545–64 by permission of M. E. Sharpe Publishers.

Chapter 3 was originally published under the pseudonym "J. Philmore" in *The Philosophical Forum* 14, no. 1 (Fall 1982): 43–58. Reprinted by permission of the publisher.

Chapter 4 is reprinted from *Journal of Economic Issues* 22, no.4 (December 1988): 1109–22 by special permission of the copyright holder, the Association for Evolutionary Economics.

British Cataloging in Publication Information Available

Library of Congress Cataloging-in-Publication Data

Ellerman, David P.
Intellectual trespassing as a way of life : essays in philosophy, economics, and mathematics / by David P. Ellerman.
p. cm. — (Worldly philosophy)
Includes bibliographical references and index.
1. Economics—Philosophy. 2. Economics—Mathematical models.
3. Paradigms (Social sciences) I. Title. II. Series.
HB72.E45 1995 330'.01'51—dc20 94-33878 CIP

ISBN 0-8476-7931-4 (cloth: alk. paper)
ISBN 0-8476-7932-2 (pbk.: alk. paper)

Printed in the United States of America

∞™ The paper used in this publication meets the minimum requirements of American National Standard for Information Sciences—Permanence of Paper for Printed Library Materials, ANSI Z39.48–1984.

Contents

Figures

Equations

Sapere Aude!

To those who have the courage to think critically
and to trespass across the boundaries of orthodoxy.

Introduction: Intellectual Trespassing as a Way of Life

Intellectual Trespassing as an Engine of Discovery

The essays in this collection illustrate a certain method or style of thought that might be called "intellectual trespassing." The domain of the intellect is divided into a number of distinct sciences and disciplines. A practitioner in any particular field must learn the styles of thought of that discipline. The person must apply himself or herself diligently, making the patterns of thought in the field second nature, until finally a frontier has been reached and the person can make an original contribution. That is the method of "normal science." If there are shortcomings, limitations, or mistakes involved in the defining thought patterns of the field, it is unlikely that a normal practitioner would escape them. By the time the person becomes an "expert" the errors would be second nature. Mastery of the mistaken thought patterns is part of what counts for proficiency and expertise. To break with the patterns would be to devalue one's own human capital and to undermine the basis of one's own professional competence.

Thus dramatic changes or revolutions in a field of science are often made by outsiders or "trespassers" who do not define their expertise as mastery of the old methods or by newcomers who are not yet beholden to the old ways. That is one of the principal reasons why intellectual trespassing between fields should be promoted as a way of thought.

There are other reasons for intellectual trespassing. The Polish mathematician Stefan Banach described mathematics as the science of analogies between analogies. Analogical reasoning is one of the most powerful engines of discovery. Trespassing is often inspired by noticing a new analogy between two different fields. Often the analogies are easily spotted because the same mathematics (which captures the analogies in abstract form) is used or can be used in both fields. Sometimes only basic knowledge in two seemingly disparate fields is needed to discover happy collisions of concepts that betray some common underlying structures. These cross-fertilizations may lead to new developments in one or the other of the fields, or they may only provide some intellectual amusement at the unexpected connections.

Example: The Additive-Multiplicative Engine of Discovery

Four of the essays in this book exploit one particular analogy that is mathematically captured in group theory. The real numbers with the operation of addition is an example of a group. The positive reals (excluding zero) with the operation of multiplication is another example of a group (indeed, the mapping of $x \rightarrow e^x$ from the reals to the positive reals shows that the two groups have the same mathematical structure). In some domains of science an additive group will have a key role, while in others a multiplicative group will capture the important relationships.

One simple engine of discovery is to systematically transfer some structure developed for the additive case over into the multiplicative case in another field, or to go the other way. This type of transfer between fields is illustrated in the essays on double-entry bookkeeping, arbitrage, valuation rings, and series-parallel duality.

Brief Introductions to the Essays

The essays in this collection fall into two distinct groups. The first five essays are concerned directly and indirectly with controversial questions at the foundation of political economy—namely questions about the employer-employee relationship. These are not just abstract intellectual issues. The essays critically analyze and attack the legitimating ideology of our current economic system of production. Since power and wealth are ultimately at stake in the economic system, it is "infinitely" more difficult to break the norm and to trespass against orthodoxy in political economy than in the natural or mathematical sciences. Hence, the first essay is devoted to the questions of trespassing against economic orthodoxy. The other essays consider a wide range of questions, including

• Has modern economics fulfilled the Enlightenment Project of developing an objective and rational science of society, or has economics more often clothed the bare bones of applied mathematics with myths and metaphors that obscure rather than illuminate basic questions in political economy?

• What can we learn from the old debates about slavery, particularly voluntary slavery, and about the basic questions in our society such as the institution of voluntarily renting people (the employment relationship)?

• How can the labor theory of property and the Enlightenment theory of inalienable rights be integrated in a coherent theory together with Kant's categorical imperative in its formulation always to treat people as ends, never merely as means?

• Since a unit of a factor of production cannot "produce its marginal product" without using some other factors, how can marginal productivity (MP) theory be reformulated to take that into account, and how does that reformulation affect the heavy ideological baggage of MP theory?

• What is the connection between the two-sidedness of fractions (numerator and denominator) and the two-sidedness of the T-accounts (debit and credit) in double-entry bookkeeping?

• How does the syntax/semantics distinction of elementary logic help us to understand the mind/machine controversy?

• What does category theory (a mathematical theory that was formulated only in the 1940s) have to do with Plato's theory of ideas?

• What does the Japanese *keiretsu* (ownership group) have to do with proportional representation in voting systems?

• What are the connections among Lagrange multipliers in optimization theory, the second law of thermodynamics, the laws of probability, and Kirchhoff's voltage law in electrical circuit theory?

• Is there a better ring-theoretic basis for treating logic than Boolean rings; can Boolean duality be generalized beyond the 0-1 two-valuedness usually associated with Boolean algebras; and how can propositional logic be reduced to polynomial rings?

• How does the parallel between parallel-connected resistors and loan payments reveal a new form of duality in financial arithmetic?

or "enterprise." We define the "firm" as the legal party that is the residual claimant for some given productive or business activity—the legal party that owns the outputs and pays for the inputs of the activity.

If one always identifies the firm with a corporation, then a corporation is, of course, owned as a piece of property. But a given corporation need not be the "firm" with respect to some given productive or business activity. When a corporation does function as the residual claimant for a certain activity, then that is the result of the current pattern of contracts (e.g., the fact that the corporation hires in the labor instead of hiring out its capital). If the pattern of contracts changed (e.g., when labor hires capital instead of vice versa), then the residual claimant in the productive activity changes, but the ownership of the corporation is still the same. Thus the identity of the firm is determined by the contractual fact-pattern (principally, the direction of the hiring contracts—"Who hires what or whom?") even though the ownership of corporations is determined by the distribution of property rights. Firmhood is a creature of contract, not of property.

When a nonbankrupt corporation has customarily undertaken a given productive activity, then it is "unthinkable" to consider a change in residual claimancy through a mere change in the hiring contracts. In addition to being "unthinkable," there might be high barriers of transaction costs that would hinder rewriting and reversing the hiring contracts. The corporation might also have monopoly ownership of certain of the inputs. These mental and cost barriers conspire to give the customary contractual fact-pattern the appearance of a "property right"—the "ownership of the firm."

The "discovery" of the contractual determination of firmhood (residual claimancy) opens up the question of property appropriation in production. If not the "ownership of the firm," then just what is it that gives one legal party rather than another the ownership of the produced outputs as well as the symmetrical set of liabilities for the used-up inputs? The answer given by the institution of private property is quite simple; the legal party that bears the costs of the used-up inputs has the defensible legal claim on the produced outputs.

That is the way the institution of private property does operate, but how should it operate? Of course, the legal party that bears the costs of the inputs should also own the outputs—but who should that party be? The old labor theory of property, usually associated with John Locke, answers that people should legally appropriate the (positive and negative) fruits of their labor. The people who work in the firm (the productive activity) are the people who jointly use up the inputs ignoring such an "obviously nonsensical book." Why take the time and effort to read the book just to put yourself in the position of being ostracized as a pariah or being a hypocrite (for keeping quiet about an argument you accept or for rejecting the argument on the basis of superficial official counterarguments)? There is simply no "incentive" to take the risk of impaling oneself on the pariah-hypocrite dilemma.

The "church" in this parable is the orthodox economics profession. The parable points out some of the exceedingly powerful but rather mundane institutional reasons why it is so hard to trespass against the dogmas of orthodoxy in economics. Even "heresy" has been co-opted and pigeonholed in the worldview of the church. While there is much active debate about shades of divergence within orthodoxy, any fundamental dissent "must" come from those who are assigned the role of being the official heretics, the Western Marxist or crypto-Marxists of various stripes. It is simply inconceivable that one could attack liberal capitalism on the non-Marxist grounds that it violates the moral basis of private property ("getting the fruits of your labor") or that it violates the basic principles of democracy (in the workplace governed by the economic *pactum subjectionis,* the employment contract). Orthodoxy is blessed with the Happy Consciousness that liberal capitalism has no basic structural violations of human rights and that, far from violating the principles of private property and democracy, it is based on those principles.

Chapter 2: Myth and Metaphor in Orthodox Economics

Discussion of the fundamental questions of political economy is today almost completely clouded and distorted by a number of basic myths and metaphors. Deconstruction is necessary before constructive discussions can begin. The myths and metaphors are concerned with basic conceptions about property and contract, not with prices and markets. As layer upon layer of distortions are removed, new facts and new perspectives on old facts will emerge. These facts have fairly direct normative implications, but the disagreements and controversies are about the facts, not about norms or prescriptions.

There is one myth that is so basic to the perception of the capitalist system in both the East and West that we call it the "Fundamental Myth" of the capitalist system. That myth is the whole idea that a firm or enterprise is owned as a piece of property in the capitalist system. This claim is, of course, sensitive to exactly how one defines "firm" is a simple restatement of an old argument about inalienable rights (called the "de facto theory of inalienability") that dates back to the Enlightenment if not to the Reformation and before. The argument was originally applied against the contract to sell all of one's labor, the self-enslavement contract, but it applies as well to the contract to sell one's labor piecemeal, the modern employer-employee contract [see Ellerman 1992].

Much of modern economic theory is a brilliantly executed piece of applied mathematics served up with a thick sauce of myths and metaphors. But when this "sauce" is brushed away, much older and long-forgotten concepts reemerge, such as people's claim to the fruits of their labor, naturally invalid contracts, and inalienable rights.

Chapter 3: The Libertarian Case for Slavery

Liberalism is living a lie. It pretends that the contract to sell all of one's labor, the self-enslavement contract, is an invalid contract beyond the pale while the contract to sell one's labor piecemeal (by the hour, day, month, or year) is a perfectly valid contract above reproach. The self-enslavement contract is one of the skeletons in liberalism's intellectual closet. Defenders of liberal capitalism are quick to accept even the most superficial arguments against voluntary slavery just to shove the issue back in the closet—just so long as the arguments do not carry over to the current contract to rent oneself out, the employer-employee contract. Who wants to be seen as, in effect, defending voluntary slavery by showing how most arguments against the self-sale contract are baseless (aside from one "J. Philmore")?

A closer look at the intellectual history reveals a different story. The inalienable rights arguments developed from the Reformation and Enlightenment against various forms of religious, economic, and political enslavement were based on certain facts of human nature (e.g., the de facto inalienability of responsibility for one's actions). Those facts do not change when the proposed contractual alienation is only piecemeal or part-time. The old inalienable-rights arguments, once understood, run against the self-rental contract as well as against the older self-sale contract.

But how can these points be made to a modern audience that no longer considers slavery to be an issue worthy of sustained thought (aside from the racial aspects) and that tends to accept most any critique of voluntary slavery that will keep the issue relegated to the and produce the outputs so, by the labor theory of property, they are the people who should constitute the legal party that is the firm. That is, by the labor theory of property, people should always be jointly self-employed in their firm (i.e., the firm should be "employee-owned," to use a common but somewhat misleading terminology).

The labor theory of property, commonly thought to be the basis for private ownership, is thus at odds with the current system, which allows any legal party to make the contracts to be the residual claimant or firm. But actually the conflict is only with one contract, the employment or hired labor contract. The conflict is not with the system of property appropriation that imputes the outputs to the party that bore the costs. The conflict is with the contract that allows any outside legal party to hire or rent the people working in a productive activity so that the outside party then appears as the legally responsible party. Thus the employment contract is at odds with the labor principle of private-property appropriation.

The analysis therefore shifts to contracts. The contract to hire or rent human beings is a free and voluntary contract, but should all free and voluntary contracts be allowed? Liberalism often pretends that the answer is "Yes" but a moment's thought reveals otherwise. For instance, one free and voluntary contract that is legally forbidden is the self-enslavement contract that was legally valid in antebellum days. The intellectual history of some arguments about the self-sale contract is traced in Chapter 3, "The Libertarian Case for Slavery." The individual contract to sell voting rights, and the collective contract to sell or forfeit the rights of self-determination (the *pactum subjectionis*) are other examples of contracts that might be free and voluntary but are not currently legally valid.

There is a simple example of an invalid contract, namely the contract to transfer responsibility for one's actions to another person when those actions are criminous. We use the intuition pump of the criminous employee wherein an employee who commits a crime at the behest of the employer is promoted by the legal authorities to the status of a partner with the employer. It is easy to understand how a person is still de facto responsible for the results of his or her actions (i.e., for the fruits of his or her labor) in spite of the contract—at least when those actions are criminous. But it is difficult to see how the factual status of one's responsibility could change when the legal status of the actions is noncriminous (as in ordinary work performed by employees). It is hard to see how employees can suddenly become instruments, tools, or robots in fact when their actions are lawful. This of political, economic, and social subjugation based on voluntary contracts [see particularly her Chapter 3, "Contract, the Individual and Slavery"].

The main purpose of the Philmore article was to resurrect the classical arguments for a civil slavery based on contracts and to show the superficiality of the standard liberal arguments against contractual slavery. Only by grasping the inadequacy of the standard arguments will one perhaps be led to appreciate the genuine case against voluntary slavery that descends from the Enlightenment (i.e., the de facto inalienability argument). The "problem" with that appreciation is that the same argument also applies against the contract to rent oneself out, the employment contract, which is the basis of liberal capitalism.

Professor Pateman indeed cites the de facto inalienability argument as the antidote to the liberal forms of contractual subjugation.

> The contractarian argument is unassailable all the time it is accepted that abilities can "acquire" an external relation to an individual, and can be treated as if they were property. To treat abilities in this manner is also implicitly to accept that the "exchange" between employer and worker is like any other exchange of material property. [Pateman 1988, 147]
>
> The answer to the question of how property in the person can be contracted out is that no such procedure is possible. Labour power, capacities or services, cannot be separated from the person of the worker like pieces of property. [150]

Unlike Professor Pateman, the philosophers of liberal capitalism have unfortunately not risen to the challenge laid down by J. Philmore that civilized forms of contractual slavery and the *pactum subjectionis* are in the same basket as the employment contract (which Philmore ironically presented as a defense of the former rather than a critique of the latter). Pateman accepts the consequences; the Enlightenment de facto inalienability critique of voluntary slavery and constitutional autocracy applies as well to the renting of human beings, the employer-employee relationship. It is little surprise that liberal philosophers seem to be "constitutionally" incapable of facing up to that line of argument. For instance, upon reading the Philmore article, the response of a prominent liberal philosopher was only to inquire into the origin of Philmore's leading quip that "free-market libertarianism is derived from liberalism by taking the limit as common sense goes to zero." For the record, it is an adaptation of Alexander Gray's "an anarchist is merely the limiting case of a liberal individualist whose commonsense has become infinitesimal" [1968, 246].

dustbin of intellectual history? The occasion to address these issues anew arose with the publication in 1974 of Robert Nozick's *Anarchy, State, and Utopia*. Nozick's work represented a quantum leap over traditional liberalism in conceptual clarity and intellectual courage to follow an argument to its logical conclusions. Accordingly, Nozick accepted that the self-sale contract and the political analogue (the *pactum subjectionis*) were no different in principle from the employment contract, and that all these contracts should, with suitable safeguards, be legally valid in a free society.

Therefore, the author published "A Note on Nozick" showing the superficiality of all the usual liberal arguments to rule out the self-sale contract (while accepting the self-rental contract). The article was written in an ironic style under a pseudonym [Philmore 1982] as if the author agreed with Nozick's conclusion that the contract to sell oneself should be allowed. The pseudonym "J. Philmore" was originally used by the unknown author of a radical 1760 antislavery pamphlet [see Davis 1971].

My purpose was to drag the issue of the voluntary slavery contract back out of the closet so that liberals would eventually have to face the arguments that descend in the inalienable-rights tradition from the Enlightenment against the contract—arguments that apply as well to the self-rental contract. These genuine arguments against the self-enslavement contract were unmentioned in the Philmore article. Indeed, most referees and apparently most readers did not realize that the article was ironic in spite of its rather outlandish stated goal (accepting the self-enslavement contract) and a few intellectual jokes sprinkled through the text. One follow-up article [Callahan 1985] in the same journal agreed with and tried to strengthen the conclusions, but noted that the self-enslavement contract might be more useful in the Third World than in the industrialized countries. Was that an attempt to trump irony with further irony, or did it illustrate that no position is too bizarre to attract some following (as if Nozick's reputation had not proven the point)?

The best response to date to the Philmore article was Carole Pateman's remarkable book *The Sexual Contract* [1988]. Citing Philmore, she argued that basing male-female relationships on voluntary contracts was not necessarily a solution since contracts could be the basis for a "civil slavery." Following many of the scholarly leads uncovered by Philmore (e.g., Reverend Samuel Seabury's liberal contractarian defense of antebellum slavery), Professor Pateman shone the spotlight on the dark underbelly of liberalism by highlighting the liberal defenses

We have also noted that shares in the product are not actually imputed or assigned to the various factor suppliers. One legal party appropriates the whole product of a firm, 100 percent of the output assets and 100 percent of the input liabilities.

There is another flaw in the orthodox treatment of MP theory that is of interest. The ideological baggage being carried by MP theory forces it to be presented in a factually implausible way. The factually implausible part of the orthodox view is the picture of a unit of a factor as producing its marginal product *ex nihilo* (even assuming we personify the factors with responsible agency). Other factors must be used, and when the value of these used-up factors is subtracted from the value of the marginal product, the result will no longer equal the value of the unit of the factor.

In this essay, we give the mathematically equivalent presentation of MP theory, which is based on the more plausible picture that a unit of labor can only produce more of the outputs by using up more of the other inputs. The "problem" with this version of MP theory is that it does not lend itself to the ideologically appealing picture of each unit of a factor as producing its marginal product. Thus we have a central example about how the ideological baggage being towed by orthodox economics affects even the mathematical presentation of the standard theories.

Chapter 6: Double-Entry Bookkeeping: Mathematical Formulation and Generalization

The essay on double-entry bookkeeping (DEB) is intellectually interesting for several reasons in spite of the well-known soporific aspects of bookkeeping. Several of the essays in the volume explicitly employ the analogy between additive and multiplicative operations (i.e., the common group-theoretic properties of additive groups of numbers and multiplicative groups of nonzero numbers). For instance, given the system of multiplying whole numbers or integers, there is no operation inverse to multiplication (i.e., there is no division). But there is a standard method of enlarging the system to allow division. Consider pairs of whole numbers a/b (with b ≠ 0) and define multiplication in the obvious way: (a/b)(c/d) = (ac)/(bd). These ordered pairs of integers are the "fractions" and they allow the operation of division ("multiply by the reciprocal").

Now substitute addition for multiplication. We start with the additive

Chapter 4: The Kantian Person/Thing Principle in Political Economy

Ethical theories can be broadly grouped into utilitarian theories and rights-based theories. Modern economics is so thoroughly utilitarian that most economists would be hard-pressed to cite the application of a rights-based argument to economic institutions. Yet the normative principles outlined in the first two chapters, the labor theory of property and the de facto theory of inalienability, are squarely within the rights-based tradition. The democratic principle of self-determination is also a closely allied rights-based theory [see Ellerman 1992].

Immanuel Kant occupied the pinnacle of the philosophical tradition of rights-based theorists. His categorical imperative, particularly in the form of the "personhood principle" always to treat human beings as persons rather than as things, seems to be quite fruitful when coupled with institutional analysis of property rights and governance rights. The purpose of this essay is to use the institutional analysis outlined in the first two chapters to show how the labor theory of property, the de facto theory of inalienability, and the democratic principle coherently fit into a Kantian framework (in the sense of the personhood principle).

Chapter 5: Are Marginal Products Created *ex Nihilo*?

When an orthodox economist considers the principle of people getting the fruits of labor, he or she will invariably interpret it in terms of marginal productivity. The orthodox claim is that under the conditions of competitive equilibrium, each unit of labor "gets what it produces." Well-meaning capitalist liberals emphasize that actual capitalism may be neither competitive nor in equilibrium, and in any case, there are enormous difficulties in measuring the "marginal product of each factor of production." In other words, they accept that interpretation of marginal productivity theory in principle but fuss about its applicability in practice.

We have argued that competitive capitalism does not even remotely satisfy in principle the norm of people getting the fruits of their labor. The orthodox view of marginal products is flawed on several counts. In previous essays, it was noted that the fallacy of personification was involved in imputing responsible agency to the nonhuman actors. Tools and machines do not "produce" their marginal product or anything else. Tools and machines are used by people to produce the outputs.

mathematically explicate it. The real question lies on the accounting side. How, over the last century, could professional accountants and accounting professors have failed to find the mathematical basis for DEB even though it was part of undergraduate algebra? The mathematical treatment of double-entry bookkeeping (and generalization to multidimensional vectors [Ellerman 1982, 1985]) will take years, if not decades, to become known and understood in the field of accounting.

Chapter 7: The Semantics Differentiation of Minds and Machines

The watershed event in the philosophy of mind (particularly as it relates to artificial intelligence or AI) during the last decade was John Searle's 1980 article "Minds, Brains and Programs." This chapter was written about the same time and independently of Searle's but it was updated in 1985 to take Searle's work into account. Searle's exposition was based on his now-famous "Chinese Room Argument"—an intuition pump that boils down to a nontechnical explanation of the difference between syntax (formal symbol manipulation) and semantics (using symbols based on their intended interpretation). Searle argues, in opposition to "hard AI," that computers can at best only simulate but never duplicate minds because computers are inherently syntactical (symbol manipulators) while the mind is a semantic device.

The syntax-semantics distinction is hardly new; it was hammered out in philosophical logic during the first part of this century and it is fundamental in computer science itself. The purpose of our paper is to analyze the minds-machines question using simple arguments based on the syntax-semantics distinction from logic and computer science (sans "Chinese Room"). I arrive at essentially the same results as Searle—with some simplification and sharpening of the argument for readers with some knowledge of logic or computer science.

This essay illustrates how a pattern or habit of thought, here called the "intentionalist fallacy," that is very useful and almost necessary for most work with computers, can become fatally misleading in the philosophical analysis of minds and machines. Clarity on the mind-machine question begins with breaking the thought pattern of the intentionalist fallacy, and we attempt to do that using examples from elementary logic. Changing a well-ingrained mode of thought is much more difficult than comprehending some complicated new technical result. Although examples from basic logic suffice to show the fallacy system of positive numbers along with zero (i.e., the non-negative numbers) where there is no inverse operation to addition (i.e., there is no subtraction). To enlarge the domain of non-negative numbers to include subtraction, consider ordered pairs [a // b] and define addition in the analogous way: [a // b] + [c // d] = [a+c // b+d]. This enlarged system of additive operations on ordered pairs of non-negative numbers allows subtraction ("add on the reversed pair"). The origin of the intellectual trespassing into DEB was the observation that these ordered pairs were simply the T-accounts of DEB.

Aside from illustrating the interplay of additive-multiplicative themes, the essay illustrates one of the most astonishing examples of intellectual insulation between disciplines, in this case, between accounting and mathematics. Double-entry bookkeeping was developed during the fifteenth century and was first recorded as a system by the Italian mathematician Luca Pacioli in 1494. Double-entry bookkeeping has been used as the accounting system in market-based enterprises of any size throughout the world for several centuries. Incredibly, however, the mathematical basis for DEB is not known, at least not in the field of accounting.

The mathematical basis behind DEB (algebraic operations on ordered pairs of numbers) was developed in the nineteenth century by Sir William Rowan Hamilton as an abstract mathematical construction to deal with complex numbers and fractions. The particular example of the ordered pairs construction that is relevant to DEB ("group of differences," in technical terms) is the one used in undergraduate algebra courses to construct a number system with subtraction by using operations on ordered pairs of non-negative numbers. All that is required to see the connection with DEB is to identify these ordered pairs with the two-sided T-accounts of DEB (debits on the left side and credits on the right side). Yet with the exception of a paragraph in a semipopular book by D. E. Littlewood, the author has not been able to find a single mathematics book, elementary or advanced, popular or esoteric, which notes that the group of differences construction has been used in the business world for about five centuries. And the mathematical basis for DEB is totally unknown in the separate world of accounting.

This almost complete lack of cross-fertilization between mathematics and accounting is a topic of some interest for intellectual history and the sociology of knowledge. The story is rather simple from the mathematics side. Double-entry bookkeeping is apparently too simple and mundane to inspire any modern mathematician to learn it and then or example represented the "essence" of a property. It would be the "paradigm example" that sets the "standard" for all the other instances of the property. The main theme of the essay is the interpretation of category theory essentially as the mathematical theory of concrete universals.

In philosophical logic, these themes can be traced back to Plato's theory of ideas, forms, or universals. The sets of set theory are often taken as the mathematical explication of Plato's universals (i.e., the symbol ∈ for set membership was taken from the Greek word ειδη for Plato's ideas). But in view of the set theoretical antinomies discovered at the turn of the century, we know that sets cannot be self-predicative (i.e., cannot belong to themselves). The set representing a property must always be more "abstract" than the entities having the property. Thus set theory is the theory of "abstract universals." Yet there was a definite self-predicative strand in Plato's theory of universals [see Malcolm 1991]. Some universals were also concrete ideal instances of the property (i.e., concrete universals). Set theory could not be the mathematical model for that type of self-predicative universal. We show that category theory is that mathematical theory, and also argue that this recognition throws some light back on the antinomies since they resulted from trying to use one mathematical theory for both abstract and concrete universals.

The Third Man Argument against self-predication in Platonic scholarship is that if "whiteness itself" is white alongside all other white objects, then there must be a "One over the Many" (a super whiteness) by virtue of which they are all white, and so on in an infinite regress. But with the rigorous modeling of concrete universals in category theory, we see that the flaw in the Third Man Argument is the assumption that the "One over the Many" is distinct from the "Many." In the example cited above, the process of forming the "One over the Many" is the process of taking the union of all the sets with the property of being a subset of both A and B. But the "One" that was the result of taking this union, namely $A \cap B$, was also one of the "Many" (one of the subsets of both A and B taken in the union).

The interpretation of category theory as the theory of concrete universals again raises the question of category theory's relation to the foundation of mathematics. Lawvere and Tierney's theory of topoi is an elegant category-theoretic generalization of set theory so it generalizes the set-theoretic foundations of mathematics in many new directions. We argue that category theory is also relevant to foundations in a different way, as the theory of concrete universals. Category theory provides the framework to identify the concrete universals in mathein the intentionalist habit of thought, it is for a computer scientist like a painful and threatening withdrawal from a very satisfying addiction.

Chapter 8: Category Theory as the Theory of Concrete Universals

This essay deals with a connection between a relatively recent (1940s and 1950s) field of mathematics, category theory, and a hitherto vague notion of philosophical logic usually associated with Plato, the self-predicative universal or concrete universal. Consider the following example of "bad Platonic metaphysics."

> Given all the entities that have a certain property, there is one entity among them that exemplifies the property in an absolutely perfect and universal way. It is called the "concrete universal." There is a relationship of "participation" or "resemblance" so that all the other entities that have the property "participate in" or "resemble" that perfect example, the concrete universal.

All of this and much more "bad metaphysics" turns out to be precisely modeled in category theory.

While category theory can be quite forbidding to the nonspecialist, simple examples can be used based on inclusion between sets [see Ellerman 1988 for a bit more category theory]. Given two sets A and B, consider the property of being a set X that is contained in A and is contained in B. In other words, the property is the property of being both a subset of A and a subset of B. In this example, the "participation" relation is the subset relation. There is a set, namely the intersection, meet, or overlap of A and B, denoted $A \cap B$, that has the property (so it is a "concrete" instance of the property), and it is universal in the sense that any other set has the property if and only if it participates in the universal example:

concreteness: $A \cap B$ is a subset of both A and B, and
universality: X is a subset of $A \cap B$ if and only if X is contained in both A and B.

Thus the intersection $A \cap B$ is the concrete universal for the property of being a subset of A and a subset of B.

The idea of a concrete universal is frequently found in ordinary thought and language. For instance, we might say that some instance against, the majoritizing board would vote all the owned shares in favor, while the pass-through board would vote 60 percent of the owned shares in favor and 40 percent against.

The pass-through board is the corporate version of proportional representation (PR), while the majoritizing board corresponds to the system of districts with single representatives representing a majority of the voters in the district. It is well known that the system of majoritizing districts can lead to violations of majority rule. If the districts did not majoritize but only passed through the proportions for and against the proposal, then the result would be the same as in the direct referendum without districts. Thus the pass-through system gives a correct representation of the electorate while "premature majoritization" at the district level can allow manipulation of the results. The PR system with large districts and many party representatives for each district to roughly represent the voters' party preferences is an attempt to reproduce the pass-through system in a system of party representatives.

Pyramidal holding-company schemes are the corporate versions of the premature majoritization. We construct an example of an ownership federation with five companies. Using premature majoritization, the external majority shareholder of one of the companies can control the other four companies through a pyramidal structure. But with pass-through voting, that majority shareholder in one firm controls only that firm and the other four firms are controlled by their own direct external shareholders.

It is clear that a corporation of any size could be controlled by any small amount of capital with enough intermediate layers of holding companies. Why use a voting rule that makes the fundamental questions of corporate governance and control sensitive to the mere legal repackaging of capital through intermediaries? Pass-through voting for intermediaries would make control independent of legal repackaging. These questions of premature majoritization versus proportional representation (or pass-through voting) have not received much attention in the literature on corporate law. The chapter concludes with a discussion of the light these arguments shed on proportional representation in political theory.

Chapter 10: Finding the Markets in the Math: Arbitrage and Optimization Theory

One of the fundamental insights of mainstream neoclassical economics is the connection between competitive market prices and the matics, the concrete instances of a mathematical property that exemplify the property in such a perfect and paradigmatic way that all other instances have the property by virtue of participating in the concrete universal.

Chapter 9: *Keiretsu*, Proportional Representation, and Input-Output Theory

This essay grew out of an attempt to model mathematically the possible cross-ownership arrangements that might arise between privatizing firms in the former Yugoslavia [see Ellerman 1991]. The cross-ownership arrangements resemble the groups of Japanese companies called *keiretsu*. There is cross ownership between the companies in the group as well as some ownership outside the group that is traded on the stock market. In spite of the partial outside ownership, the *keiretsu* often behave as "self-owning" groups. If firm A owns shares in B, then the management in A usually signs over its proxy on shares in B to the management in firm B. And the management in B does likewise with respect to the managers in A. Thus, within certain constraints, each firm can act like a "self-owning" firm, not totally unlike the self-managing firms of the former Yugoslavia.

In this essay we investigate the opposite alternative to this proxy assumption. We make the more classical assumption that the managers act only as "transmission belts" for the wishes of the shareholders. But with cross ownership, the shareholders are in part other corporations whose managers also pass along the wishes of their shareholders. Thus the determination of the votes on a question put to a corporation can generate an infinite regression of the type familiar from input-output theory. As long as some external shareholders exist, the infinite regression is benign and decisions would ultimately be made by the external shareholders. A similar "pass-through" or "transmission-belt" assumption is made for dividends. Each company passes through to its own shares any dividends received on shares it owns. Thus the dividends will also eventually trickle into the hands of the external shareholders.

Given the votes of the shareholders (external and other companies in the group), there are two ways that the board can vote on the owned shares. The board could majoritize and vote all the owned shares as a block according to the majority outcome, or the board could simply pass along the percentages for and against on the owned shares. For instance, if the shareholders vote 60 percent in favor and 40 percent

This Cournot-Kirchhoff law has many applications outside of electrical circuit theory and economics. For instance, the second law of thermodynamics can be formulated as the impossibility of a certain form of "heat arbitrage" between temperature reservoirs, and the "prices" that emerge in this case are the Kelvin absolute temperatures of the reservoirs. Yet another application of the arbitrage framework is to probability theory. Profitable arbitrage in the market for contingent commodities is called "making book." A person's subjective probability judgments satisfy the laws of probability if they are "coherent" in the sense of not allowing book to be made against the person. Thus arbitrage on the market for contingent commodities enforces the laws of probability.

The arbitrage interpretation of the first-order necessary conditions for classical optimization problems suggests a research program to extend the arbitrage reasoning to other parts of optimization theory (e.g., nonlinear and linear programming, calculus of variations, and optimal control theory). In the appendix, we sketch the interpretation of the sufficient conditions for a classical optimum in terms of "arbitrage operating to eliminate its own possibility."

Chapter 11: Valuation Rings: A Better Algebraic Treatment of Boolean Algebras

Let B be a Boolean algebra such as the set P(u) of all subsets of a set u. The usual method of interpreting B as a ring is to define:

addition	= exclusive or (= non-equivalence)
multiplication	= intersection (= meet)
unity (1)	= u
zero (0)	= z (null set).

The resulting ring was a Boolean ring. But there was always the asymmetrical oddity of an alternative way to render a Boolean algebra as a Boolean ring, namely with the definitions:

addition	= equivalence
multiplication	= join
unity (1)	= z
zero (0)	= u.

The usual Boolean ring-theoretic treatment of Boolean algebras made no particular sense out of this alternative definition; it was just an odd footnote.

Lagrange multipliers of optimization theory in mathematics. Yet this insight has not been well developed. In the standard theory of markets, competitive prices result from the equilibrium of supply and demand schedules. But in a constrained optimization problem, there seems to be no mathematical version of supply and demand functions so that the Lagrange multipliers would be seen as equilibrium prices. How can one "find the markets in the math" so that Lagrange multipliers will emerge as equilibrium market prices?

We argue that the solution to the "find the markets in the math" problem is to reconceptualize equilibrium as the absence of profitable arbitrage instead of the equating of supply and demand. With each proposed solution to a classical constrained optimization problem, there is an associated market. The maximand is one commodity, and each constraint provides another commodity on this market. Given a marginal variation in one commodity, one can define the marginal change in any other commodity so the market has a set of exchange rates between the commodities. The usual necessary conditions for the proposed solution to solve the maximization problem are the same as the conditions for this mathematically defined "market" to be arbitrage-free. The prices that emerge from the arbitrage-free system of exchange rates (normalized with the maximand as numeraire) are precisely the Lagrange multipliers. We also show that the cofactors of a matrix describing the marginal variations can be taken as the prices (before being normalized) so the Lagrange multipliers can always be presented as ratios of cofactors. The results about cofactors also allow an economic interpretation of inverse matrices and of Cramer's Rule.

The basic mathematical result, which dates back to Augustin Cournot in 1838, is that:

> there exists a system of prices for the commodities such that the given exchange rates are the price ratios if and only if the exchange rates are arbitrage-free (in the sense that they multiply to one around any circle).

This simple graph-theoretic theorem is known in its additive version as Kirchhoff's Voltage Law:

> there exists a system of potentials at the nodes of a circuit such that the voltages on the wires between the nodes are the potential differences if and only if the voltages sum to zero around any cycle.

Kirchhoff's work was published after Cournot in 1847, so the result might be called "the Cournot-Kirchhoff law."

Chapter 1: Trespassing against the Happy Consciousness of Orthodox Economics

The first chapter addresses the problems of trespassing involved in understanding the arguments presented in the first five "controversial" chapters of the collection. These chapters challenge the whole idea of the employer-employee relationship that is the institutional basis for our present version of a private-property market economy. The problems of trespassing against fundamental orthodoxy in the social and moral sciences are of a completely different order of magnitude than the problems of trespassing in the natural and mathematical sciences.

Perhaps a parable will illustrate the point. You are a member of the hierarchy in some church (sacred or profane). A book is published that argues against some basic dogma of your church (e.g., the dogma that the Sun, the planets, and the stars revolve around the Earth). You are explicitly or implicitly faced with several choices.

1. Read the book, accept the arguments, and advocate them in your church—which would probably lead to being ostracized and losing your job.
2. Read the book and accept the arguments but keep quiet so that you "live a lie" the rest of your tenure in the church.
3. Read the book and reject the arguments based on any number of convenient counterarguments supplied by the church.
4. Ignore the book.

The first two options, open your mouth and be punished or close your mouth and live a lie, are the two rather unpalatable options that result from taking seriously and understanding the arguments against the dogma. Therefore, quite aside from the merits of the arguments, one should not expect to find too many church functionaries taking seriously any arguments against their basic dogmas. One would expect to find some variation on the last two options. No counterargument is too superficial to be accepted as "settling the issue." A responsible church member would not want to be seen as indirectly attacking the sacred dogma and defending the heretical arguments by showing the superficiality of some counterargument against the heresy. Thus church intellectuals are very comfortable with accepting the most banal counterarguments so they can redirect their time and energy on other, more "promising," issues. The last option is also very attractive. Few of your superiors within the church would attack you for

In the approach using Gian-Carlo Rota's valuation rings, a new ring V(B,2) is defined from the Boolean algebra B and the two-element ring 2 ($=Z_2$). On this valuation ring V(B,2) with multiplication defined using the meet, the "universe" u of B is the unity (1) of the ring but the "null set" z of B is distinct from the zero 0 of the ring. The alternative join-multiplication can be defined using the same addition so V(B,2) is a module with two ring multiplications defined on it. With the join-multiplication, z serves as the unity for that ring structure. The usual Boolean ring is obtained from V(B,2) cum meet-multiplication by taking the quotient setting z equal to 0, and the other Boolean ring is obtained by taking the quotient of V(B,2) cum join-multiplication by setting u equal to 0. Thus V(B,2) contains the information and structure of the two Boolean rings that can be obtained as quotients.

A Boolean algebra satisfies the Boolean duality principle that any theorem remains valid under the interchange of the meet and join, and the interchange of the null element z and the unit u. Boolean duality generalizes to valuation rings as the "complementation" anti-isomorphism between the two ring structures that interchanges the two multiplications and the two elements u and z. This formulation of Boolean duality is much more general since it applies to all valuation rings, and a valuation ring V(L,A) can be constructed starting with any distributive lattice L and any commutative ring A with unity. Thus "Boolean" duality generalizes far beyond the two-valued case where the ring of coefficients is 2 = Z_2. For instance, the valuation ring V(B,Z_n) might prove useful for an algebraic treatment of multi-valued logic.

The usual Boolean algebraic treatment of propositional logic uses the free Boolean algebra B on a set P of propositional variables. We characterize the valuation rings for the free Boolean algebras as a certain class of special polynomial rings. The polynomials are augmented with an extra variable z, which has the special property that it "acts like zero" with respect to the other variables in the sense that $xz = z$. The unit 1 is the "u" of the valuation ring. Thus each polynomial can have a "co-constant" term $a_z z$ in addition to the usual constant term $a_u u = a_u 1 = a_u$ where the scalars a_z and a_u are from the ring of coefficients A. In addition, all the variables are idempotent in the sense the $x^2 = x$ and $z^2 = z$. We show that the ring of augmented polynomials with idempotent variables and coefficients from a commutative ring A is isomorphic to the valuation ring of the free Boolean algebra on the set of variables (without z) with coefficients from A.

That characterization means that all the duality machinery of valuations rings can be defined on these augmented polynomial rings. In particular, there is the second join-multiplication (with z as the ring unity) and the complementation anti-isomorphism between the two ring structures. Thus we have a duality theory for these augmented polynomials. Furthermore, propositional logic (i.e., free Boolean algebras) can be recast and generalized using these augmented polynomial rings. We prove a generalization of the completeness theorem using elementary polynomial reasoning.

Chapter 12: Parallel Addition, Series-Parallel Duality, and Financial Mathematics

Boolean duality can be algebraically represented on Rota's valuation rings, which have two ring multiplications and one addition, as the complementation anti-isomorphism on the ring that interchanges the two multiplications (see previous chapter). The work in this last chapter arose by extending the same type of treatment to series-parallel duality. The roles of addition and multiplication are reversed. Series-parallel algebras are defined with two additions (the usual series addition and parallel addition) and one multiplication. Duality on series-parallel algebras that allow division (such as the positive rationals) is represented by the reciprocity anti-isomorphism that interchanges the two additions.

Series-parallel duality has been previously studied in electrical circuit theory and combinatorial theory. The parallel sum arose naturally when resistors are connected in parallel instead of series. Given two resistors with the positive real resistances of a and b, their combined resistance is $a + b$ when connected in series and $(1/a + 1/b)^{-1}$ when connected in parallel. The full colon (:) notation will be used for the parallel sum, $a{:}b = (1/a + 1/b)^{-1}$.

Any equation on the positive reals concerning the two sums and multiplication, can be "dualized" by applying the "take-reciprocals" map to obtain another equation. Each number is replaced by its reciprocal and the two additions are interchanged. The following equation

$$1 = (1 + x) : \left(1 + \frac{1}{x}\right)$$

holds for any positive real x. Add any x to one and add its reciprocal to one. The results are two numbers larger than one and their parallel sum is exactly one. Dualizing yields the equation

$$1 = \left(1 : \frac{1}{x}\right) + (1 : x)$$

for all positive reals x. Taking the parallel sum of any x and its reciprocal with one yields two numbers smaller than one that sum to one. For instance, taking x = 2, we have that

$$(1+2):(1+(1/2)) = 3:(3/2) = 1 \text{ and } (1:(1/2)) + (1:2) = (1/3) + (2/3) = 1.$$

The principal application considered in the essay is series-parallel duality in financial arithmetic. The basic result is that the parallel sum of the one-shot "balloon" payments at different times that would pay off a given loan is the equal amortization payment that would pay off the loan if paid at each of those times. This interpretation is not restricted to financial arithmetic. For example, suppose a forest of initial size PV (in harvestable boardfeet) grows at the rate r_i in the ith period. Let

$$P_m = PV \prod_{i=1}^{m} (1 + r_i)$$

Then P_m would be the one-shot harvest that could be obtained at the end of the mth period. For instance, P_3, P_{17}, and P_{23} are the amounts that could be harvested if the whole forest was harvested at the end of the 3rd, 17th, or the 23rd period. But what is the smooth or equal harvest PMT so that if PMT was harvested at the end of the 3rd, 17th, and 23rd periods, then the forest would just be completely harvested at the end of that last period? That equal harvest amount is just the parallel sum of the one-time harvests:

$$PMT = P_3 : P_{17} : P_{23}.$$

In the standard application to financial arithmetic, PV is the principal value of a loan, r_i is the interest rate for the ith period, and PMT is the equal amortization payment. Ordinarily, the amortization payments are made at equal time intervals, but this example showed that equal intervals are not necessary.

Since the parallel sum has a natural interpretation, any equation in financial arithmetic can be dualized and interpreted in the field. Suppose the constant interest rate is 20 percent per period. Then the discounted present value of two amortization payments of 1 at the end of the first and second period is principal value of the loan paid off by those payments, i.e.,

$$\frac{55}{36} = \frac{1}{(1.2)^1} + \frac{1}{(1.2)^2}.$$

The equation dualizes to:

$$\frac{36}{55} = (1.2)^1 : (1.2)^2.$$

The amounts $(1.2)^1 = 1.2$ and $(1.2)^2 = 1.44$ are the compounded principal values of a one-dollar loan so they are the one-shot or balloon payments that would pay off the loan if paid, respectively, at the end of the first or the second period. Their parallel sum, 36/55, is the equal amortization payment that would pay off the loan if paid at the end of both the first and second periods.

These facts can be arranged in the following dual format.

Primal Fact:	**Dual Fact:**
The series sum of the discounted amortization payments for a loan is the principal of the loan.	The parallel sum of the compounded principals of a loan is the amortization payment for the loan.

In this manner, each equation can be paired with a dual equation to reveal the structure of series-parallel duality within financial arithmetic.

In the appendix to the essay, commutative series-parallel algebras are defined that are to series-parallel duality as Rota's valuation rings are to

Boolean duality. In a series-parallel algebra where every element has a multiplicative inverse, called a "series-parallel division algebra," the take-reciprocals map is an anti-isomorphism that interchanges the two additions. It is easy to find such algebras since every group generates a series-parallel division algebra. For instance, the trivial group {1} (written multiplicatively) generates the positive rationals $\mathbf{Q}^+$. This means that an electrical circuit of any given rational resistance can be constructed solely from series and parallel connections of one-ohm resistances.

Non-commutative series-parallel algebras are also defined, and every non-commutative group also has a series-parallel completion. The principal model for a non-commutative series-parallel algebra is the algebra of monotonic increasing real functions on a single real variable. Series and parallel sums are respectively the vertical and horizontal sums of functions. Multiplication is functional composition, so the reciprocal of an element is its functional inverse.

In the move from commutative to non-commutative series-parallel algebras, the standard models change from an algebra of numbers such as $\mathbf{Q}^+$ to an algebra of functions such as the monotonic increasing real functions. That is important because it allows us to see the connection to convex duality.

In modern economics, duality on convex functions has an important role. Duality in linear programming is a well-known special case of convex duality. We argue informally that convex duality is related to series-parallel duality as a function is related to its derivative. The derivatives of differentiable strictly convex functions of one variable are the monotonic increasing functions used in the standard model of a non-commutative series-parallel algebra. The "series" and "parallel" sums of convex functions are, respectively, the usual sum and the infimal convolution. The derivatives of these two sums of convex functions are, respectively, the vertical and horizontal sums of the derivatives. Each convex function has a dual or convex conjugate. The derivative of the convex conjugate of a convex function is the functional inverse of the derivative of the original convex function.

In this manner, the operations expressing duality on convex functions map via differentiation into the operations of the series-parallel algebra of increasing monotonic functions. In that sense, series-parallel duality can be seen as the "derivative" of convex duality.

References

Callahan, J. 1985. "Enforcing Slavery Contracts: A Liberal View." *The Philosophical Forum* 16 (Spring):223–36.

Davis, David Brion. 1971. "New Sidelights on Early Antislavery Radicalism." *William and Mary Quarterly* 28 (October):585–94.

Ellerman, David. 1982. *Economics, Accounting, and Property Theory*. Lexington, Mass: D.C. Heath.

———. 1985. "The Mathematics of Double Entry Bookkeeping." *Mathematics Magazine* 58 (September):226–33.

———. 1988. "Category Theory and Concrete Universals." *Erkenntnis* 28:409–29.

———. 1990. "An Arbitrage Interpretation of Classical Optimization." *Metroeconomica* 41, no. 3:259–76.

———. 1991. "Cross Ownership of Corporations: A New Application of Input-Output Theory." *Metroeconomica* 42, no. 1:33–46.

———. 1992. *Property and Contract in Economics: The Case for Economic Democracy*. Oxford: Basil Blackwell.

Gray, Alexander. 1968. *The Socialist Tradition: Moses to Lenin*. New York: Harper.

Malcolm, John. 1991. *Plato on the Self-Predication of Forms*. Oxford: Clarendon Press.

Pateman, Carole. 1988. *The Sexual Contract*. Stanford: Stanford University Press.

Philmore, J. 1982. "The Libertarian Case for Slavery: A Note on Nozick." *The Philosophical Forum* 14 (Fall): 43–58.

Searle, John R. 1980. "Minds, Brains and Programs." *Behavioral and Brain Sciences* 3:417–24.

Chapter 1

Trespassing against the Happy Consciousness of Orthodox Economics

Introduction

All stable societies are basically happy with themselves. Any stable, self-reproducing society must educate its people to the consciousness that "all is essentially well" with the society. There are no structural flaws, only the problems of implementing the sound principles at the foundation of the society. This self-reproducing and self-congratulatory state of mind might be called the "Happy Consciousness."

Any attempt to develop a critique of the basic structures and principles of a society involves of necessity transgressing and trespassing against the Happy Consciousness. There are not only glass ceilings but glass walls that define the accepted corridors of thought. Young, aggressive professors in economics and the other social sciences are usually equipped with uncanny radar so they can roar down the corridor of orthodox thought without ever getting close to breaking through the walls—all the while seeing themselves as brash free thinkers exploring the vast unknown. This radar-like instinct, inbred by the ambient society as a part of the Happy Consciousness, constantly and almost unconsciously warns them away from the glass walls—away from irresponsible speculations (except perhaps in the pink of youth) and down the avenues of sound and serious research.

Breaking through the invisible walls of orthodoxy and trespassing against the Happy Consciousness has little to do with intellectual insight. It took no great brain power to "see" that slaves were persons and not things, but where were the abolitionists among the intellectual elites of ancient Greece or the antebellum South? Trespassing against orthodoxy requires a willingness to follow lines of thought wherever they might lead, a willingness to ignore the warning signals sent by one's inbred monitor of orthodoxy ("Is it serious responsible work?", "Is it publishable?", "Is it scientific?", "Will it adversely affect my job prospects?", and so forth). Those who choose to develop unorthodox theories must develop their own strategies for bearing the adverse consequences. For instance, Charles Darwin trespassed against the religious orthodoxy of his day, so he tried to postpone the publication of his theory but was forced to publish by the challenge of Alfred Wallace's work.

When one breaks through the glass walls of orthodoxy, then one may enter a topsy-turvy world where the customary guideposts of normality are missing. What was previously "normal" now appears as surreal and absurd. How can this be communicated to those who are still in the embrace of the Happy Consciousness?

This essay is an introduction to the intellectual trespassing involved in the essays of the collection about certain fundamental normative and positive questions of political economy. These essays boil down to an attack on one and only one institution of our society, the institution of hiring or renting people (i.e., the employer-employee contract). The employment relation lies at the foundation of our present form of a market economy, just as the master-slave relationship lay at the foundation of the society of the antebellum South. The alternative is a market economy without the employment relation, an economy where all people are self-employed (perhaps individually but usually jointly) in the firms known variously as worker-owned firms, labor-managed firms, industrial partnerships, or democratic firms. Self-employment is the economic version of political self-government, so the alternative system is sometimes called "economic democracy" [Ellerman 1992].

A number of expository devices and intuition pumps will be used to try to break through the walls of conventional thought. For instance, we have already used one. We have called the employment relationship the "renting" of people. This is an intentionally jarring use of words. One rents, hires, or leases a car or an apartment, but one only "hires" a person. Yet the relationship is basically the same. In each case, one buys a certain type of services provided by the entity (measured in car-days, apartment-months, or man-hours) for a specified time period. While the characterization of the employment relationship as the "renting" of people may sound at first like a contentious accusation, it is actually not a bone of contention. Orthodox economists fully accept the characterization although they would prefer to use other language.

> One can even say that wages are the rentals paid for the use of a man's personal services for a day or a week or a year. This may seem a strange use of terms, but on second thought, one recognizes that every agreement to hire labor is really for some limited period of time. By outright purchase, you might avoid ever renting any kind of land. But in our society, labor is one of the few productive factors that cannot legally be bought outright. Labor can only be rented, and the wage rate is really a rental. [Samuelson 1976, 569]

The "renting people" characterization of the employer-employee relationship is perhaps the simplest example of the invisible boundaries of orthodox language and thought. That characterization is a "surprise" to most people. How is it that people can live their whole lives in a society based on the renting of people and yet when it is pointed out to them, they confess that they "never thought of it that way." If a person lived their whole life in the antebellum South and then said he or she "never thought of it" as being based on owning people, then we would conclude that he or she was firmly in the grip of false consciousness. Yet today most people who never considered employment as the renting of people would not see themselves as being in the grip of social thought control or false consciousness. They just "never considered it in that way."

And that is just the simple matter of changing one word to a synonym. It is much more difficult to trespass over the other boundaries that demarcate the Happy Consciousness.

Surreality and the Happy Consciousness

Political-economic research can be an alienating experience. From being "at home" and "seeing the obvious" like everyone else, one can end up feeling like a visitor from Mars wondering why everyone else cannot or will not see the obvious.

Suppose that a person of modern moral sensitivities could be taken back by a time machine and dropped in the middle of a slave society such as the American antebellum South at the beginning of the nineteenth century. One might think that surely the distinguished professors, the celebrated thinkers, and the religious leaders of the society would be leading a struggle against slavery. But one would be quite disappointed. For centuries slavery had hardly been a topic of debate. Slavery was a "given" part of the social universe. Morally sensitive educated thinkers would go through their entire careers with hardly a word about slavery except for a few thoughtful criticisms of the various abuses of the system by unscrupulous and brutish individuals.

Our time traveler might well feel a stranger, a visitor from another planet. He or she might ask: "Why don't the intellectual and moral leaders raise their voice in protest? Why do the people of this slave society seem to have this strange "moral blind spot"? Aren't they aware that the slaves are human beings like you and me? Don't they believe in basic inalienable human rights?" And so forth.

The truth of the matter is quite simple; it does not call for some complicated and convoluted theory. The slave society might seem surreal to our modern time traveler, but it was quite normal to its inhabitants. Societies do not promote to positions of status and influence those individuals who are likely to attack the foundations of the society. And any individuals who aspire to positions of status and influence are unlikely to harbor "unsound" opinions. There is no need for any "conspiracy." It is based on simple, self-regarding common sense. The moral and intellectual leaders of a slavery society did not secretly develop what we would take as a modern critique of slavery and keep it hidden in the back of their minds. Instead they "grew up" with a "moral sense" endowed by their ambient society as to what opinions were sound and unsound. Any line of inquiry that looked like it would lead in the wrong direction was quickly abandoned as "unfruitful." There is no need for a conspiracy to hide or express such thoughts. Substantive men and women have neither the time nor inclination to pursue "irresponsible" speculations.

Let us now change the example. Instead of being deposited in a society based on owning other human beings, let us suppose that our time traveler has landed in a society based on the renting of other human beings. Instead of buying a lifetime of services (as when buying a car), one could buy services for specified limited time period (as when one rents or leases a car).

That journey needs no time machine because that society is our society. The renting of people is the employment relationship. We prefer to use the word "hired" or "employed" or various other expressions when a person is rented.

> Since slavery was abolished, human earning power is forbidden by law to be capitalized. A man is not even free to sell himself; he must **rent** himself at a wage. [Samuelson, 1976, 52 (emphasis in the original)]

Again one might think that surely the distinguished professors, the celebrated moral philosophers, and the religious leaders of our present society would at least *discuss* the appropriateness of a whole society based on the renting of human beings. But it is not even a topic of debate. It is a "given" part of the social universe.

One standard argument is that the employment relation cannot be considered merely a limited version of slavery because slavery was involuntary. But that is not the comparison being made. I am considering the voluntary rental relationship as the limited version of the *voluntary* sale of oneself (i.e., as part-time *voluntary* slavery). When slavery was abolished, voluntary contractual slavery was abolished along with involuntary servitude. As Samuelson noted, "A man is not even free to sell himself." It does seem a bit surreal that voluntarily selling all of one's labor should be seen as fundamentally against our jurisprudence while selling only part of one's labor is so taken for granted that social and moral thinkers do not even bother to discuss it. One might wonder about the borderline between perfectly normal rentals and fundamental violation of inalienable rights. Does it occur after 5-year contracts? After contracts of 8.5 years, 15 years, 25 years, . . . ?

There is no conspiracy to avoid or hide these questions. There is no need. Conventional intellectuals see no promise or payoff in thinking along such lines so there are no secret thoughts to be hidden behind a cloak of conspiracy. Instead of estrangement, there is the Happy Consciousness that all is fundamentally well in our institutions—the consciousness that one is "at home" in this society. There are only the difficult and seemingly intractable problems of implementing the sound principles embodied in our institutions. But on the question of there being something *structurally* wrong with a socioeconomic system based on renting people, no shadow of doubt darkens the brow of our intellectual and moral leaders—although there is much hand-wringing and anguished distress concerning those in the bottom layers of society who have to rent themselves out for such a low wage or who cannot find anyone to rent them at all.

The Schizophrenic Nature of Modern Democracy

Suppose that our modern time traveler was transported back to a "predemocratic" time such as the Middle Ages. Religious and secular autocrats vied for political sovereignty; democracy was not one of the options. The people were hardly aware of any such notions as democratic self-government; they sought a wise, strong, and good master.

Our traveler from modern society might find this situation rather perplexing. Democracy was known at least from ancient Greece. Why weren't courageous intellectuals and spiritual leaders of the Middle Ages raising the issue? If there was too much oppression, then the moral leaders might at least write about democratic rights in secret for posthumous publication. But there is little evidence that such thoughts were harbored by the elites. They were formed by a society that inculcated views as to what was sound and unsound. Responsible thinkers who shaped the opinions that carried weight saw no reason to veer off into iconoclastic speculations about inalienable democratic rights.

Someone from the distant or perhaps not so distant future who traveled back to our time might be similarly perplexed. Today we are steeped in the language of inalienable rights such as the inalienable right of self-government or self-determination. The right to self-determination is not seen as an ownership right like the property right to a car that we may have today and sell tomorrow. It is inalienable in the sense that we may not give up the right even with consent. A *pactum subjectionis,* a social contract to give up and transfer the right of self-government to some sovereign person or body, is considered inherently invalid. This is part of the conventional wisdom reinforced in serious political speeches about our basic rights and reiterated in the philosophical tomes that record the fundamental inalienable rights that undergird our morally advanced civilization.

Or so it seems at first. But then our time traveler from the future asks about "what people do all day long," namely about their work. The time traveler finds that almost all people work as employees under the legal contract known as the employment contract. In that contract, the employee gives up and transfers to the employer the right of self-determination within the scope of the contract (i.e., concerning the work). It is not a contract of representation or delegation as is contemplated in democratic theory. The employer is not the representative or delegate of the employees. The employment contract transfers and alienates the right to control the employee's actions within the scope of the contract to the employer who then exercises that right in his or her own name, not in the name of the employees.

This may seem strange indeed to our time traveler who might come from a world where people are recognized as having an inalienable right of self-determination in *all* spheres of life—political, economic, and private family life.

How is it that human beings are seen to be neatly partitioned so that in a person's life as a citizen the right to self-determination is sacred, inviolate, and inalienable, but in a person's life as a worker the right to self-determination is routinely bought and sold as a matter of ordinary commerce? Are people perhaps seen as moral minotaurs, half-human and half-beast, so that the human half enjoys inalienable rights while the beastly half can be rented out in the employment contract? Or perhaps people are amphibious creatures alternating between a "public world" that enjoys inalienable rights and a "private world" where such rights fall into eclipse?

Our time traveler from the future might have some difficulty understanding today's mindset. We now find it strange that people in the past could have been denied fundamental rights to self-determination simply due to the color of their skin or their sex. Yet even stranger is today's view that the self-same person can have an inalienable natural right to self-determination in one sphere of life (the "public sphere" or life as a citizen) but have no trace of this inalienability survive in another sphere (the "private sphere" or life as a worker).

Our time traveler might search the political, economic, and philosophical texts and treatises of today to find some recognition, discussion, and explanation of this curious split personality of modern man. But the traveler would be largely disappointed. In the orthodox texts that express the conventional wisdom, one will find no discussion of the matter. The legal alienation of the right of self-determination in "what people do all day long" is not deemed a worthy topic of debate by responsible intellectual and moral leaders. Since the (political) democratic revolutions of the eighteenth and nineteenth centuries, the rather contrived public/private distinction has functioned to "explain" the failure to recognize democratic rights in the economic sphere. The public/private distinction serves as an intellectual prophylactic to guard the economic sphere against being "infected" with the democratic germ. The Happy Consciousness is trained to be placated with "It is private" as a sufficient explanation for the alleged inapplicability of democratic principles to what people do all day long.

Deep Metaphors versus Superficial Facts in the Scientific Search for Symmetry

Symmetry in the Rights of the Factors

Science wants to be "deep," not superficial. In the social sciences where the Happy Consciousness is the customary guide, the facts often "get in the way." But unwelcome facts can often be avoided through metaphorical reinterpretation. This is viewed as an advance in the social sciences. The serious and responsible researcher must delve beneath the superficial facts to probe the deep metaphors that will finally bring "science" in line with the pre-analytical vision of the Happy Consciousness.

This process of "scientific" explanation and reconciliation is nowhere more evident than in the treatment of the firm, particularly in the structure of property rights within the firm. Let us consider an ultra-simple description of a production opportunity. The managerial and nonmanagerial labor symbolized by L uses the services of capital and the other inputs symbolized by K to produce the outputs Q during a certain time period. No conceptual clarity would be added to our discussion by using a more complicated and realistic description. Who will be the "firm" that undertakes this production process:

- the suppliers of the capital services K as in the capitalist firm (Capital hires labor),
- the people who carry out the labor services L as in the democratic firm (Labor hires capital), or
- the state as in the socialist firm (the state hires or owns both)?

In each case, what are the property rights enjoyed by the firm? The facts can be easily stated. In each case, the legal party that is the firm owns all (100 percent) of the produced outputs Q and holds all (100 percent) of the liabilities for the used-up services of capital and labor. If the liabilities for the used-up capital and labor services were indicated by negative signs, then we could say that the firm has the bundle of property rights and obligations $(Q, -K, -L)$, that can be called the "whole product" to distinguish it from the simple product Q. The other parties hold none of these assets and liabilities.

For instance, in the capitalist firm, Labor (the suppliers of the labor services L) owns none (0 percent) of the outputs Q, and none (0 percent) of the liabilities for the used-up capital and labor services are charged against Labor. Similarly, in the democratic firm, Capital (the suppliers of the capital services K) owns none (0 percent) of the outputs Q and has none (0 percent) of the input liabilities charged against it. Of course the same individuals might both supply capital and labor, but we are considering the functional roles separately.

The facts are that the property rights held by the various parties are totally asymmetrical (100 percent versus 0 percent). The Happy Consciousness is unhappy with these facts. The capitalist firm needs to be presented as a picture of symmetry and harmony so the facts need to be reinterpreted. The first step is to change the topic from property flows (assets and liabilities per time period) to income flows. Let p, r, and w respectively stand for the unit prices of the outputs, capital services, and labor services. In view of the above-mentioned property flows, it follows that the legal party that operates as the firm gets all (100 percent) of the revenues pQ and is liable to pay all (100 percent) of the capital and labor expenses rK and wL. The other parties do not own the revenues and are not liable for the expenses. But these facts are again "superficial" because they are still completely asymmetrical. Science, under the guidance of the Happy Consciousness, must probe for deeper symmetries.

The move from property flows to income flows does represent some progress since the income flows are stated in the commensurate monetary units. The firm is liable to the factor supplier for the expense of that factor. One can "jump over" the firm and "picture" this right of the factor supplier "as if" it were a direct right on that share of the revenue. Of course, as long as the firm exists (i.e., is not bankrupt), the factor supplier does not actually own that share of the revenue (since the firm owns all the revenue). But the Happy Consciousness is not satisfied with such superficial legalistic facts; it prefers the deep metaphor of picturing the factor suppliers as getting their "distributive share of the product." Since the size of the distributive share is determined by the price and equilibrium demand of the factor, the touchy question of "what each factor gets" is now reduced to price theory. The original questions about property rights and "who is to be the firm" have been marginalized if not eliminated. The Happy Consciousness is happier.

Since the factor suppliers are pictured as "sharing" the (income stream of the) product, the firm is left out of the picture unless there is some "residual" left over after each factor takes its distributive share. The firm (which has 100 percent of the whole product from the "superficial" factual viewpoint) is thus reduced to the cameo role of the "residual claimant" in the new metaphorical drama, and even that role is squeezed out in the long-run competitive equilibrium with zero residual profits.

The symmetrical "distributive shares" picture of production has passed into popular consciousness. In the context of broader social discussions, it serves to derail any discussion of property rights to the whole product and to shunt the discussion over to the topic of "income distribution."

One key to the distributive shares picture is that the firm is excluded from the main picture as holder of asset and liability flows. The factor suppliers are pictured as having direct claims on the revenue. In one recent variant on this set of metaphors, the factor suppliers are pictured as "contracting" for a share of the revenue and the "firm" itself is pictured as just this "nexus of contracts." The "residual claimant" is just another party that contracts for the "residual share" of the income.

> This is the set of contracts theory of the firm. The firm is viewed as nothing more than a set of contracts. One of the contract claims is a residual claim (equity) on the firm's assets and cash flows. [Ross and Westerfield 1988, 14]

Thus even the residual claim—ordinarily pictured as getting what is left after contractual claims are satisfied—is depicted as "one of the contract claims." Thus the newfangled "nexus of contracts" metaphor improves on the old-fashioned distributive shares metaphor by treating the residual claim or equity as another contractual relationship. All trace of the complete asymmetry in the actual property rights is eliminated in this picture. The army of metaphors marches on. The Happy Consciousness is even happier.

The high priests of neoclassical economics often challenge those who have alternative views to express them in a precise mathematical form. How can the actual structure of property rights and income flows in a firm be put into a mathematical form and be brought to the attention of sophisticated economists? Perhaps this could be "revealed" in a new application of game theory, control theory, or catastrophe theory, and thus get published in some serious scientific journal. But, alas, a mathematical theory already exists that describes the actual stocks and flows of property and income in a firm. This theory is not chaos theory or nonlinear analysis. Unfortunately, this theory is called "accounting." Ordinary accounting deals with the stocks and flows of value. Accounting can be mathematically formulated and generalized also to deal directly with the multidimensional stocks and flows of property in a firm [see Ellerman 1982, 1986, or the essay on double-entry accounting in this volume]. It would be difficult to imagine any subject matter more boring and uninteresting to the refined mathematical sensibilities of modern economists than accounting. Thus there seems to be little immediate hope of weaning sophisticated economists away from their deep metaphors and exposing them to the superficial facts—even when the superficial facts are expressed in precise mathematical form.

Symmetry in the Activities of the Factors

Jurisprudence does not recognize "symmetry" between the actions of persons and the services of things. The services rendered by things have a causal effect, but things cannot be "responsible" for their services. Only persons can be responsible. Thus jurisprudence recognizes a deep and fundamental asymmetry between L and K, between the actions of human beings and the services of capital.

The basic juridical principle of imputation is to assign legal or de jure responsibility in accordance with factual or de facto responsibility. Since only persons can be de facto responsible for anything, the imputation of legal responsibility goes back through any tools or other things used by people to the people themselves as the responsible agents. In the production opportunity considered above, the managerial and nonmanagerial people by performing the labor services L use up the capital services K and produce the outputs Q. Thus the juridical principal of imputation implies that those people should have those legal responsibilities (i.e., should be legally liable for the capital services K and have the legal ownership of the outputs Q). Since we are following the practice of conceptualizing this productive activity as also producing and using up the "labor" L, it also follows that those people should be liable (to themselves) for the labor services. Thus elementary jurisprudence implies that Labor ought to legally appropriate the whole product; the firm should be a democratic firm. Thus democratic theory and elementary jurisprudence arrive at the same result.

The simple jurisprudential fact that "only labor can be responsible" is obviously rather inconvenient for the Happy Consciousness in general and for orthodox economic theory in particular. It also "requires" metaphorical reinterpretation. There are two ways metaphorically to restore the much-wanted symmetry between the actions of persons and the services of things: (1) promote things to the level of responsible agents, or (2) demote persons down to the level of non-responsible things. The first metaphor will be called the "active poetic view" of production while the second metaphor will be called the "passive technological view" of production.

The older economic literature favored the active poetic view. The non-human factors are personified with responsible agency so that they can rise up and cooperate with labor to jointly produce the product. For example, "Together, the man and shovel can dig my cellar" or "land and labor together produce the corn harvest" [Samuelson, 1976, 536–37]. While this view has great poetic charm, economists generally think that it is more "scientific" (in the sense of "physics envy") to demote persons down to the level of things. Production becomes a "technological process," not a human activity. Given the inputs K and L, the outputs Q are produced (but not produced "by anyone").

With either the active or passive metaphors the crucial symmetry between labor and the other factors is restored. The unique and fundamental jurisprudence role of the actions of persons (as opposed to the services of things) is hidden from the penetrating scrutiny of orthodox social scientists.

Symmetry and the R-word

"Responsibility" is the R-word that economics cannot utter. The reader is invited to find a single economics text that mentions that only human actions, not the services of things, can be de facto responsible. Apparently, economics exists in simply a different world than jurisprudence.

The basic juridical principle of imputation ("Impute de jure responsibility according to de facto responsibility") can also be restated in the language of property theory ("Assign to people the positive and negative fruits of their labor") and then it is usually called the "labor theory of property." The labor theory of property (which has nothing to do with prices) is often confused with the various "labor theories of value." The confused treatment of the two theories might be called the "labor theory."

The studied incapacity of orthodox economics to recognize the unique de facto responsibility of labor is nowhere more evident than in the conventional discussion of the "labor theory." Orthodox economics depicts adherents of the so-called "labor theory" as not understanding that land (and capital) is "productive" in the sense of being causally efficacious. They "seemed to deny that scarce land and time-intensive processes can also contribute to competitive costs and to true social costs . . ." [Samuelson 1976, 545]. Happily, neoclassical economists have taken a tip from farmers and have discovered that scarce land is useful in producing the harvest—so economics can finally move beyond the "labor theory." In the Happy Consciousness of neoclassical theory, there is no inkling that some other unmentionable attribute might be involved in addition to causal productivity.

In their defense, neoclassical economists might reply that it not *their* job to provide a "non-silly" interpretation to "the labor theory." That should be the job of the economists officially designated as the heretics, namely the Marxists. Why have the Marxists also been completely unable to utter the R-word and thus unable to provide a non-silly interpretation to "the labor theory"? One needs to understand the different social roles of Marxist economists in the West and in the East. In the West, Marxist economists are maintained in the universities essentially as nonthreatening but occasionally annoying gadflies to prove the liberalism and open-mindedness of the economics profession. In the East, Marxist economists were priests who had to adhere to their own orthodoxy. Marx could not find the R-word, and after Marx, the genetic code of Marxism was fixed. Mutations in the direction of interpreting "the labor theory" in terms of "bourgeois jurisprudence" had no survival value in the Marxist environment of the East or West.

One seemingly has to go back to the roots of marginal productivity to find any recognition in economics of the usual juridical principle of imputation. Friedrich von Wieser, the economist who introduced the word "imputation" (*Zurechnung*) into the economics vocabulary, understood that ordinary jurisprudence operates on the assumption that only people, not things, can be responsible for anything.

> The judge . . . who, in his narrowly-defined task, is only concerned with the *legal imputation,* confines himself to the discovery of the legally responsible factor,—that person, in fact, who is threatened with the legal punishment. On him will rightly be laid the whole burden of the consequences, although he could never by himself alone—without instruments and all the other conditions—have committed the crime. The imputation takes for granted physical causality. . . . If it is the moral imputation that is in question, then certainly no one but the labourer could be named. Land and capital have no merit that they bring forth fruit; they are dead tools in the hand of man; and the man is responsible for the use he makes of them. [Wieser 1930, 76–79]

Wieser was clearly aware that "only labor can be responsible" even though all the factors are causally efficacious. At least he could not claim that he "just never thought about" ordinary jurisprudence. But Wieser was not in the business of determining whether production based on renting people was consistent with jurisprudence. As any serious and substantive economist could see, normal production was obviously correct. If some principle was not in accord with ordinary production, then clearly the principle begged to be reinterpreted.

Therefore there must be some metaphorical reinterpretation to render ordinary jurisprudence "inapplicable" to the world of economics. Jurisprudence deals with legalistic matters such as property rights and ownership. Economics must probe for deeper realities. Thus the notion of responsibility used in ordinary jurisprudence would have to be replaced by an appropriate notion of "economic responsibility."

> In the division of the return from production, we have to deal similarly . . . with an imputation—save that it is from the economic, not the judicial point of view. [Wieser 1930, p. 76]

Thus deep metaphors make ordinary jurisprudence inapplicable to the world that economists live in. By defining "economic responsibility" in terms of marginal productivity, Wieser could finally draw the desired conclusion that capitalist production "economically" imputes the product in accordance with "economic responsibility."

In addition to metaphorically reinterpreting "responsibility," Wieser and later neoclassical economists also misunderstood the logical structure of the imputation question. The usual notions of responsibility and imputation are not relevant to the question about the division of shares of the product since the ownership of the product is not "shared" in the first place—except metaphorically. But if we set aside the deep metaphors and consider for a moment the superficial facts, then we will see that one legal party gets the de jure responsibility for the whole product (i.e., gets the legal ownership for 100 percent of the produced outputs and is legally liable for 100 percent of the used-up inputs). The question of imputation is whether or not that imputation of legal or de jure responsibility is in accordance with factual or de facto responsibility.

The facts about de facto responsibility are that all the people working in the enterprise, management and labor, are de facto responsible for producing the outputs by using up the inputs—so by the ordinary principle of imputation, they should receive the imputation of that legal responsibility for the whole product. That is the ordinary jurisprudential argument for the type of firm known as a worker-owned firm, labor-managed firm, or democratic firm.

The tactics of Wieser and innumerable other economists illustrate one of the basic methodological principles of the economic sciences.

Economics must not be left vulnerable to being invaded or "blind-sided" from some other field. Important questions about economics cannot be left to the domain of noneconomists. One defensive tactic is to try to immunize any invading concept by developing an "economic" version of the concept. If the ordinary notion of responsibility seems threatening, then invent a new notion of "economic responsibility" that will be the sole domain of economics. If legal notions of ownership seem inconvenient in economics (e.g., one legal party's 100 percent ownership of the whole product of a firm), then economists can retaliate by developing notions of "economic ownership." Since economic ownership and economic responsibility are defined to deal with the deeper questions facing economics, economists do not have to worry about their theories being inconsistent with jurisprudence, which, after all, deals "only" with the legal version of those notions.

Symmetry and Asymmetry in Marginal Productivity Theory

The symmetrical picture of all the factors being in the same sense "productive" is nowhere more prominent than in marginal productivity (MP) theory. The basic paradigm is that the marginal unit of a factor produces its marginal product and each unit can be taken as the marginal unit. Hence each unit produces its marginal product. MP theory is particularly weighty in the annals of the social sciences because it is mathematically formulated.

The orthodox view of marginal products is flawed on several counts. We have already noted the fallacy of personification involved in imputing responsible agency to the nonhuman actors. Tools and machines do not "produce" their marginal product or anything else. Tools and machines are used by people to produce the outputs. We have also noted that shares in the product are not actually imputed or assigned to the various factor suppliers. One legal party appropriates the whole product of a firm, 100 percent of the output assets and 100 percent of the input liabilities.

There is another flaw in the orthodox treatment of MP theory that is of interest. The ideological baggage being carried by MP theory forces it to be presented in a factually implausible way. An entirely plausible and mathematically equivalent way of presenting the theory is ignored because it does not lend itself to the same ideologically inspired interpretation.

The factually implausible part of the orthodox view is the picture of a unit of a factor as producing its marginal product *ex nihilo* (even assuming we personify the factors with responsible agency). Other factors must be used, and when the value of these used-up factors is subtracted from the value of the marginal product, then the result will no longer equal the value of the unit of the factor.

Suppose that the marginal product of a man-year in a tractor factory is two tractors. The usual treatment of MP theory would show that in competitive equilibrium, the value of the man-year was equal to the value of its marginal product so that each worker could be said to "get what he produces." That equation would hold if the annual wage was $20,000 and each of the two tractors sold for $10,000. But steel and a variety of other inputs are usually required to produce tractors. When the cost of those other inputs is subtracted, the equation no longer holds. Something has to give.

The matter can be resolved by reformulating MP theory into a mathematically equivalent vectorial form that does not picture the marginal unit of labor as producing its marginal product [see Chapter 5]. Instead, the marginal unit is pictured as producing a list or vector of positive and negative quantities. The positive quantities are the extra outputs produced and the negative quantities are the extra inputs used up when an extra unit of labor is employed (and output is produced at minimum cost). The net value of that vector is equal to the value of a unit of labor when profits are maximized in the competitive firm.

Since this mathematically equivalent vectorial reformulation of MP theory uses the empirically plausible picture that outputs require inputs, why do all the conventional texts use the rather implausible picture of each factor as producing its marginal product *ex nihilo*? The answer seems to lie in the symmetry of the implausible picture. The vector picture breaks the symmetry. Once one has told the story of the marginal worker as using up so much steel to produce so many tractors, then one cannot turn around and present the opposite picture of the marginal ton of steel as using up so much labor and producing so many tractors (leaving aside the fallacy of personification). But one can symmetrically picture both the marginal worker as producing so many tractors and the marginal ton of steel as producing so many other tractors (which then "add up" to yield the product). The vector picture leads one to break the symmetry by picking an "active" factor that is viewed as using up the passive factors to produce the output. In the orthodox view, each factor can be symmetrically viewed as being "active" and producing its own marginal product (out of nothing).

Understanding the Nontransferability of Labor

One can buy a long-lived asset or rent the asset (i.e., buy a car or rent a car). When one rents an asset, one buys the services provided by the asset within the scope of the rental contract. But what counts as fulfilling the rental contract on the part of the asset owner? To fulfill the rental contract, the services provided by the asset are transferred from the owner to the lessee by turning over the use and control of the asset to the lessee. For instance, the use and possession of a rented apartment or a rented car is turned over by the owner to the lessee or renter for the duration of the rental contract.

The employment contract is the contract for the renting or hiring of human beings—for buying the services of human beings (labor services). For human beings, one does not today have the buy-or-rent option since the voluntary sale of labor by the lifetime was forbidden along with involuntary slavery. Self-ownership is legally mandatory. We have commented previously on the oddity of the usual view that the long-term renting of humans is a fundamental violation of human rights while short-term rentals are the foundation of our economic system.

We now seek to make a different point concerning what counts as fulfilling a rental contract for human beings (i.e., as fulfilling a contract for the purchase of labor services). What in fact fulfills the contract?

If the owner of a car or an apartment rented out the asset but then refused to deliver it even though the rent was paid (e.g., refused to give the keys to the lessee), then the owner would have violated the contract. The owner would not have fulfilled his or her half of the contract. Notice that it is a factual question whether or not the owner turned over the possession and use of the rented asset to the lessee. When the use of the asset is factually transferred to the lessee in fulfillment of the contract, then the lessee can use the asset on his or her own and be responsible for the results.

This whole legal framework of the rental, leasing, or hiring contract is carried over and applied to persons in the employment contract. But the problem is that the factual question of fulfilling the contract by turning over the possession and use of the rented asset from the owner to the renter (employer) is entirely different when the rented entity is a person. Labor is not in fact interpersonally transferable. A person can at most agree to cooperate with another person (e.g., by following the latter's instructions) but then they are in fact jointly responsible for the results of their joint activity.

The nontransferability of labor is easy to "see" using the intuition pump of the hired criminal. An entrepreneur hires a person to work in his business and he also hires a van. In addition to normal business activities, the entrepreneur "employs" his employee and the van to rob a bank. When caught, the employer and the employee are both charged with the crime. But the van owner, who was not involved other than as owner of the rented asset, was not charged in the crime. The employee might argue in court that he is as innocent as the van owner. He too rented an asset to the entrepreneur and he turned over the employment of the rented entity to the employer in fulfillment of the contract. What the entrepreneur did with his hired entities was his business.

But this defense would not be accepted in court. The judge would point out that the van owner could indeed turn over the use and possession of the van to the entrepreneur and not be personally involved in the use of the van. But a person cannot as a matter of fact do the same with his own self. He is inextricably involved in the "employment" of his labor and thus he is inherently jointly responsible for the results of the joint activity.

This is a point of fact, not a point of law. Of course, the legal doctrine is that when the employer and employee turned to illicit activities then the employment relation ceased and they became de facto partners. But that is only a question of legal doctrine. The point is the facts, and the facts are not changed by the legal doctrine. If the worker is de facto co-responsible when he or she obeys the employer in the commission of a crime, then the worker is also de facto co-responsible in the commission of ordinary work. The worker does not suddenly become a machine or automaton in fact when the work is legally permitted and when the employment contract is legally accepted. Alternatively, if the employee was really an instrument devoid of responsible capacity, then it is hard to see how he or she could suddenly burst into responsible agency when the labor stepped over the boundaries of the law.

When the law is broken, then the law rejects the contractual superstructure, the law looks at the facts, and the law sees responsible cooperation. The servant in work suddenly becomes the partner in crime.

> All who participate in a crime with a guilty intent are liable to punishment. A master and servant who so participate in a crime are liable criminally, not because they are master and servant, but because they jointly carried out a criminal venture and are both criminous. [Batt 1967, 612]

When the "venture" being "jointly carried out" is noncriminal, then the servant or employee is just as de facto co-responsible for the results of the venture. It is the reaction of the law that changes. When no illegality is involved the same de facto responsible cooperation of the employee is then "accepted" by the law as "fulfilling" the contract for the transfer and alienation of the labor services from the employee to the employer—as if the employee had been "employed" as an instrument.

None of this is new. The law, of course, exhibited the same inconsistency when the workers were owned instead of merely being rented. The slaves, who normally had the legal role of beasts of burden, suddenly burst into responsible agency when they committed crimes.

> The slave, who is but *"a chattel"* on all *other* occasions, with not one solitary attribute of personality accorded to him, becomes *"a person"* whenever he is to be *punished*! [Goodell 1853, 309]

The "talking instrument" in work becomes the responsible person in crime.

Did the law of the antebellum South ever recognize this inconsistency? Sometimes. One antebellum court in Alabama held that slaves

> are rational beings, they are capable of committing crimes; and in reference to acts which are crimes, are regarded as persons. Because they are slaves, they are . . . incapable of performing civil acts, and, in reference to all such, they are things, not persons. [Catterall 1926, 247]

It is an interesting question whether or not the legal authorities of today have achieved this level of consciousness about the similar problem involved in the renting of human beings—the problem that was illustrated by the example of the criminous employee.

From the precedent of slavery we can draw lessons about today's peculiar institution of renting human beings. Since the antebellum law recognized that the slaves were in fact persons, the whole legal superstructure that treated them as things (when they did not break the law) was really a "fiction." In less kind terms, it was a massive fraud on an institutional scale. And that is the lesson that can be applied, *mutatus mutandis,* to the renting of people.

We have seen that the law is perfectly aware that the employee cooperates with the employer in a venture they jointly carry out and they are de facto co-responsible for the results of the venture—at least when the venture is criminous. And we have seen no inkling of an argument that the facts change when the venture is noncriminous. But the law then "pretends" that the responsible cooperation of the employee constitutes the alienation and transfer of the labor services from the employee to the employer in "fulfillment" of the labor contract. With the labor contract legally accepted as both valid and fulfilled, the employer has borne the costs of all the inputs including labor, so the employer has the legally defensible claim on the outputs. Thus it is that the employees have 0 percent legal ownership of the produced outputs and 0 percent liability for the used-up inputs in spite of their de facto co-responsibility for using up the inputs and for producing the outputs. And thus it is that by pretending the employees' responsible cooperation "fulfilled" the labor contract (when no crime is committed), the law sets up and allows the violation of the basic juridical principle of assigning legal responsibility in accordance with de facto responsibility.

When the law pretends that responsible human actions ("labor") can be transferred from one person to another (when no crime is committed), that is a legal fiction. It is a fiction that is set aside in favor of the uncontested facts when the law is broken. Since the employment contract is based on the fictional transferability of responsible human action, it is what would commonly be called a "fraud"—a fraud executed on an institutional scale. And, as usual, a fraud allows a theft or injustice (the misimputation of legal responsibility) to take place behind the guise of a voluntary contract.

It might well be asked: "If the responsible cooperation of the employees does not fulfill the employment contract, then what does?" Nothing does. Labor is de facto nontransferable (as was seen in the case of the criminous employee). To change that would be to change human nature. We can, in the spirit of science fiction, consider how human nature might be changed to allow the resulting "persons" to fulfill the employment contract. Suppose that some sort of computer chip could be implanted in a person's brain so that the person would become a part-time robot. When the control chip was turned on, the "person" would temporarily lose the capacity for responsible action and self-control and would be controlled as a robot through a computer. The "actions" or rather behaviors of such an individual would indeed be transferred from the original owner of the entity to the employer. Then the worker would be on a par with the owner of the rented van. "Labor" would then be de facto transferable, and the employment contract would no longer be based on a fiction or fraud.

This example can also be viewed the other way around. The contract for renting people treats people *as if* they already were such part-time robots—*as if* they were part-time things. Thus we again have the unsurprising result that renting people is treating people as things (on a part-time basis within the scope of the employment). But the reasoning and analysis that lead to these unsurprising results are unavailable to the Happy Consciousness. There is no point, no profit, and no payoff in asking such questions, pursuing such lines of thought, and indulging such speculations. It is "obvious" that the cooperation of the employee with the employer "fulfills" the employment contract.

Conclusion

Someday, the Happy Consciousness of today may not seem so "normal." Someday it will seem strange that there could be a whole society based on the renting of human beings—a society with an "advanced" social consciousness—in which that was not even considered a topic worthy of discussion by the moral and intellectual leaders of the day.

It might seem strange that a "democratic society" could be so schizophrenic and bifurcated in its vision of democratic rights that a person could be seen as having an inalienable right to self-determination as a citizen but could at the same time be routinely alienating the right to self-determination in the workplace.

We have a whole system of jurisprudence based on the fundamental distinction between persons and things—where only persons can be responsible and where responsibility can only be imputed through things back to the responsible person (regardless of the causal efficacy of the tools or things). Thus it might seem odd that we also have a "science" of economics where this distinction is unheard of, where the R-word cannot be spoken (except metaphorically), and where textbook upon textbook, for decades upon decades, present "the labor theory" as a patently implausible theory denying the causal efficacy of things without ever broaching the thought that the distinction between labor and the services of things might have something to do with the R-word.

Today, we perhaps understand the irony that the law of slavery only treated the slaves with the respect and dignity that was their due as persons when the law punished the slaves for crimes. Someday the analogous irony of today's legal system might be understood. The law only recognizes the inherent de facto responsibility of the employees for the fruits of their labor when the employees break the law. Then the law—with unintended irony—correctly recognizes that the employment contract was fictional, correctly recognizes that all who carried out the venture are jointly de facto responsible for the results, and correctly reconstructs the venture as a partnership of all who worked in the venture. Thus just as the antebellum law ironically recognized the case for the abolition of slavery in favor of self-ownership, so today's law, when it sets aside the fictions in favor of the facts, inadvertently trespasses against the Happy Consciousness and sets forth the case for the abolition of the employment contract in favor of people being universally self-employed in the types of firms called industrial partnerships, labor-managed firms, and democratic firms [see Ellerman 1990, 1992].

References

Batt, Francis. 1967. *The Law of Master and Servant.* Fifth edition. London: Pitman.

Catterall, Helen T. 1926. *Judicial Cases Concerning Slavery and the Negro.* Vol. III. Washington, D.C.: Carnegie Institute.

Ellerman, David P. 1982. *Economics, Accounting, and Property Theory.* Lexington, Mass.: D.C. Heath.

Ellerman, David. 1986. "Double Entry Multidimensional Accounting." *Omega, International Journal of Management Science* 14, no. 1: 13–22.

Ellerman, David. 1990. *The Democratic Worker-Owned Firm.* London: Unwin Hyman.

Ellerman, David. 1992. *Property & Contract in Economics: The Case for Economic Democracy.* Cambridge, Mass.: Blackwell Publishers.

Goodell, William. 1853. *The American Slave Code in Theory and Practice.* Reprinted in 1969. New York: New American Library.

Ross, Stephen A., and Randolph W. Westerfield. 1988. *Corporate Finance.* St. Louis: Times Mirror/Mosby.

Samuelson, Paul A. 1976. *Economics.* Tenth edition. New York: McGraw-Hill.

Wieser, Friedrich von. 1930 (Orig. 1889). *Natural Value.* Trans. C. A. Malloch. New York: G. E. Stechert and Company.

Chapter 2

Myth and Metaphor in Orthodox Economics*

End of the Pseudo-Debate between Capitalism and Socialism

These are interesting times to think anew about orthodox neoclassical economics. With the collapse of communism, the bipolar economic-political order is breaking down.

Suppose that the proslavery writers had managed to get "The Slavery Question" posed as the question of whether slave plantations should be publicly or privately owned. Instead of being privately owned and exploited for private greed (the "Athens model"), shouldn't the slave plantations be publicly owned and operated for the public good (the "Sparta model")?

Public ownership of plantations would, however, be inefficient. Publicly owned slaves would be "owned by everyone and thus by no one." Without clear-cut property rights and claims to the residual in the hands of an effective monitor, the slaves would shirk their duties and the plantation assets would be mismanaged. Eventually the public plantations would collapse under the weight of their own inefficiency and would thus prove the superiority of "Athenian" private ownership of slave plantations.

The Great Debate between the public or private ownership of slave plantations would finally be over. Athens and private ownership would have won. Pundits would declare "the end of history." So-called abolitionists might speak of a "Third Way" involving self-ownership but the slaves who have been reduced to near-starvation on the public plantations would not be able to afford some other "experiment."

---

*Reprinted with minor editing from *Journal of Post-Keynesian Economics* 13, no. 4 (Summer 1991): 545–64 by permission of M. E. Sharpe Publishers.

Across the long sweep of human history, the economic system with the greatest longevity and stability is slavery under private ownership. That is the verdict of history. The slaves should forget any half-baked dreams of an untried and untested Third Way. The public plantations should be straightaway privatized.

This hypothetical "Great Debate" about slavery has a familiar ring to it. With the end of that pseudo-debate, the ground would be cleared for the recognition that the real question was not whether slaves should be privately or publicly owned but whether people should always be "self-owning."

Today, the economic systems of the world are based not on owning workers but on hiring, employing, or renting workers. Today's pseudo-debate is over whether workers might be privately employed for private interests or should always be publicly employed for the public good. However, the real question is whether people might be rented at all (by a public or private party) or should always be jointly self-employed in their place of work [see Dahl 1985 or Ellerman 1990 for a discussion of an economic democracy with democratic worker-owned companies]. Now that the pseudo-debate between capitalism and socialism is over, perhaps the real question can be addressed.

Conventional economics—after over a century of the Great Debate with Marxist socialism—has developed a number of bad habits of mythical and metaphorical thought, particularly when applied to the capitalist firm (i.e., the firm based on the employer-employee relationship). Since the socialist firm is also based on the employment relationship, socialist economics has not been an effective critic.

Neoclassical economic models often seem to possess a bare skeleton of applied mathematics (various models of constrained optimization) with an overlay of shifting metaphors that obscure rather than elucidate the underlying reality. The postmodernist philosopher Richard Rorty has argued against the traditional notion of an "underlying reality" in favor of seeing "truth" along with Nietzsche as "a mobile army of metaphors" [1989, 17]. We shall argue that much of neoclassical economics already is "a mobile army of metaphors" so, by those standards, it may be very near to the "truth."

The Liabilities-Cancellation Metaphor

Applied to Stocks on the Balance Sheet

Stocks of property (three apples and five oranges) and flows of property (an apple a day) can be described in physical terms. Given a set of prices, the stocks and flows of property can be reduced to stocks and flows of value. Values are commensurate. One cannot subtract apples from oranges, but one can subtract the value of apples from the value of oranges.

Suppose an individual owns five oranges as an asset and holds a debt or liability of three apples to another person. It would not be meaningful to subtract the liability of three apples from the assets of five oranges and to conclude that the person has "net assets" of two "fruit." The individual does not just own two oranges; he or she owns all five oranges and *also* owes a liability of three apples to another party. The liabilities do not somehow cancel part of the property rights.

Given prices for the apples and oranges, the values can indeed be canceled. If oranges are $1.00 each and apples are $1.30 each then the net worth is $1.10 (but there are no "net assets").

Assets	Liabilities
5 Oranges @ $1 = $5.00	3 Apples @ $1.30 = $3.90
	Net Worth $5.00 - 3.90 = $1.10

Figure 2.1. Balance Sheet

"Liabilities cancellation" is the practice of metaphorically reinterpreting the perfectly valid value cancellation as some type of *property* cancellation so that the debtor is viewed as only owning two "fruit."

Assets	Liabilities
5 Oranges	3 Apples
	"Net Assets" 2 "Fruit"

Figure 2.2. Incorrect "Liabilities Cancellation"

Applied to Flows on the Income Statement: Distributive Shares Metaphor

The liabilities cancellation metaphor can be applied to property flows as well as to property stocks, e.g., to the income statement as well as to the balance sheet [for the physical versions of these accounting statements, see Ellerman 1982, 1986a]. Consider the usual stylized description $Q = f(K,L)$ of a production opportunity, which means that the workers and managers perform certain human activities described by the labor services L that use up the capital services K and produce the outputs Q during a given time period. If the fixed unit prices of Q, K, and L are respectively P, R, and W, then the net income or profit is $\pi = PQ - RK - WL$. The liabilities cancellation metaphor applied to the income statement yields the "distributive shares" metaphor.

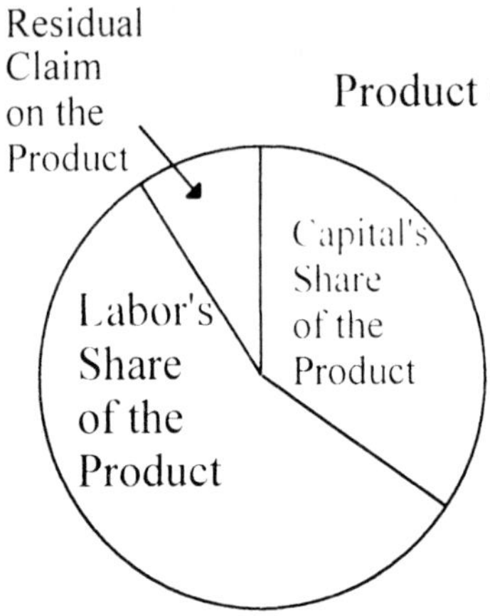

Figure 2.3. Distributive Shares Metaphor

Each input supplier receiving an expense payment is depicted as a co-claimant on a share of the product with the "residual claimant" claiming any remaining residual. The distributive shares metaphor presents the capitalist firm as some type of partnership. Each input supplier shares in the product with the residual claimant taking what is left. Attention is directed away from the structure of property rights toward the array of input prices that in part determine the "relative shares" of the product.

The value cancellation used to compute the net income is perfectly legitimate, but the metaphorical extension to a property cancellation is illegitimate. The input suppliers—qua input suppliers—do not own a share of the product. The "residual claimant" owns *all* of the product Q, not just some residual share. How can this be consistent with the income to the input suppliers? The point is that the residual claimant also holds *all* the liabilities for the used-up inputs. In addition, the residual claimant also has *all* the discretionary control rights over the work process within the confines of the input supply contracts.

The residual claimant claims not just the residual but a bundle of incommensurate rights and liabilities (Q, −K, −L) consisting of the produced assets Q *and* the liabilities for the used-up inputs symbolized by −K and −L. In the modern nonmetaphorical treatment of property rights, this bundle of property rights and obligations is called the "whole product" [Ellerman 1982]. Technically feasible whole product vectors are the production vectors used in the modern production set representation of technical opportunities. In the economics literature, a whole product vector is also called a "production possibility vector" [Arrow and Debreu 1954, 267], an "activity vector" [Arrow and Hahn 1971, 59], a "production" [Debreu 1959, 38], or an "input-output vector" [Quirk and Saposnik 1968, 27].

The Metaphor of the Firm as a "Nexus of Contracts"

The latest fashion in the "mobile army of metaphors" is the idea of the firm as "a nexus of contracts" or "a nexus of treaties" [see Aoki et al., 1989]. This should not be confused with the trivial truth that the firm lies *in* a nexus of contractual and quasi-contractual relationships with employees, input suppliers, output demanders, and governmental authorities. The idea is that the firm *is* just a nexus of contracts, a relational entity like a weekend flea market that vanishes on weekdays.

> This is the set of contracts theory of the firm. The firm is viewed as nothing more than a set of contracts. One of the contract claims is a residual claim (equity) on the firm's assets and cash flows. [Ross and Westerfield 1988, 14]

It is not easy to imagine the stocks and flows of property in a corporation like General Motors as "nothing more than a set of contracts," but apparently the idea is a wholesale application of the liabilities-cancellation metaphor. Like a liquidation bankruptcy carried out at the metaphorical level, the assets and revenues are divvied up between the creditors and suppliers. Even the residual claim—ordinarily pictured as getting what is left after contractual claims are satisfied—is depicted as "[o]ne of the contract claims." Thus the newfangled "nexus of contracts" metaphor improves on the old-fashioned distributive shares metaphor by treating the residual claim or equity as another contractual relationship.

An actual nonmetaphorical firm is a legal party that owns 100 percent of the produced outputs, holds 100 percent of the liabilities for the used-up inputs, and has 100 percent of the discretionary control rights over the work process. A legal party that only supplies inputs—such as the workers in a capitalist firm—owns 0 percent of the produced outputs, holds 0 percent of the liabilities for the used-up inputs, and has 0 percent of the discretionary control rights over the work process. Those are the actual institutional facts—not the metaphors. It is not a picture of symmetry; it is total asymmetry.

The fundamental question about production—which is the fundamental question of political economy—is the question of "Who is to be the Firm?" Capital (suppliers of equity capital), the State, or Labor (the people working in the enterprise)?

The distributive shares metaphor obfuscates the question by picturing all the input suppliers in symmetrical roles as contractual claimants on shares of the product. But the noncontractual residual claimant's role still hints that one party is not symmetrical with the others. The nexus of contracts picture mops up that untidy detail by presenting the residual claim as just another contractual claim. Then the fundamental question of "Who is to be the Firm?" has *completely* vanished; the firm is "nothing more than a set of contracts." The "mobile army of metaphors" marches on.

Laissez-Faire Appropriation

Markets transfer property rights. But to be transferred, a property right must first be "born" or initiated, and it will eventually "die" or be terminated. The birth of property rights is called "appropriation" and the death of property rights is the original meaning of "expropriation" (as opposed to the acquired meaning involving eminent domain).

In a production process, new property is created and old property is used up. In the stylized example, the property rights to the outputs Q are created and the property rights to the input services K and L are terminated. In order to avoid confusion with the acquired sense of "expropriation," we will rephrase the "termination of the rights to K and L" as the "appropriation of the liabilities $-K$ and $-L$." Thus in the stylized production example, the output assets Q *and* the liabilities $-K$ and $-L$ are *all* appropriated, i.e., the whole product (Q, $-K$, $-L$) is appropriated.

What is the legal mechanism of appropriation? When a law is

broken, the liabilities are assigned by the legal authorities through the court system. But when no law is broken, a "laissez-faire" system of appropriation is the default. One legal party buys or already owns all the (exclusively owned) inputs needed for production, and that party "swallows" or bears those costs when the inputs are consumed in production. Then that party has the legally defensible claim on the produced outputs. Hence that party legally appropriates the whole product of production.

How is the question "Who is to be the Firm?" answered descriptively in a private-property market economy? First we must define "firm" so as not to beg the question. Consider a production process that is noninstitutionally described in the usual manner by a production function $Q = F(K,L)$. Take "firm" to mean the legal party that legally appropriates the whole product $(Q, -K, -L)$ of the production process in the institutional setting of a private-property market economy. Then the laissez-faire mechanism of appropriation provides an answer to the descriptive question of "Who is to be the Firm?"—namely, the hiring party.

The Fundamental Myth about Capitalist Property Rights

The Neglect of Appropriation

Conventional economics does not even recognize that appropriation takes place in production. The nonrecognition of appropriation in production is one of the remarkable oversights of the field called the "economics of property rights."

Philosophers follow Locke and discuss appropriation as the birth of private-property rights in some primordial state where goods were held in common or were unowned. Economists follow suit and discuss the formation of private property rights out of common ownership. For instance, Harold Demsetz [1967] considers how private property in land with fur-bearing animals was established as a result of the growth of the fur trade. John Umbeck [1981] considers how rights to gold deposits were created during the 1848 California gold rush on land recently ceded from Mexico. Yoram Barzel [1989] considers how the common property rights to minerals under the North Sea were privatized. But in Barzel's book [e.g., his Chapter 5, "The Formation of Rights"] as elsewhere in the economics of property rights literature, there is no recognition of the appropriation of the outputs and the symmetrical termination of rights to the used-up inputs in the normal production process. That omission, like "the dog that didn't bark," calls for an explanation.

The Fundamental Myth

There is a "fundamental myth" accepted by both sides in the Great Debate between capitalism and socialism. The myth can be crudely stated as the belief that "being the firm" is part of the bundle of property rights referred to as "ownership of the means of production." Any legal party that operates as a capitalist firm (e.g., a conventional company) actually plays two distinct roles:

- the *capital-owner role* of owning the means of production (the capital assets such as the equipment and plant) used in the production process; and
- the *residual claimant role* of bearing the costs of the inputs used up in the production process (e.g., the material inputs, the labor costs, and the used-up services of the capital assets) and of owning the produced outputs.

The Fundamental Myth can now be stated in more precise terms. It is the myth that the residual claimant's role is part of the property rights owned in the capital owner's role, i.e., part of the "ownership of the means of production." *That* is why "appropriation" does not appear in the conventional treatment of production; the ownership of the (whole) product is taken as part of the "ownership of the means of production."

It is simple to show that the two roles of residual claimant and capital owner can be separated without changing the ownership of the means of production. *Rent out the capital assets.* If the means of production such as the plant and equipment are leased out to another legal party, then the lessor retains the ownership of the means of production (the capital-owner role) but the lessee renting the assets would then have the residual claimant's role for the production process using those capital assets. The lessee would then bear the costs of the used-up capital services (which are paid for in the lease payments) and the other inputs costs, and that party would own the produced outputs. Thus the residual claimant's role is *not* part of the ownership of the means of production.

The separation of the two roles has become clear even in the Soviet Union. Over a thousand firms in the Soviet Union are organized as "lease firms," wherein the worker collective leases the needed physical assets from the ministry [see Ellerman 1990]. Thus residual claimancy switches to the workers while the ministry maintains the ideological fetish of "ownership of the means of production."

The "Miracle" of Incorporation

This "rent-out-the-capital" argument is very easy to understand. But it is astonishing how many economists fail to understand the argument when the capital owner is a corporation. If an individual owns a machine, a "widget maker," then that ownership is independent of the residual claimant's role in production using the widget maker. The capital owner could hire in workers to operate the widget maker and to produce widgets—or the widget maker could be hired out to some other party to produce widgets.

Now suppose the same individual incorporates a company and issues all the stock to himself in return for the widget maker. Instead of directly owning the widget maker, he is the sole owner of a corporation that owns the widget maker. Clearly this legal repackaging changes nothing in the argument about separating capital ownership and residual claimancy. The corporation has the capital owner's role and—depending on the direction of the hiring contracts—may or may not have the residual claimant's role in the production process using the widget maker. The corporation (instead of the individual) could hire in workers to use the widget maker to manufacture widgets, or the corporation could lease out the widget maker to some other party. The process of incorporation does not miraculously transubstantiate the ownership of a capital asset into the ownership of the net production vector produced using the capital asset.

The Fundamental Myth in Economic Theory

The Fundamental Myth in Theory of the Firm

In the early models of perfectly competitive equilibrium, constant returns to scale in production was assumed. This implied zero economic profits in equilibrium, so from the viewpoint of value theory, it was immaterial who was the firm, i.e., who appropriated the whole product vector (since it had zero net value). In 1954, Professors Kenneth Arrow and Gerard Debreu published a paper [Arrow and

Debreu 1954] in which they claimed to show the existence of a competitive equilibrium under the general conditions of nonincreasing returns to scale, i.e., decreasing or constant returns to scale. Under decreasing returns to scale, there would be positive economic or pure profits. Hence the Arrow-Debreu model alleges to show the existence of a perfectly competitive equilibrium with *pure profits*. In the following passage, Professor Arrow contrasts the Arrow-Debreu model with the model by Professor Lionel McKenzie [1959] which used constant returns to scale.

> The two models differ in their implications for income distribution. The Arrow-Debreu model creates a category of pure profits which are distributed to the owners of the firm; it is not assumed that the owners are necessarily the entrepreneurs or managers. . . .
>
> In the McKenzie model, on the other hand, the firm makes no pure profits (since it operates at constant returns); the equivalent of profits appears in the form of payments for the use of entrepreneurial resources, but there is no residual category of owners who receive profits without rendering either capital or entrepreneurial services. [Arrow 1971, 70]

Since the whole product vectors could have a positive value in the Arrow-Debreu model, the model had to face the question as to how these vectors got assigned to people. The Arrow-Debreu model does not answer the question by postulating "hidden factors" since that would compromise the model in a number of ways [see Ellerman 1982, Chapter 13; or McKenzie 1981]. Arrow explicitly states that "pure profits" are distributed to "the owners of the firm," and that, in contrast, the McKenzie model does not have this "residual category of owners who receive profits without rendering either capital or entrepreneurial services."

The Arrow-Debreu model answers the question by assuming that there is a property right such as the "ownership" of the production sets of technically feasible whole product vectors. The train of reasoning is that production sets represent the production possibilities of "firms" and "firms" are (mistakenly) identified with specific corporations, which, of course, are owned by their shareholders.

In a private-enterprise capitalist economy, there is no such property right as the "ownership" of production sets of feasible whole product vectors. In the Arrow-Debreu model each consumer-resourceholder is endowed prior to any market exchanges with a certain set of resources and with shares in corporations. However, prior to any market activity, ownership of corporate shares is only an indirect form of ownership of resources such as widget maker machines. It is the subsequent contracts in input markets that will determine whether a corporation, like any other resource owner, successfully exploits a production opportunity by purchasing the requisite inputs.

The Arrow-Debreu model mistakes the whole logic of appropriation. The question of who appropriates the whole product of a production opportunity is not settled by the initial endowment of property rights. It is only settled in the markets for inputs by who hires what or whom. In other words, the determination of who is to be the "firm" (the whole product appropriator) is not exogenous to the marketplace; it is a *market-endogenous* determination. This adds a degree of freedom to the model that can only be ignored in the special case of universal constant returns to scale when it doesn't matter (for income determination) who is the firm. This degree of freedom eliminates the possibility of a competitive equilibrium with positive economic profits (e.g., with decreasing returns to scale in some production opportunity). Any profit seeker would bid up the price of the inputs that could be engaged in any opportunity with pure profits.

The symmetry is restored between decreasing and increasing returns. Competitive equilibrium fails under decreasing returns because everyone tries to be the firm (positive profits)—just as it fails under increasing returns because no one wants to be the firm (negative profits). Competitive equilibrium can only exist under constant returns where profits are zero. Our point is not that the idealized model is unrealistic. Our point is that the Arrow-Debreu model (with decreasing returns) does not correctly model an *idealized* competitive private property market economy. The structural modeling error is the assumed "ownership" of production set—which in turn disallows profit-seeking arbitrageurs from bidding on inputs to undertake production. Idealized competitive models should allow all forms of arbitrage [see Ellerman 1984]—including the "production arbitrage" of buying the inputs and selling the outputs.

The Imputation Fallacies of Capital Theory

Broadly speaking, capital has two types of uses, "active" or passive. Capital is used passively when it is sold or rented out in return for some market price or rental. Capital is used "actively" when, instead of being evaluated directly on the market, it is used up in production, usually along with other resources. Then the liabilities for the used-up resources and the rights to any produced assets are appropriated. Thus appropriation is involved in the active use, not in the passive use of capital.

One of the basic concepts of capital theory is the notion of the capitalized value of an asset. The definition is usually stated in a rather general fashion; owning the asset "yields" a future income stream and the discounted present value of the income stream is the capitalized value of the asset. But there are quite different ways in which "owning an asset" can "yield" an income stream. In particular, there are the "active" and the passive uses of capital. The capitalized value concept is unproblematic in the passive case where the income stream is the stream of net rentals plus the scrap value. The capitalized value of that stream is, under competitive conditions, just the market value of the asset. Bonds and annuities provide similar examples of income streams generated by renting out or loaning out capital assets (i.e., by the passive use of capital).

The capitalized value definition is, however, applied to the quite different active case where, instead of hiring out the capital, labor is hired in, a product is produced and sold, and the net proceeds are all imputed to the capital assets. When the discounted profits are included in the "capitalized value *of the capital asset*," then the role of appropriation is overlooked. One might then think that by purchasing the asset or the "means of production," one is thereby purchasing the outputs and the net proceeds—so there is no need to appropriate the outputs.

> When a man buys an investment or capital-asset, he purchases the right to the series of prospective returns, which he expects to obtain from selling its output, after deducting the running expenses of obtaining that output, during the life of the asset. [Keynes 1936, 135]

But that is a factually incorrect description of property rights. A man thereby purchases only the asset. Any further return will depend on his contracts. If he rents out the asset and sells the scrap, then he receives only the rental-plus-scrap income stream. If, instead, he hires in labor, bears the costs of the used-up labor and capital services, and claims and sells the outputs, then he receives the net proceeds mentioned by Keynes.

Another example of assigning the whole product to the capital asset is involved in the notions of "marginal efficiency of capital" or "net productivity of capital." The discount rate that discounts all the future returns (including the profits) back to the market cost of the capital asset is sometimes called an internal rate of return or average rate of return over cost. However, it is also presented as the yield rate *of the capital asset* and then it is called the marginal efficiency of capital [Keynes 1936, 135] or the net productivity of capital [Samuelson 1976, 600—where Samuelson correctly notes that it is not a marginal concept]. This usage presents the profit stream *as if* it were part of the return to owning the capital asset when in fact it is the return to being the hiring party. Thus the "net productivity of capital" is actually the net rate of return to the combined role of owning the capital *and* having the contractual role of being the residual claimant.

Professor Samuelson asserts that "capital goods have a 'net' productivity" [1976, 661] (while the other factors have only a marginal productivity), as a "technological fact" [1976, 600]. That is a clear-cut case where the *social* role of Capital as the hiring party in capitalist society is presented as a *technological* characteristic of capital goods. It is a capital theoretic version of the Fundamental Myth. Unfortunately, the Cambridge controversy in capital theory failed to uncover these basic imputation fallacies, which have nothing to do with "reswitching and all that."

Labor in Conventional Economics: Uttering the R-word

One of the most astonishing aspects of neoclassical economics is its studied inability to meaningfully differentiate the actions of persons (a.k.a. "labor") from the services of things. When burglaries are committed, it is the alleged burglars—not the burglary tools—who are hauled into court. Burglary tools are nonetheless useful ("productive") for the burglar. But only people can be *responsible*. Things cannot be responsible for anything.

"Responsibility" is the R-word that conventional economists cannot utter (except, of course, metaphorically). For instance, Alfred Marshall [1920, Chapters IV and V of Bk. VI] went to unusual lengths to note a number of peculiarities of labor: (1) workers may not be bought and sold, only rented or hired, (2) the seller must deliver the service himself, (3) labor is perishable, (4) labor owners are often at a bargaining disadvantage, and (5) specialized labor requires long preparation time. Yet none of these "peculiarities" explain why people, not things, are charged in court. Marshall could not find the R-word.

Another example of this studied incapacity is the conventional treatment of the "labor theory of value" in the textbooks. Orthodox economics depicts adherents of the so-called "labor theory of value" as not understanding that land (and perhaps capital) is "productive" in the sense of being causally efficacious. They "seemed to deny that scarce land and time-intensive processes can also contribute to competitive costs and to true social costs . . ." [Samuelson 1976, 545]. Happily, neoclassical economics has discovered that land is useful in producing the harvest so economics has finally moved beyond the "labor theory." In the "Happy Consciousness" of neoclassical theory, there is no inkling that some other unmentionable attribute might be involved in addition to causal productivity. "Responsibility" is not a concept of physics. From the viewpoint of physics, human actions are simply causally efficacious services like the services of things. In view of the physics envy of modern economics [see Mirowski 1989], economists can ignore the R-word and thereby be even more "scientific."

One of the original developers of marginal productivity theory, Friedrich von Wieser, found the R-word. Wieser even admitted in print that, of all the factors of production, only labor is de facto responsible. Thus the usual imputation of legal responsibility in accordance with de facto responsibility will go back through the instruments solely to the human agents.

> The judge, . . . , who, in his narrowly-defined task, is only concerned with the legal imputation, confines himself to the discovery of the legally responsible factor,—that person, in fact, who is threatened with the legal punishment. On him will rightly be laid the whole burden of the consequences, although he could never by himself alone—without instruments and all the other conditions—have committed the crime. The imputation takes for granted physical causality. . . . If it is the moral imputation that is in question, then certainly no one but the labourer could be named. Land and capital have no merit that they bring forth fruit; they are dead tools in the hand of man; and the man is responsible for the use he makes of them. [Wieser 1889, 76–79]

These are astonishing remarks. Wieser at last sees the explanation of the old radical slogans "Only labor is creative" or "Only labor is productive," which the classical radicals could never explain clearly. Since labor is the only responsible factor, capitalist apologetics clearly requires that "responsibility" be metaphorically reinterpreted. Simple causal efficacy must be animistically interpreted as the special type of "responsibility" needed by economic theory.

> In the division of the return from production, we have to deal similarly . . . with an imputation,—save that it is from the economic, not the judicial point of view. [Wieser 1889, 76]

By defining "economic responsibility" in terms of the animistic version of marginal productivity, Wieser could finally draw the conclusion demanded by his ideological goal: to show that competitive capitalism "economically" imputes the product in accordance with "economic" responsibility. Then neoclassical economists could use words such as "imputation" and even the dreaded R-word—metaphorically.

Metaphors are like lies; one requires others to round out the picture. The ideological interpretation of marginal productivity theory (pioneered by Friedrich von Wieser and John Bates Clark) uses one metaphor to justify another metaphor. We previously considered the distributive shares metaphor which pictured each factor as getting a share of the product. The Wieser-Clark interpretation of MP theory metaphorically pictures each factor as being "responsible" for a share of the product. And, lo, under appropriate competitive conditions, the two metaphors match; each factor "gets what it produces." By justifying one metaphor with another metaphor, capitalist apologetics can "slip the surly bonds" of reality and soar freely in the metaphorical void.

It is, however, the actual property relations of capitalist production (i.e., the employer's appropriation of the whole product) that need to be judged, and the notion of responsibility relevant to the structure of legal property rights is the normal nonmetaphorical juridical notion of responsibility that is used every day from "the judicial point of view."

Labor and Inalienability

We warm to the modernity of Immanuel Kant's call for "universal suffrage" until we see the jarring footnote "except, of course, for women, children, and lunatics"—not to mention servants (now called "employees" in our newspeak). The Founding Fathers' proclamation that "All men are created equal" similarly excluded slaves and women. When a society is based on an institutional form of dehumanization, the people born and raised in that society will see it as "natural." It is "hard-wired" into their social perceptions of reality—into their "happy consciousness."

We live in a society based on the renting of human beings, and that is perceived as being totally natural. The recent "alternative" was a society where all workers were rented by the government. That was the choice: capitalism or socialism.

Yet, something is amiss. Labor is peculiar. Being the sole responsible factor is only one of labor's peculiarities. This can be illustrated by using the case of the criminous employee as an "intuition pump." Suppose that an entrepreneur hired an employee for general services (no intimations of criminal intent). The entrepreneur similarly hired a van, and the owner of the van was not otherwise involved in the entrepreneur's activities. Eventually the entrepreneur decided to use the factor services he had purchased (man-hours and van-hours) to rob a bank. After being caught, the entrepreneur and the employee were charged with the crime. In court, the employee argued that he was just as innocent as the van owner. Both had sold the services of factors they owned to the entrepreneur. The use the entrepreneur made of these commodities was "his own business."

The judge would, no doubt, be unmoved by these arguments. The judge would point out it was plausible that the van owner was not responsible. He had given up and transferred the use of his van to the entrepreneur, so unless the van owner was otherwise personally involved, his absentee ownership of the factor would not give him any responsibility for the results of the enterprise. Absentee ownership of a factor is not itself a source of responsibility.

The judge would point out, however, that the worker could not help but be personally involved in the robbery. Man-hours are a peculiar commodity in comparison with van-hours. The worker cannot "give up and transfer" the use of his own person, as the van owner can the van. Employment contract or not, the worker remained a fully responsible agent knowingly cooperating with the entrepreneur. The employee and the employer share the de facto responsibility for the results of their joint activity, and the law will impute legal responsibility accordingly. The servant in work becomes the partner in crime.

> All who participate in a crime with a guilty intent are liable to punishment. A master and servant who so participate in a crime are liable criminally, not because they are master and servant, but because they jointly carried out a criminal venture and are both criminous. [Batt 1967, 612]

It should be particularly noted that the worker is *not* de facto responsible for the crime *because* an employment contract which involves a crime is null and void. Quite the opposite. The employee is de facto responsible because the employee, together with the employer, committed the crime (not because of the legal status of the contract). It was his de facto responsibility for the crime that invalidated the contract, not the contractual invalidity that made him de facto responsible.

When the venture being carried out is not criminous, the facts about the nontransferability of de facto responsibility do not change. It is the reaction of the legal system that changes. When no law has been broken, the law does not intervene, so laissez-faire appropriation takes over. When the employee cooperates in the same manner with the employer, that now "counts" as fulfilling the labor contract to "deliver" the labor services to the buyer. The hiring party has then borne the costs of the labor and the other inputs, so the hiring party has the defensible legal claim on all the outputs produced. Thus the employer receives the legal or de jure responsibility for the whole product.

But workers do not suddenly turn into non-responsible things when their actions are not criminous. The working employer and employees are still de facto responsible for the fruits of their joint labor (i.e., for using up the inputs and producing the outputs). Labor is de facto nontransferable and inalienable. The whole idea of a "labor contract" to buy and sell labor as a commodity—the contract to rent human beings—is fraudulent at its very roots.

Modernity and the Enlightenment Project

None of this is new. It is part of the Enlightenment project. Consider, for instance, the Enlightenment doctrine of inalienable rights based on the de facto inalienability of a person's capacity for responsible decisions and actions. One source was Martin Luther's Reformation doctrine of the liberty of conscience. It is de facto impossible for a person to alienate his decision-making power to the church on matters of faith.

> Furthermore, every man is responsible for his own faith, and he must see it for himself that he believes rightly. As little as another can go to hell or heaven for me, so little can he believe or disbelieve for me; and as little as he can open or shut heaven or hell for me, so little can he drive me to faith or unbelief. [Luther 1942, 316]

Francis Hutcheson, a teacher of Adam Smith, developed this inalienability argument as a part of the Scottish Enlightenment. Hutcheson is important for another reason. The American Declaration of Independence is one of the high points in the praxis of the inalienable rights tradition. The conventional scholarly view has been that "Jefferson copied Locke" [Becker 1958, 79]. But Locke had no serious theory of inalienability, and he in fact condoned a limited voluntary contract for slavery, which he nicely called "Drudgery."

In his important study, *Inventing America*, Garry Wills reinvented Jeffersonian scholarship concerning the intellectual roots of the Declaration of Independence. Wills convincingly argued that the Lockean influence was more indirect and even to some extent resisted by Jefferson, while Hutcheson's influence was central and pervasive. In particular, "Jefferson took his division of rights into alienable and unalienable from Hutcheson, who made the distinction popular and important." [Wills 1979, 213]

In Hutcheson's *An Inquiry into the Original of Our Ideas of Beauty and Virtue* [1725], he first distinguished between alienable and inalienable rights. The de facto inalienability argument is developed in Hutcheson's influential *A System of Moral Philosophy* [1755]. He followed Luther in showing how the "right of private judgment" or "liberty of conscience" was inalienable. He focused on the *factual* nontransferability of private decision-making power. In the case of the criminous employee, the employee ultimately makes the decisions himself in spite of what is commanded by the employer. Short of physical coercion, an individual's faculty of judgment cannot in fact be short-circuited by a secular or religious authority.

> A like natural right every intelligent being has about his own opinions, speculative or practical, to judge according to the evidence that appears to him. This right appears from the very constitution of the rational mind which can assent or dissent solely according to the evidence presented, and naturally desires knowledge. The same considerations shew this right to be unalienable: it cannot be subjected to the will of another: tho' where there is a previous judgment formed concerning the superior wisdom of another, or his infallibility, the opinion of this other, to a weak mind, may become sufficient evidence. [Hutcheson 1755, 295]

This inalienable-rights doctrine, based on the de facto inalienability of a person's capacity for thought and action, developed into the Enlightenment critique of the contract to sell all of one's labor at once (the voluntary self-enslavement contract) and of the Hobbesian *pactum subjectionis* [see Ellerman 1986b, 1990]. Adam Smith did not follow his teacher, Francis Hutcheson, in this doctrine—and the rest is the intellectual history of modern economic thought.

Postmodern criticism should not give modern economics credit for fulfilling the Enlightenment project in the social sciences. Quite to the contrary, economics has betrayed the ideals of the Enlightenment in order to better serve an economic system based on renting human beings. Economics has offered up applied mathematics smothered with a thick sauce of myths and metaphors in order to obfuscate the structure of property rights, to justify treating the inalienably responsible actions of persons as the transferable non-responsible services of things, and to apologize for the limited *pactum subjectionis* of the workplace, the employment contract.

References

Aoki, Masahiko, Bo Gustafsson, and Oliver Williamson. 1989. *The Firm as a Nexus of Treaties*. London: Sage Publications.

Arrow, K. J. 1971. "The Firm in General Equilibrium Theory." In *The Corporate Economy*. R. Marris and A. Woods, eds. Cambridge, Mass.: Harvard University Press.

Arrow, K. J., and G. Debreu. 1954. "Existence of an Equilibrium for a Competitive Economy." *Econometrica* 22: 265–90.

Arrow, K. J., and F. H. Hahn. 1971. *General Competitive Analysis*. San Francisco: Holden-Day.

Barzel, Yoram. 1989. *Economic Analysis of Property Rights*. New York: Cambridge University Press.

Batt, Francis. 1967. *The Law of Master and Servant*. Fifth edition. London: Pitman.

Becker, Carl. 1958. *The Declaration of Independence*. New York: Vintage Books.

Dahl, Robert. 1985. *Preface to Economic Democracy*. Berkeley: University of California Press.

Debreu, G. 1959. *Theory of Value*. New York: John Wiley & Sons.

Demsetz, Harold. 1967. "Toward a Theory of Property Rights." *American Economic Review* 57 (May): 347–59.

Ellerman, David P. 1982. *Economics, Accounting, and Property Theory*. Lexington, Mass.: D. C. Heath.

———. 1984. "Arbitrage Theory: A Mathematical Introduction." *SIAM Review* 26: 241–61.

———. 1986a. "Property Appropriation and Economic Theory." In *Reconstruction in Economic Theory*, ed. Philip Mirowski, 41–92. Boston: Kluwer-Nijhoff.

———. 1986b. "The Employment Contract and Liberal Thought." *The Review of Social Economy* 44 (April): 13–39.

———. 1990. *The Democratic Worker-Owned Firm*. London: Unwin and Hyman.

Hutcheson, Francis. 1725. *An Inquiry into the Original of Our Ideas of Beauty and Virtue*. London.

———. 1755. *A System of Moral Philosophy*. London.

———. 1969. *Collected Works of Francis Hutcheson*. Hildesheim: Georg Olms Verlangsbuchhandlung.

Keynes, J. M. 1936. *The General Theory of Employment, Interest, and Money*. New York: Harcourt, Brace & World.

Luther, Martin. 1942. "Concerning Secular Authority." In *Readings in Political Philosophy*, ed. F. W. Coker, 306–29. New York: Macmillan.

Marshall, Alfred. 1920. *Principles of Economics*. New York: Macmillan.

McKenzie, L. 1954. "On Equilibrium in Graham's Model of World Trade and Other Competitive Systems." *Econometrica* 22 (April): 147–61.

———. 1959. "On the Existence of a General Equilibrium in a Competitive Market." *Econometrica* 27: 54–71.

———. 1981. "The Classical Theorem on Existence of Competitive Equilibrium." *Econometrica* 49, no. 4 (July): 819–41.

Mirowski, Philip. 1989. *More Heat than Light*. New York: Cambridge University Press.

Quirk, J., and R. Saposnik. 1968. *Introduction to General Equilibrium Theory and Welfare Economics*. New York: McGraw-Hill.

Rorty, Richard. 1989. *Contingency, Irony, and Solidarity*. Cambridge: Cambridge University Press.

Ross, Stephen A., and Randolph W. Westerfield. 1988. *Corporate Finance*. St. Louis: Times Mirror/Mosby.

Samuelson, Paul A. 1972. *The Collected Scientific Papers of Paul A. Samuelson. Vol. III*. Edited by Robert C. Merton. Cambridge, Mass.: MIT Press.

———. 1976. *Economics*. Tenth edition. New York: McGraw-Hill.

Umbeck, John. 1981. "Might Makes Right: A Theory of the Formation and Initial Distribution of Property Rights." *Economic Inquiry* 19, no. 1: 38–59.

Wieser, Friedrich von. 1889. *Natural Value*. Trans. C. A. Malloch and published in 1930. New York: G. E. Stechert and Company.

Wills, Garry. 1979. *Inventing America*. New York: Vintage Books.

Chapter 3

The Libertarian Case for Slavery*

Our property in man is a right and the title to human labor. And where is it that this right and title does not exist on the part of those who have money to buy it? The only difference in any two cases is the tenure.[1]

Introduction

A prominent economist has quipped that free-market libertarianism is derived from liberalism by taking the limit as common sense goes to zero. There is an element of truth in this because what liberals take as "common sense" often turns out to be only a shared prejudice. The Harvard philosopher Robert Nozick has carried out this limiting process of taking liberalism to its only logical conclusion: libertarianism.[2] Nozick's uncompromising statement of the libertarian credo represents something of a watershed in modern social and moral philosophy because of its explicit acceptance of voluntary contractual slavery.

> The comparable question about an individual is whether a free system will allow him to sell himself into slavery. I believe that it would.[3]

It seems to be a basic shared prejudice of liberalism that slavery is inherently involuntary, so the issue of genuinely voluntary slavery has received little scrutiny. The perfectly valid liberal argument that involuntary slavery is inherently unjust is thus taken to include voluntary slavery (in which case, the argument, by definition, does not

---

*Originally published under the pseudonym "J. Philmore" in *The Philosophical Forum* 14, no. 1 (Fall 1982): 43–58. Reprinted by permission of the publisher.

apply). This has resulted in an abridgment of the freedom of contract in modern liberal society.

> Since slavery was abolished, human earning power is forbidden by law to be capitalized. A man is not even free to sell himself: he must *rent* himself at a wage.[4]

People are only allowed the temporary security afforded by capitalizing a portion of their earning power (i.e., by renting or hiring themselves out for a specified time period), but are denied the freedom of obtaining a maximum of security by selling all of their human capital. The owners of nonhuman capital (e.g., money, machines, buildings, etc.) enjoy the contractual freedom of either hiring out their capital or selling it, but state interference in the marketplace prevents the owners of human capital from exercising the same liberty. And yet the principal difference between selling and only hiring out an entity is that of selling all or only a part of the services provided by the entity (i.e., the tenure of the contract).

> The labourer, who receives wages sells his labour for a day, a week, a month, or a year, as the case may be. The manufacturer, who pays these wages, buys the labour, for the day, the year, or whatever period it may be. He is equally therefore the owner of the labour, with the manufacturer who operates with slaves. The only difference is, in the mode of purchasing. The owner of the slave purchases, at once, the whole of the labour, which the man can ever perform: he, who pays wages, purchases only so much of a man's labour as he can perform in a day, or any other stipulated time.[5]

For the worker's viewpoint, the "only difference" is not just the mode of selling if the slavery is involuntary, as in the customary juxtaposition of "free labor" and (involuntary) "slave labor." But we are discussing voluntary self-enslavement, i.e., people's sale of their labor by the "lifetime" (that is, up to some specified retirement age) instead of just by the hour, day, week, or year.

Warranteeism

Since the voluntary contracts to rent oneself out or sell oneself differ primarily in their extent and duration, what are the relative advantages of the slavery contract? People enter the marketplace with different attitudes and preferences about the holding of responsibility and authority. In the colorful but blunt language of George Fitzhugh:

> It would be far nearer the truth to say, "that some were born with saddles on their backs, and others booted and spurred to ride them."[6]

This needlessly abrasive (and illiberal) formulation of the insight should be recast in terms of the technical language used by the Chicago school of libertarian economics to explain the social function of the wage contract. People enter the marketplace with risk-preference differentials: some are risk averters and others are risk takers.

> This fact is responsible for the most fundamental change of all in the form of organization, the system under which the confident and venturesome "assume the risk" and "insure" the doubtful and timid by guaranteeing to the latter a specified income in return for an assignment of the actual results. . . . The result of this manifold specialization of function is the enterprise and wage system of industry. Its existence in the world is a direct result of the fact of uncertainty.[7]

This specialization in the risk-bearing function is, however, incomplete in modern liberal societies.

A principal failure of liberal capitalism has been its inability to provide maximal "cradle-to-grave" economic security to those who desire it. This failure has been an important force behind the development of welfare-state capitalism (not to mention socialism), where the state forces everyone to provide security to those who cannot or will not provide it for themselves. A standard liberal argument against many free-market libertarians is that the laissez-faire market does not provide adequate security for the needy. But Robert Nozick, by strictly adhering to libertarian principles, has shown that there is a free-market solution to the problem of providing a maximum of economic security to those who desire it, namely, voluntary contractual slavery. As any libertarian would expect, the problem may be solved not by increasing government interference and coercion (as in welfare-state capitalism/socialism), but by removing the legal restrictions on the lifetime sale of labor.

If contractual slavery were legally permitted, then risk averters with little nonhuman capital could utilize the free market to obtain lifetime security by capitalizing all of their earning power. American slavery, in the antebellum era, was typically not based on an explicit contract. However, some proslavery writers, such as Reverend Samuel Seabury, gave a liberal contractarian defense of antebellum slavery by interpreting it as being based on an implicit contract like the implicit social contract of liberal political theory.

> What is a competent consideration for the labor of the poor if it be not nurture in infancy, maintenance in health, support in sickness and old age, and a relief from the uncertainty and mental anxieties inseparable from the lot of those who are compelled to provide for themselves?[8]

Reverend Seabury's liberal arguments are far more sophisticated than the feudalistic appeals given by George Fitzhugh, and thus Reverend Seabury has received far less attention than Fitzhugh from liberal historians of thought.

Many proslavery writers have emphasized the risk-bearing and risk-averting roles of the master and slave. Some considered the insurance provisions to be so central to the institution that they suggested it be renamed "warranteeism."

> Slavery is the duty and obligation of the slave to labor for the mutual benefit of both master and slave, under a warrant to the slave of protection, and a comfortable subsistence, under all circumstances. The person of the slave is not property, no matter what the fictions of the law may say; but the right to his labor is property, and may be transferred like any other property. . . . Nor is the labor of the slave solely for the benefit of the master, but for the benefit of all concerned; for himself, to repay the advances made for his support in childhood, for present subsistence, and for guardianship and protection, and to accumulate a fund for sickness, disability, and old age. The master, as the head of the system, has a right to the obedience and labor of the slave, but the slave has also his mutual rights in the master; the right of protection, the right of counsel and guidance, the right of subsistence, the right of care and attention in sickness and old age. . . . Such is American slavery, or as Mr. Henry Hughes happily terms it, "Warranteeism."[9]

No one would take this seriously as a description of antebellum slavery, but recent research[10] indicates that the standard histories of the institution should also not be taken at face value. In any case, since so many people are slaves to the connotation of involuntariness in the word "slavery," it may be better to refer to voluntary contractual slavery as "warranteeism."

Some Historical Precedents

Contractual slavery existed from antiquity up to the Civil War. In Roman law, as codified in the *Institutes* of Justinian, the self-sale contract was one of the three legal means of becoming a slave. Jurists also saw some of the incidents of contract in the other two legal means of becoming a slave: being taken prisoner of war and being born of slave parentage. If the alternative was execution, a prisoner might choose instead a lifetime of servitude in return for his life. And servitude was seen as the recompense to the master for the food, clothing, and shelter advanced to the children of slaves.

In feudal times, the homage contract was a warranty arrangement whereby the vassal acquired security and protection in return for lifetime service.

> While slavery is widely accepted as being an involuntarily achieved status (although there were cases of voluntary entry and sales of children in ancient and medieval Europe), other forms of what are sometimes called "forced labor" are the result of voluntary agreement. Recently economic historians have reopened the discussion of whether European serfdom represented a voluntary exchange—protection for labor services—or whether it was a form of forced labor imposed from above.[11]

In the antebellum South, a number of voluntary contractual enslavements were secured by the passage of private bills in the state legislatures. For example, in 1858 the North Carolina legislature passed "A Bill for the Relief of Emily Hooper of Liberia," which provided

> That Emily Hooper a negro, and a citizen of Liberia, be and she is hereby permitted, voluntarily, to return into a state of slavery, as the slave of her former owner, Miss Sally Mallet of Chapel Hill. . . .[12]

In the period just before the Civil War, general legislation was passed in six states "to permit a free Negro to become a slave voluntarily."[13] For instance in Louisiana, legislation was passed in 1859 "which would enable free persons of color to voluntarily select masters and become slaves for life."[14] The racist character of these laws—and of antebellum slavery in general—would have no place in a libertarian society where the freedom contractually to alienate one's labor for any time period would extend to everyone regardless of race, creed, color, or sex.

The Classical Liberal Case Against Voluntary Slavery

What are the liberal arguments against voluntary contractual slavery? There are none that are substantial. The whole subject of voluntary slavery is usually passed over in an embarrassed silence. When liberal thinkers do attempt to argue against the permissibility of voluntary slavery, their arguments are surprisingly superficial and inconsistent with other liberal tenets. Indeed some "arguments" against voluntary slavery seem more like special pleas to the effect: "Let's just agree to rule it out for whatever reason." It quickly becomes clear that the general disapprobation of voluntary slavery is based less on rational argumentation than on an emotional reaction to the word "slavery" (with its connotation of involuntariness).

Many liberal philosophers and legal theorists have argued against voluntary slavery only because they construed slavery as entailing the master's power of life and death over the slave.

> For a Man, not having the Power of his own Life, *cannot,* by Compact, or his own Consent, *enslave* himself to any one, nor put himself under the Absolute, Arbitrary Power of another, to take away his Life, when he pleases.[15]

Locke construes such slavery as a state of war continued between conqueror and captive. There is no need to evaluate these objections since they would not apply to a civilized form of contractual slavery where both parties had certain rights as well as obligations.

> For, if once *Compact* enter between them, and make an agreement for a limited Power on the one side, and Obedience on the other, The State of War and *Slavery* ceases, as long as the Compact endures. . . . I confess, we find among the *Jews,* as well as other Nations, that Men did sell themselves; but, 'tis plain, this was only to *Drudgery, not to Slavery.* For, it is evident, the Person sold was not under an Absolute, Arbitrary, Despotical Power.[16]

Montesquieu attempts to criticize the self-sale contract on legalistic grounds.

> Neither is it true that a freeman can sell himself. Sale implies a price; now, when a person sells himself, his whole substance immediately devolves to his master; the master, therefore, in that case, gives nothing, and the slave receives nothing.[17]

Blackstone introduced this argument into English common law.

> Every sale implies a price, a quid pro quo (value for value); can an equivalent be given for life, and liberty, both of which (in absolute slavery) are held to be in the master's disposal? His property also, the very price he seems to receive, devolves to his master, the instant he becomes a slave. In this case, therefore, the buyer gives nothing, and the seller receives nothing: of what validity, then can a sale be, which destroys the very principles upon which all sales are founded?[18]

This *quid pro quo* argument is, at best, a shallow legalism (and, at worst, just a special plea). The *quid pro quo* in the warrantee contract is a lifetime guarantee of food, clothing, and shelter (or equivalent money income) in return for the lifetime right to one's labor services. Moreover, there is no more need for a warrantee to give up his personal property and political rights in the lifetime labor contract than there is for an employee to do the same in the short-term labor contract.

A closer examination of Montesquieu's and Blackstone's arguments shows that they—like Locke—objected not to the lifetime labor contract but only to the absolute slavery that permits the master to kill the slave (e.g., early Roman slavery). When Montesquieu says "To sell one's freedom," he refers to "slavery in a strict sense, as it formerly existed among the Romans, and exists at present in our colonies."[19] Blackstone makes a similar distinction when he discusses the contract whereby "one man sells himself to another."

> This, if only meant of contracts to serve or work for another is very just: but when applied to strict slavery, in the sense of the laws of old Rome or modern Barbary, is . . . impossible.[20]

Blackstone then states that the law of England abhors slavery, and that a slave becomes a freeman the instant he lands in England.

> Yet, with regard to any right which the master may have lawfully acquired to the perpetual service of John or Thomas, this will remain exactly in the same state as before: for this is no more than the same state of subjection for life, which each apprentice submits to for the space of seven years, or sometimes for a longer term.[21]

Locke, Montesquieu, and Blackstone (as a representative of the English common-law tradition) are among the founders of modern liberal thought. The case against voluntary slavery is often based on their authority. Yet we have seen that, upon closer examination, they only objected to a rather extreme form of slavery, and that they did not object to a civilized contract for the sale of labor services by the lifetime instead of by the day, month, or year.

Modern Arguments Against Voluntary Slavery

One modern legal argument against contractual slavery is based on the doctrine of specific performance. This doctrine holds that, except as an occasional equitable remedy, the law will generally require only material damages for breached contracts and will not enforce specific performance. It is argued that the slavery contract is null and void because it is unenforceable. It should be noted that the doctrine of specific performance applies to all contracts, not just to labor contracts. Hence, if a contract is to be void because it is unenforceable (in the sense of specific performance), then all contracts that require some future performance (i.e., all contracts) would be invalid. The doctrine, of course, implies nothing of the sort. In the case of the lifetime labor contract, the doctrine only implies that if the warrantee chooses to breach the contract then he or she must pay appropriate material damages (possibly over a period of time as in alimony payments), i.e., restore to the warrantor a portion of the purchase price and human capital investment.

> Thus, if A has agreed to work for life for B in exchange for 10,000 grams of gold, he will have to return the proportionate amount of property if he terminates the arrangement and ceases to work.[22]

This is effectively self-manumission, and it would be a legal possibility at any point in time.

Another argument is that a lifetime labor contract should be invalid because it involves a lifetime personal commitment. The principal counterexample to this argument is, of course, the marriage contract ("till death do us part"). Moreover, the slavery contract compares favorably with the marriage contract since the former could be dissolved at any time by the mutual agreement of both parties whereas the marriage contract cannot.

The last resort, in the liberal case against voluntary slavery, is pure and simple paternalism. People must be protected against their own judgment; people must be forced to be free.

> A . . . basic policy that is justified this way in part is the prohibition against a person's selling or mortgaging himself: Freedom is a paramount value, and whenever a person feels that he wants to sell himself for something else offered in return, he should be protected against his own poor judgment.[23]

Security—the freedom from want—is also a paramount value. By what right does the liberal state forbid the full range of voluntary trade-offs between freedom (risk bearing) and security (risk aversion) in the marketplace? Why is it good judgment for the risk-adverse human capital owner to sell his labor day by day—never knowing if he will have his job the next day, and yet "poor judgment" to finally obtain security and insure his future by selling his labor all at once?

Some reflective liberals point to an alleged analogy with suicide. Although they have no valid theoretical case against genuinely voluntary suicide, they would nevertheless be willing to coercively prevent any given suicide attempt on a paternalistic basis. But the suicide analogy is faulty because of the irreversibility of a successful attempt. As mentioned above, the slavery contract, like any contract, could be breached at any point in time by either party if that party was willing to incur the material damages.

Another reason why the paternalistic argument is given particular credence, in the case of voluntary slavery, is that slavery is only thought of in terms of the involuntary slavery of the past. That is only a failure of the imagination. It is surely not beyond the wit of man to design a civilized contract for the sale of labor by the lifetime that would contain the same safeguards as the present contract for the sale of labor by the day, week, or year.

There already exists a de facto system of lifetime employment in at least one capitalist country, Japan. This system includes many aspects of warranteeism even though it is not based on an explicit lifetime contract. For example, there are de facto penalities of social disapprobation against either party if the party "breaches" the agreement. It is most interesting that almost all observers agree that the Japanese system of lifetime employment is based on paternalism. It thus seems somewhat ironic that Western liberals should cite "paternalism" as the reason for exactly the opposite policy of prohibiting lifetime labor contracts. One suspects that the root of the matter is not "paternalism'' at all but the conditions of supply and demand on the labor market. Japan had an abnormal labor shortage in the postwar years, whereas the other liberal capitalist countries have a relative surplus of labor—or, at least, of the type of labor that would be offered by potential warrantees. Why assume the risks and responsibilities involved in buying workers when they can always be rented by the day, week, month, or year?

If there are no valid legal or moral arguments against genuinely voluntary slavery, then perhaps it can be condemned on grounds of economic inefficiency. Quite to the contrary, the competitive capitalist system cannot be shown to be allocatively efficient without permitting voluntary slavery in the system. In their celebrated general equilibrium model[24] of a competitive capitalist economy, Kenneth Arrow and Gerard Debreu prove the basic efficiency theorem that a competitive equilibrium is allocatively efficient (Pareto optimal). The Arrow-Debreu model utilizes complete future markets in all goods and services. Thus the model assumes that a person is legally permitted to sell all of his or her future labor services. If it was legally prohibited to sell certain commodities—such as future dated labor service—then the efficiency theorem for competitive capitalism would fail.

Given the conventional liberal prejudice against voluntary slavery, it is not surprising that neoclassical economists are loath to admit that their fundamental efficiency theorem for competitive capitalism requires the assumption that voluntary slavery is permitted. But some economists have been courageously frank about the matter.

> Now it is time to state the conditions under which private property and free contract will lead to an optimal allocation of resources. . . . The institution of private property and free contract as we know it is modified to permit individuals to sell or mortgage their persons in return for present and/or future benefits.[25]

Hence, far from voluntary slavery being condemnable on efficiency grounds, its permissibility is a necessary condition for the efficient functioning of the system of private property and free contract—as any consistent free-market libertarian would expect.

When all serious arguments fail, modern liberals are reduced to procedural fussing about the "quality of the consent." It should be clear by now that there are no valid libertarian arguments against genuinely voluntary slavery on moral, legal, or economic grounds. There are no valid reasons for prohibiting acts of enslavement between consenting adults. It must be concluded that the prohibition of contractual slavery in modern liberal societies is based on little more than an irrational and emotional reaction to the historical connotations of the word "slavery." If voluntary slavery is to be outlawed because of the violence and coercion that was a part of involuntary slavery, then shouldn't voluntary sexual intercourse be outlawed because of the violence and coercion involved in rape? The logic is the same in either case.

Constitutional Dictatorship

There is an analogous problem in political theory that should be mentioned. Just as liberals always tend to interpret slavery as being inherently involuntary, so they also tend to construe nondemocratic forms of government as being coercively imposed. But that is only another shared prejudice. A dictatorship, an autocracy, an oligarchy, or some other form of nondemocratic government could be based on the consent of the governed just as well as democracy. Grotius, not to mention Hobbes, was quite explicit on this point.

> A man may by his own act make himself the slave of any one: as appears by the Hebrew and the Roman law. Why then may not a people do the same, so as to transfer the whole Right of governing it to one or more persons? . . . But as there are many ways of living, one better than another, and each man is free to choose which of them he pleases; so each nation may choose what form of government it will: and its right in this matter is not to be measured by the excellence of this or that form, concerning which opinions may be various, but by its choice.[26]

The voluntaristic principles of liberalism and libertarianism do not entail that the form of government should be democratic. Rousseau saw the analogy with voluntary slavery and tried to respond.

> If an individual, says Grotius, can alienate his liberty and make himself the slave of a master, why could not a whole people do the same and make itself subject to a king?[27]

Rousseau inveighed against these contractual freedoms on the basis of the *quid pro quo* and the "poor judgment" arguments (which we have already considered). He concluded that people should be forced to be "free." But such coercion cannot be justified on libertarian grounds.

Democracy is only one among an indefinite number of voluntary forms of government, each of which embodies a different social division of authority, responsibility, and risk bearing. People should not be forced to "consent" to one form of government and thus be denied the freedom to make alternative voluntary arrangements. There is no necessary connection between libertarian principles and democracy (and thus the word "democracy" does not even appear in the index of Nozick's book).

The Employer-Employee Contract

In the free-market private enterprise system, most work is performed under the auspices of the "legal relationship normally called that of 'master and servant' or 'employer and employee.' "[28] In order to give the "essentials of this relationship," the Chicago free-market economist Ronald Coase quotes from a legal reference book.

> The master must have the right to control the servant's work, either personally or by another servant or agent. It is this right of control or interference, of being entitled to tell the servant when to work (within the hours of service) or when not to work, and what work to do and how to do it (within the terms of such service), which is the dominant characteristic in this relation and marks off the servant from an independent contractor, or from one employed merely to give to his employer the fruits or results of his labor.[29]

Coase concludes: "We thus see that it is the fact of direction which is the essence of the legal concept of 'employer and employee.' "

The free-enterprise or capitalist firm is based on the employment relation (as Coase points out). A capitalist firm is not a democracy. In the employment contract, the employees voluntarily transfer to the employer the right of government or management of their labor (within the limits of the contract). Thus the employment contract establishes a nondemocratic form of industrial government or management—a limited Hobbesian *pactum subjectionis* for the workplace—that is based on the consent of the governed. In a constitutional but nondemocratic form of government, the citizens would similarly make a voluntary transfer of the general right of government to the person or persons constituting the sovereign body. Hence a constitutional nondemocratic form of political government, a peacetime constitutional dictatorship, could be seen as an extension of the existent contractual basis for the free-enterprise firm to the overall political sphere.

It was noted above that the warrantee contract for voluntary contractual slavery would be a sale of labor services by the lifetime (or up to retirement) instead of by the hour, week, or year. It would allow human capital[30] to be purchased as well as rented like the other forms of capital.

> By outright purchase, you might avoid ever renting any kind of land. But in our society, labor is one of the few productive factors that cannot legally be bought outright. Labor can only be rented, and the wage rate is really a rental.[31]

The warrantee contract would remove this labor market imperfection by extending the duration and extent of the employer-employee contract. By allowing both the self-ownership and the absentee ownership of human capital, the full powers of free markets could be used to obtain an optimal allocation of human and nonhuman resources.

We are finally in a position to see why classical and modern liberals have not been able to express any serious arguments (*ad hoc* special pleas aside) against voluntary contractual slavery and its political analogue of nondemocratic government. Contractual slavery and constitutional nondemocratic government are, respectively, the individual and social extensions of the employer-employee contract. Any thorough and decisive critique of voluntary slavery or constitutional nondemocratic government would carry over to the employment contract—which is the voluntary contractual basis for the free-market free-enterprise system. Such a critique would thus be a *reductio ad absurdum*.

Final Remarks

There are many types of human activity that occur in both a voluntary and an involuntary form, such as the voluntary transfer of property and theft, or voluntary intercourse and rape. Since both forms occur, it is easy to separate and distinguish them, and to understand that a libertarian society would permit the voluntary form and prohibit the involuntary form. However, there are certain human institutions, such as slavery and nondemocratic government, which have, as a matter of historical fact, almost always occurred in an involuntary and coercive form. These uniformities of historical experience have led to the common liberal prejudice that those institutions are somehow intrinsically coercive. The coercive forms of these institutions have been appropriately prohibited. But the prohibition has been carried over, by the inertia of prejudice, to voluntary and noncoercive forms of the institutions.

This situation has led to what might be termed the fundamental contradiction of modern liberalism: it claims to lay the foundation for a free and just society and yet it coercively prohibits certain voluntary contractual arrangements. This basic contradiction is best summarized in the Rousseauian dictum that people must be "forced to be free."

The problem of voluntary slavery and its political analogue is the fundamental paradigmatic problem of modern social philosophy. The time has come for liberal economic and political thinkers to stop dodging this issue and to critically re-examine their shared prejudices about certain voluntary social institutions. Under the leadership of the Harvard philosopher Robert Nozick and the Chicago school of free-market economists, this critical process will inexorably drive liberalism to its only logical conclusion: libertarianism that finally lays the true moral foundation for economic and political slavery.

Notes

1. Edward B. Bryan, *Letters to the Southern People* (Charleston, S.C.: 1858), p. 10. Quoted in W. S. Jenkins, *Pro-Slavery Thought in the Old South* (Chapel Hill: University of North Carolina Press, 1935), p. 109.
2. Robert Nozick, *Anarchy, State, and Utopia* (New York: Basic Books, 1974).
3. Nozick, p. 331.
4. Paul Samuelson, *Economics,* 9th ed. (New York: McGraw-Hill, 1973), p. 52.
5. James Mill, *Elements of Political Economy,* 3rd ed. (London: 1826), Chapter I, Section 11.
6. Quoted in C. Vann Woodward, "George Fitzhugh, Sui Generis," which is the Foreword to George Fitzhugh, *Cannibals All! Or, Slaves Without Masters* (Cambridge, Mass.: Belknap, 1960), p. xix.
7. Frank H. Knight, *Risk, Uncertainty and Profit* (1921; rpt. New York: Harper & Row, 1965), pp. 269–71.
8. Samuel Seabury, *American Slavery Justified by the Law of Nature* (1861; rpt. Miami: Mnemosyne, 1969), p. 150.

9. E.N. Elliott, *Cotton is King and Pro-Slavery Arguments* (Augusta, Ga.: 1860), p. vii.

10. Robert Fogel and Stanley Engerman, *Time on the Cross* (Boston: Little, Brown and Co., 1974).

11. Stanley Engerman, "Some Considerations Relating to Property Rights in Man," *Journal of Economic History* 23, no. 1 (1973), 44.

12. John Hope Franklin, *The Free Negro in North Carolina 1790–1860* (New York: Russell & Russell, 1969), quoted on p. 219.

13. Lewis Cecil Gray, *History of Agriculture in the Southern United States to 1860,* Vol. I (Gloucester, Mass.: Peter Smith, 1958), p. 527.

14. H. E. Sterkx, *The Free Negro in Ante-Bellum Louisiana* (Cranbury, N.J.: Associated University Presses, 1972), p. 149.

15. John Locke, *Two Treatises of Government,* ed. P. Laslett (New York: Mentor, 1965), p. 325 (Second Treatise, section 23).

16. Locke, p. 326 (Second Treatise, section 24).

17. Montesquieu, *The Spirit of the Laws,* Vol. I (New York: Appleton, 1912), p. 283 (Book XV, section 11).

18. William Blackstone, *Ehrlich's Blackstone,* ed. J. W. Ehrlich (New York: Capricorn, 1959), p. 71 (Book 1, Master and Servant).

19. Montesquieu, p. 284.

20. Blackstone, p. 71.

21. Blackstone, p. 72.

22. Murray Rothbard, *Man, Economy, and State,* Vol. I (Los Angeles: Nash, 1962), p. 441.

23. Carl F. Christ, "The Competitive Market and Optimal Allocative Efficiency," in John Elliott and John Cownie, eds., *Competing Philosophies in American Political Economics* (Pacific Palisades, Calif.: Goodyear, 1975), pp. 337–38.

24. Kenneth Arrow and Gerard Debreu, "Existence of an Equilibrium for a Competitive Economy," *Econometrica* 22 (1954), 265–90; Gerard Debreu, *Theory of Value* (New York: Wiley, 1959).

25. Christ, p. 334.

26. Hugo Grotius, "The Law of War and Peace," in *The Great Legal Philosophers,* ed. Clarence Morris (Philadelphia: University of Pennsylvania Press, 1959), p. 89 (Book 1, Chapter III).

27. J. J. Rousseau, *The Social Contract and Discourses,* trans. G. D. H. Cole (New York: Dutton, 1950), pp. 7–8 (Book 1, Chapter IV).

28. Ronald Coase, "The Nature of the Firm," *Economics* 4 (1937), 403.

29. Francis Batt, *The Law of Master and Servant,* Fifth edition (London: Pitman, 1967), p. 8. Quoted in Coase, p. 403.

30. The human capital concept has been developed by Chicago economists such as T. W. Schultz and Gary Becker. For example, Gary Becker, *Human Capital* (New York: National Bureau of Economic Research, 1964).

31. Samuelson, p. 567.

References

Arrow, Kenneth, and Gerard Debreu. "Existence of an Equilibrium for a Competitive Economy." *Econometrica* 22 (1954): 265–90.

Batt, Francis. *The Law of Master and Servant*. Fifth edition. London: Pitman, 1967.

Becker, Gary. *Human Capital*. New York: National Bureau of Economic Research, 1964.

Blackstone, William. *Ehrlich's Blackstone*. Ed. J. W. Ehrlich. New York: Capricorn, 1959.

Bryan, Edward B. *Letters to the Southern People*. Charleston, 1858.

Christ, Carl F. "The Competitive Market and Optimal Allocative Efficiency." In *Competing Philosophies in American Political Economics*, ed. John Elliott and John Cownie, 332–38. Pacific Palisades, Calif.: Goodyear, 1975.

Coase, Ronald. "The Nature of the Firm," *Economics* 4, 16 (1937): 386–405.

Debreu, Gerard. *Theory of Value*. New York: Wiley, 1959.

Elliott, E. N. "Introduction," *Cotton is King and Pro-Slavery Arguments*. Augusta, Ga.: 1860.

Engerman, Stanley. "Some Considerations Relating to Property Rights in Man." *Journal of Economic History* 23, No. 1 (1973): 43–65.

Fitzhugh, George. *Cannibals All! Or, Slaves Without Masters*. 1857; rpt. Cambridge, Mass.: Belknap, 1960.

Fogel, Robert, and Stanley Engerman. *Time on the Cross*. Boston: Little, Brown, 1974.

Franklin, John Hope. *The Free Negro in North Carolina 1790–1860*. New York: Russell & Russell, 1969.

Gray, Lewis Cecil. *History of Agriculture in the Southern United States to 1860*. Vol. 1. Gloucester, Mass.: Peter Smith, 1958.

Grotius, Hugo. "The Law of War and Peace." In *The Great Legal Philosophers*, ed. Clarence Morris. Philadelphia: University of Pennsylvania Press, 1959.

Jenkins, W. S. *Pro-Slavery Thought in the Old South*. Chapel Hill: University of North Carolina Press, 1935.

Knight, Frank H. *Risk, Uncertainty and Profit*. 1921; rpt. New York: Harper & Row, 1965.

Locke, John. *Two Treatises of Government*, ed. P. Laslett. New York: Mentor, 1965.

Mill, James. *Elements of Political Economy*. Third edition. London: 1826.

Montesquieu, Michel de. *The Spirit of the Laws*. Vol. 1. New York: Appleton, 1912.

Nozick, Robert. *Anarchy, State, and Utopia*. New York: Basic Books, 1974.

Rothbard, Murray. *Man, Economy, and State*. Vol. 1. Los Angeles: Nash, 1962.

Rousseau, J. J. *The Social Contract and Discourses*. Trans. G. D. H. Cole. New York: Dutton, 1950.

Samuelson, Paul A. *Economics*. Ninth edition. New York: McGraw-Hill, 1973.

Seabury, Samuel. *American Slavery Justified by the Law of Nature*. 1861; rpt. Miami: Mnemosyne, 1969.

Sterkx, H. E. *The Free Negro in Ante-Bellum Louisiana*. Cranbury, N.J.: Associated University Presses, 1972.

Woodward, C. Vann. "George Fitzhugh, Sui Generis." Foreword to George Fitzhugh, *Cannibals All! Or, Slaves Without Masters*. 1857; rpt. Cambridge, Mass.: Belknap, 1960.

Chapter 4

The Kantian Person/Thing Principle in Political Economy*

The Kantian Person/Thing Principle

Normative ethical theories are usually divided into two broad categories: *utilitarian* theories and *rights-based* (or deontological) theories. Bergson-Samuelson welfare economics [Bergson 1966; Samuelson 1972] is a well-known example of a utilitarian normative economic theory. In Samuelson's memorable phrase, "The cash value of a doctrine is in its vulgarization," and the cash value of welfare economics is to be found in the wealth maximization of the Law and Economics approach to jurisprudence. Immanuel Kant and Ronald Dworkin [1978, 1985] are classical and modern examples of ethical and juridical thinkers using a rights-based approach. The labor theory of property and the democratic principle of self-government are rights-based theories with direct economic implications when applied to production [Ellerman 1984, 1985, 1986]. The theory sketched here integrates the labor theory of property and democratic theory into a Kantian framework.

There are at least two nonequivalent versions of "the" categorical imperative found in Kant's writings. The first version is the *generalization or universality principle:*

> Act only on that maxim through which you can at the same time will that it should become a universal law. [Kant 1964, 88]

*Reprinted from *Journal of Economic Issues* 22, no. 4 (December 1988): 1109–22 by special permission of the copyright holder, the Association for Evolutionary Economics.

The second version is the *personhood principle:*

> Act in such a way that you always treat humanity, whether in your own person or in the person of any other, never simply as a means, but always at the same time as an end. [Kant 1964, 96]

Philosophical exegesis has, for the most part, concentrated on the first version of the categorical imperative which emphasizes the generalizability or universalizability of actions [e.g., Paton 1948; Singer 1961; Gregor 1963; Wolff 1969]. But that principle is more formal than substantive. The second version of the categorical imperative, the "principle of personality" [Jones 1971], holds out more promise for substantive implications, and that is the Kantian principle developed here. The "Kantian" adjective is only for historical reference. Our purpose is not Kantian exegesis; there is no claim that the theory presented here is the "true meaning" of Kant's ethical theory.

The theory is not a utilitarian theory. It is based on the concept of persons as having intrinsic dignity, as being ends-in-themselves, as opposed (say) to being represented by inputs with certain weights in a social welfare function.

Kant used the language of "persons" and "things" to differentiate beings who were ends-in-themselves from those that might function solely as means.

> Beings whose existence depends, not on our will, but on nature, have none the less, if they are non-rational beings, only a relative value as means and are consequently called *things*. Rational beings, on the other hand, are called *persons* because their nature already marks them out as ends in themselves—that is, as something which ought not to be used merely as a means—and consequently imposes to that extent a limit on all arbitrary treatment of them (and is an object of reverence). [Kant 1964, 96; or in Wolff 1969, 53]

Therefore we will straightaway adopt the concise formulation of the Kantian categorical imperative as the following *person/thing principle:*

> Act in such a way that you always treat human beings as persons rather than as things.

The person/thing principle is sometimes used to provide side constraints on individual actions.

> Side constraints upon action reflect the underlying Kantian principle that individuals are ends and not merely means; they may not be sacrificed or used for the achieving of other ends without their consent. [Nozick 1974, 30–31]

The analysis presented here will focus on institutions, not actions, and the Kantian principle will be applied (contra Nozick) to provide a rights-based critique of institutions that treat persons as things *even with consent,* e.g., to exclude a system of contractual slavery.

Treating Persons as Things: The Paradigm Case of Slavery

Chattel slavery provided the paradigmatic example of an economic institution that treated persons as things. But what aspect of slavery constituted treating persons as things? Liberalism might answer, "the involuntariness of slavery." But the answer is inadequate. Involuntariness was a sufficient but not a necessary condition for slavery. Recent scholarship has emphasized a *hidden history of liberalism* that not only condoned voluntary contractual forms of self-enslavement or selling oneself, but reinterpreted historical slavery as being based on such implicit contracts [Philmore 1982 (ed. note: see previous chapter)].

The modern libertarian philosopher Robert Nozick argues that a free libertarian society should allow individuals to sell themselves into slavery. A people may alienate and transfer the right of self-government to some sovereign person or body such as a constitutional monarch, a body of oligarchs, or, in the parlance of modern libertarianism, a "dominant protective association" [Nozick 1974, 113].

> The comparable question about an individual is whether a free system will allow him to sell himself into slavery. I believe that it would. [Nozick 1974, 331]

Would such a system of *voluntary* contractual slavery be an institution that treated persons as things? Does neoclassical welfare economics provide an alternative critique of voluntary slavery?

An Application: Voluntary Slavery in Neoclassical Economics

The normative principles of welfare economics (e.g., Pareto optimality) do not provide an argument against voluntary slavery. The standard general equilibrium model of competitive capitalism [e.g., Arrow-Debreu 1954] allows certain forms of self-sale in order to exhibit the usual efficiency properties. The economic meaning of a self-sale contract is the sale of labor by the lifetime. In the third century, the Stoic philosopher Chrysippus noted that

> no man is a slave 'by nature' and that a slave should be treated as a 'laborer hired for life,'. . . . [Sabine 1958, 150]

In more recent times, James Mill elaborated on the distinction between buying and hiring people from the employer's viewpoint.

> The only difference is, in the mode of purchasing. The owner of the slave purchases, at once, the whole of the labour, which the man can ever perform: he, who pays wages, purchases only so much of a man's labour as he can perform in a day, or any other stipulated time. [Mill 1826, Chapter I, section II]

To display the desired efficiency results, a competitive model allows all commodities, including future-dated labor services, to be marketed. For example, the Arrow-Debreu model has complete future markets in all commodities. A consumer/worker

> is to choose (and carry out) a consumption plan made now for the whole future, i.e., a specification of the quantities of all his inputs and all his outputs. [Debreu 1959, 50]

The competitive equilibrium requires each consumer/worker to make a utility-maximizing choice of using or selling a lifetime of labor. The model thus allows contractual slavery in the sense of selling a lifetime of labor (not necessarily all to the same employer) because Pareto optimality could not be assured if certain trades were forbidden.

The theorem that a competitive equilibrium is Pareto optimal is one of the crown jewels of modern economics; it is the (first) "fundamental theorem of welfare economics." Neoclassical economists are understandably reticent to recognize that *the basic efficiency theorem for competitive capitalism presupposes a form of contractual slavery.* Some economists have been courageous enough to admit the problem.

> Now it is time to state the conditions under which private property and free contract will lead to an optimal allocation of resources. . . . The institution of private property and free contract as we know it is modified

> to permit individuals to sell or mortgage their persons in return for present and/or future benefits. [Christ 1975, 334; quoted in Philmore 1982, 52].

But such forthrightness is quite the exception. To my knowledge, the point is not admitted in a *single* economics textbook. Not one. Far from providing a critique of voluntary slavery, neoclassical "normative economics" presupposes that lifetime labor contracts are allowed to obtain the fundamental efficiency theorem.

How can a system of voluntary slavery be criticized if it really is voluntary? Liberalism has no unified answer. There are two venerable traditions of liberal thought, the *nondemocratic alienist* tradition (e.g., Hobbes and Nozick), which argued that the basic rights an individual has as a person could be voluntarily alienated, and the *democratic inalienist* tradition of liberalism, which argued that such rights were inalienable.

The Kantian principle of not treating persons as things *does* provide a critique of voluntary slavery, and it is squarely in the inalienist tradition. In brief, the argument is as follows.

> The legal role of a slave still has the characteristics of being a chattel, a nonperson, or a thing—independently of whether the legal condition of being a slave was acquired voluntarily or involuntarily. In spite of a legal contract to take on the legal role of a thing, the individual *in fact* remains a person. Being a person is not an alienable condition or characteristic; personhood as a factual status is unchanged by consent or contract. Since personhood is not factually alienable by consent, any contract pretending to legally alienate personhood would be an institutionalized fraud. Any legal system, such as Nozick's "free system," which validated such contracts would be authorizing the legal treatment of persons as things in violation of the Kantian principle.

A Kantian Analysis of the Employment Relation

If a contract selling a lifetime of labor involves treating a person as a thing, what about a twenty year contract or a contract for any shorter period? A contract to sell labor for a given period is a contract to hire or rent out the person for that period. The modern legal system has invalidated voluntary self-sale contracts, but it still permits the self-rental contract, i.e., the present employer-employee contract.

> Since slavery was abolished, human earning power is forbidden by law to be capitalized. A man is not even free to sell himself: he must *rent* himself at a wage. [Samuelson 1976, 52]

Does the Kantian analysis of the self-sale contract carry over to the self-rental contract? Is renting a person treating that person as a nonperson, a thing? This requires a more detailed analysis of what it means to possess the legal role of a nonperson or thing. The difference between the legal role of a person or a thing will be analyzed from two viewpoints: actions and decisions. The analysis of *acting* as a person versus *being employed* as an instrument is an application of the *labor theory of property* [Ellerman 1985]. The analysis of the *delegation* versus the *alienation of decision-making* is an application of the *democratic theory of government* [Ellerman 1986]. The labor theory of property and democratic theory dovetail into the Kantian person/thing principle by providing the substantive analysis of acting and deciding as a person as opposed to being used as a nonperson or thing.

Acting as a Person versus Being Employed as an Instrument

In the past, economists have wondered if labor has some unique attribute that is relevant to distributional questions and that is not shared by the services of the other factors such as capital and land. The labor theory of property is based on an answer to that question. The answer is *responsibility*. All the factors are productive in the sense of marginal productivity theory. All the factors are causally efficacious; otherwise there would be no reason to use them. But only intentional human actions, i.e., labor (in the broad sense that includes managerial actions), can be responsible. This is clear in jurisprudence. Burglars have the tools of their trade and those tools have a marginal productivity in the execution of their assigned tasks. But the tools can shoulder no responsibility for the results of their use.

> An instrument of labour is a thing, or a complex of things, which the worker interposes between himself and the object of his labour and which serves as a conductor, directing his activity onto that object. [Marx 1977, p. 285]

Thus the responsibility is imputed through the tools as a conductor or conduit solely to the person or persons using the tools.

Economists are accustomed to conceptualizing production using the distributive shares metaphor. The workers, "Monsieur le Capital and Madame le Terre" [Marx 1967, 830], are animistically pictured as "cooperating together" to produce the product. Under competitive circumstances, the product is imputed to the factors in accordance with their marginal productivity. But the animistic agency assigned to the nonhuman factors is only a metaphor (pathetic fallacy). Since the nonhuman factors lack the capacity for responsibility, the distributive shares picture cannot possibly be accurate in terms of responsibility. As in the case of the burglars and their tools, only the persons performing the activity can be responsible for the results.

One of the founders of marginal productivity theory, Friedrich von Wieser, recognized the exclusive responsibility of labor quite explicitly.

> The judge . . . who, in his narrowly-defined task, is only concerned with the *legal imputation*, confines himself to the discovery of the legally responsible factor,—that person, in fact, who is threatened with the legal punishment. On him will rightly be laid the whole burden of the consequences, although he could never by himself alone—without instruments and all the other conditions—have committed the crime. The imputation takes for granted physical causality. . . .
>
> If it is the moral imputation that is in question, then certainly no one but the labourer could be named. Land and capital have no merit that they bring forth fruit; they are dead tools in the hand of man; and the man is responsible for the use he makes of them. [Wieser 1889, 76–79]

The *labor theory of property* (not to be confused with the labor theory of value, see [Ellerman 1983]) is the application to property appropriation of the usual juridical norm of assigning or imputing *legal responsibility* in accordance with *de facto responsibility*. Legal responsibility is a creature of the law, while de facto responsibility is a question of fact. A mismatch between the two is a violation of juridical norm as, for example, when the wrong person is convicted of a burglary. In that case the legal responsibility for the burglary is assigned to one person when another person was de facto responsible for the deed.

When applied to production, the juridical principle of imputation starts with the *fact* that "no one but the labourer could be named." Only Labor (always in the inclusive sense of all the people, managers and nonmanagers, working in the firm) can be de facto responsible for the results of production. And those results must be viewed in an algebraically symmetric manner as being both positive and negative. If the outputs $Y = f(X_1,X_2)$ are produced by using up the inputs X_1 and X_2, then the positive results are the production of Y and the negative results are the using-up of X_1 and X_2. In vectorial terms, the *positive product* is (Y,0,0) and the *negative product* is $(0,-X_1,X_2)$. The total results of production are represented by the vector sum of the positive and negative products, which will be called the:

$$\begin{array}{lll} \textit{whole product} & = \text{positive product} & + \text{ negative product} \\ (Y,-X_1,-X_2) & = (Y,0,0) & + (0,-X_1,-X_2). \end{array}$$

Since "no one but the labourer could be named," the people working in the firm (Labor) are jointly de facto responsible for producing the outputs *and* for using up the inputs, i.e., for producing the whole product. Thus according to the labor theory of property (i.e., the juridical norm of imputation in property-theoretic clothing), the people working in the company should legally appropriate the positive and negative fruits of their labor (i.e., the whole product). Then the legal responsibility, both positive and negative, would be assigned according to de facto responsibility. From the legal standpoint, the "firm" by definition owns the outputs and is liable for the inputs, so the argument implies that *Labor should be the firm*. That is the pure and simple *property argument* for the labor-managed firm.

This property-theoretic argument for labor-managed firms is not a value-theoretic argument. It says nothing about prices or values. It is totally independent of neoclassical price theory or any other value theory such as the "labor theory of value" (as a value theory as opposed to an ill-formulated version of the labor theory of property). Far from implying a certain price of labor, the theory implies that Labor ought to be the residual claimant (and thus not a hired factor at all).

The argument about the appropriation of the whole product $(Y,-X_1,-X_2)$ makes no assumptions whatsoever about the prior distribution of ownership of the factors X_1 and X_2. Labor in that firm should not appropriate the assets X_1 and X_2. Instead, Labor should appropriate the liabilities $-X_1$ and $-X_2$ for using up the factors X_1 and X_2. The prior ownership of the factors X_1 and X_2 only determines to whom Labor should be liable for using up X_1 and X_2. The labor theory of property might also determine that prior ownership of factors by being applied to past production or some factors might be "gifts of nature," but that does not affect the analysis of the current production opportunity $Y = f(X_1,X_2)$.

We can establish the connection with the Kantian principle by defining how a person can have the legal role of a nonperson or thing from the viewpoint of action. Since things can have no responsibility for their services,

> persons have the *legal role of things* or nonpersons from the viewpoint of action if the persons bear no legal responsibility for the results of their actions within the scope of the role.

The previous example was the legal role of the slave regardless of whether or not the condition was acquired voluntarily. But that characteristic of the contractual slave's role is independent of the duration of the contract. It is the same if the labor is sold by the lifetime or by the day.

The employees in a capitalist firm also have the legal role of an instrument or thing within the scope of the employment. That is, the employees have no legal responsibility for, or ownership of, the produced outputs (Y,0,0), and the employees have no legal responsibility or liability for the used-up inputs $(0 - X_1, - X_2)$. The employees are "employed" by the employer (who could be individuals, artificial persons, or the state as in the socialist firm). All the legal responsibility for the positive and negative results of their actions is imputed back through the employees as a conduit or conductor to the employer. The legal "imputation takes for granted" the employees' actions *as if* they had only physical causality with no de facto responsibility. Thus the employees have the legal role of instruments or things within the scope of their employment.

Only when the people working in a firm are "the firm," i.e., when the firm is labor-managed, do those people have the joint legal responsibility for the positive and negative fruits of their labor. A simple example of a labor-managed firm would be a "self-employed" individual in a one-person business. The person owns the output (Y,0,0), holds the liabilities for the used-up inputs $(0, - X_1, - X_2)$, and has the specific decision-making control over the work process. When the output Y is a tangible appropriable product, there is no possible confusion that the self-employed person is "employed" by the customer buying Y. When Y is an intangible, nonappropriable effect, the self-employed person is usually called an "independent contractor" (e.g., lawyers, plumbers, and electricians in independent practice). When a person "hires" a plumber to fix a faucet or "hires" a lawyer to represent them, the plumber and lawyer are not employees of that person.

Agency law is concerned with cases that require differentiating independent contractors from employees. The independence test looks to who bears the costs of the liabilities $(0, -X_1, -X_2)$ and the control test looks to who has specific control over the work process (see Coase [1937]). The question of control or decision making within the employer-employee relation is considered below. Since independent contractors have legal responsibility for their outputs (Y,0,0) (albeit intangible) and their input liabilities $(0, -X_1, -X_2)$ and have decision-making control over their work, the critique developed here does not apply to independent contractors (one-person labor-managed firms), only to the employment relation.

The employee has two legal roles: the role of the owner/seller of labor services, and the role of the employee performing the labor services. When slaveowners, during a slack season, hired slaves out to work on other plantations or on the docks, it was easy to separate the two roles since they were played by different people. The same conceptual separation must be made when the labor-seller and employee roles are played by the same person. It is only in the *employee's role* that a person has the legal role of nonresponsible instrument (in the sphere of production), not in his role as a seller of labor (in the sphere of exchange).

The same person in the labor-seller's role receives the payment for the labor services. In spite of the popular but misleading distributive shares metaphor, the wage payment does not somehow "represent" an ownership share in the product. The employer legally appropriates 100 percent of the produced outputs but also holds 100 percent of the liabilities for the used-up inputs. Instead of owning a share of the product, the factor suppliers are simply the parties to whom those liabilities are legally owed. The wage payment satisfies those legal liabilities owed by the employer to the employees.

The Delegation versus the Alienation of Decision Making

We now consider how a person might have the legal role of a non-person or thing from the viewpoint of decision making. Just as a thing cannot be responsible, so a thing cannot make decisions. It is a "conduit" for decisions as for actions. Since things cannot make decisions,

> persons have the *legal role of things* or non-persons from the viewpoint of decision making if the persons are not a legal party, directly or

indirectly, to the decisions made about the services performed within the scope of their role.

When the owner of an entity hires out the entity to be used by another person, then the second person, the renter, takes over the legal responsibility and the decision making for the use of the entity within the scope of the rental contract. That is the *alienation and transfer* of decision making about the entity's use from the owner to the renter. For instance, when a person rents a car, an apartment, or a sum of money, then, within the limits of the contract, the renter decides on use. The owner and renter do *not* co-decide about use; it is the renter's decision. The owner is *not a legal party* to those use decisions.

It is important to clearly distinguish renting an entity out, where decision making is transferred, from the *delegation* of some decision making about an entity's use to another party. For example, consider the difference between loaning a sum of money to another person to invest, and delegating certain investment decisions about the money to the other person as a financial manager. In the latter case, the decision making is not alienated or transferred; it is only delegated. This means the manager acts in the name of and in the interest of the owner who has decided to follow the investment choices of the manager. From the legal viewpoint, the decisions are still ultimately the decisions of the owner. But when the money is loaned out, the borrower makes investment decisions in his own name and interests. The lender is not a legal party, directly or indirectly, to those investment decisions.

A person has the legal role of a thing from the viewpoint of decision making if the person is not a legal party to the decisions about the services performed in that role. The owner of an entity rented out is, as we have seen, not a legal party to the decisions about the entity's use. Therefore when the entity hired out is a person, the person has the legal role of a thing. The person in the role of the owner of the entity hired out (i.e., in the labor-seller's role) is not a legal party to the decisions made within the scope of the employment contract. Decision-making power is not delegated from the employees to the employer; the employer decides in his own name. The legal decision-making authority is alienated and transferred to the employer. As the decision-making power was alienated, the employees are not a legal party to those decisions and thus the employees' role is the role of nonpersons or things.

The opposite relationship between workers and the manager can be found when production is organized on a democratic basis (i.e., in the labor-managed firm). Then the decision-making power is delegated to the managers from those being managed so a democratic firm is called "self-management" just as a democratic government is an example of self-government. There is, of course, a managerial hierarchy but it is based on the democratic delegation of authority, not on the alienation and transfer of decision-making power. The managers exercise their delegated decision-making authority in the name of those managed. In delegating that authority, the workers have decided to follow the choices of the managers so the decisions are ultimately the decisions of the workers themselves. Each worker is thus *directly or indirectly a legal party* to the decision making about their actions. In a democratic organization, the decisions about the people being governed are directly or indirectly (i.e., through delegation) the decisions of those being governed; that is the basic idea of *self*-government. And that is the fundamental *democratic argument* for the labor-managed firm.

The acid test to differentiate delegated from alienated decision making is the question of in whose name does the decision maker decide. The democratic leader decides in the name of the members of the democratic polity while the employer, like a monarch or Hobbesian sovereign, decides in his own name. It may well happen that the employer will delegate some authority to the employees over the specifics of their work. That does not reverse or cancel the original alienation of authority from the employees to employer. The employee then acts in the employer's name, not in his own name.

The analysis of delegated versus alienated decision making descends from democratic theory in the inalienist tradition of liberal thought [Ellerman 1986]. The alternative alienist tradition also founded government on consent, on a voluntary contract, the *pactum subjectionis,* which alienated and transferred the right to govern to the sovereign who governed in his own name. The democratic inalienist tradition argued that the *pactum subjectionis* was only a collective version of the self-enslavement contract. Similarly, it cast people in the legal role of nonpersons without legal decision-making capacity. Since people in fact remained fully capacitated persons, the *pactum subjectionis* was invalid under natural law. The rights to self-government are inalienable. Instead of the social contract of subjugation, the inalienist tradition founded government on the democratic constitution, which secured rather than alienated the right to self-government and which delegated certain decision-making powers to duly authorized governing bodies.

Both the alienist and inalienist traditions of liberal thought based government on consent. The real debate was over whether or not the social contract could alienate basic rights. Could it alienate the decision-making powers to the government, or must it be only a delegation?

> This dispute also reaches far back into the Middle Ages. It first took a strictly juristic form in the dispute . . . as to the legal nature of the ancient "translatio imperii" from the Roman people to the Princeps. One school explained this as a definitive and irrevocable alienation of power, the other as a mere concession of its use and exercise. . . . On the one hand from the people's abdication the most absolute sovereignty of the prince might be deduced, . . . On the other hand the assumption of a mere "concessio imperii" led to the doctrine of popular sovereignty. [Gierke 1966, pp. 93–94]

This ancient *translatio*-or-*concessio* debate continues today in the workplace. There are two opposite models of production. There is the capitalist firm (including the state-socialist firm) where the legal decision-making power is alienated ("translatio") to the employer. And there is the democratic firm where the decision-making power is delegated ("concessio") to management from those being managed.

One must be careful to distinguish between a person's legal role and the person's factual role. In spite of the legal role of a nonperson, the slave in fact remained a person. The same holds for the employee's role. The employee is in fact not a conduit of responsibility; the employee inexorably remains a de facto responsible person. The employees, together with any working managers-employers, are de facto co-responsible for the results of their actions. And the same holds for decisions. The employee is not in fact a transmission belt for decisions; the employee inexorably remains a deciding agent. In performing work, the employees are in fact constantly accepting and ratifying the decisions of the employers. It is only in their *legal role* that the employees have *no legal responsibility* for their actions and are *not a legal party* to the decisions. The role mismatch between the legal and factual roles is the basis for the normative critique of the legal institution of renting human beings. There is no wrong in legally treating things as things; the problem is legally treating persons as things.

Final Remarks

Our purpose has been to outline the application of the Kantian person/thing principle to normative political economy. The Kantian principle is to treat human beings as persons rather than as things. When developed and refined, the labor theory of property and democratic theory fit precisely into the Kantian principle by analyzing, from the respective viewpoints of actions and decisions, how persons could have the legal role of nonpersons or things. The theory was applied not only to a contractual form of slavery where labor is sold by the lifetime but to our present system of production based on renting or hiring people.

Employees are not a legal party to the decisions about their actions, and the employees have no legal responsibility for the results of their actions. On both counts, when a person is rented, the person takes on the legal role of a thing. But in spite of that legal contractual role, the individual remains a person. Therefore such contracts to voluntarily take on the legal role of a nonperson or thing are inherently invalid. The rights that the contracts pretend to alienate are thus inalienable. The democratic inalienable-rights tradition of liberal thought contributes that heritage to normative political economic theory.

References

Arrow, K. J., and Debreu, G. 1954. "Existence of an Equilibrium for a Competitive Economy." *Econometrica* 22:265–290.

Bergson, Abram. 1966. *Essays in Normative Economics*. Cambridge, Mass.: Harvard University Press.

Coase, R. H. 1937. "The Nature of the Firm." *Economica* 4:386–405.

Christ, Carl F. 1975. "The Competitive Market and Optimal Allocative Efficiency." In *Competing Philosophies in American Political Economics*, ed. John Elliott and John Cownie, 332–38. Pacific Palisades, Calif.: Goodyear.

Debreu, G. 1959. *Theory of Value*. New York: John Wiley & Sons.

Dworkin, Ronald. 1978. *Taking Rights Seriously*. Cambridge, Mass.: Harvard University Press.

———. 1985. *A Matter of Principle*. Cambridge, Mass.: Harvard University Press.

Ellerman, David P. 1983. "Marxian Exploitation Theory: A Brief Exposition, Analysis, and Critique." *The Philosophical Forum* 14, nos. 3–4 (Spring-Summer): 315–33.

———. 1984. "Theory of Legal Structure: Worker Cooperatives." *Journal of Economic Issues* 18, no. 3 (September): 861–91.

———. 1985. "On the Labor Theory of Property." *The Philosophical Forum* 16, no. 4 (Summer): 293–326.

———. 1986. "The Employment Contract and Liberal Thought." *Review of Social Economy* 44, no. 1 (April): 13–39.

Gierke, Otto von. 1966. *The Development of Political Theory*. Trans. B. Freyd. New York: Howard Fertig.

Gregor, Mary J. 1963. *Laws of Freedom*. New York: Barnes & Noble.

Jones, Hardy E. 1971. *Kant's Principle of Personality*. Madison: University of Wisconsin Press.

Kant, Immanuel. 1964. *Groundwork of the Metaphysic of Morals*. Trans. H. J. Paton. New York: Harper Torchbooks.

Marx, Karl. 1977. *Capital*, Volume I. Trans. Ben Fowkes. New York: Vintage Books.

———. 1967. *Capital,* Volume III. New York: International Publishers.

Mill, James. 1826. *Elements of Political Economy*. Third edition. London.

Nozick. Robert. 1974. *Anarchy, State, and Utopia*. New York: Basic Books.

Paton, H. J. 1948. *The Categorical Imperative*. Chicago: University of Chicago Press.

Philmore, J. 1982. "The Libertarian Case for Slavery: A Note on Nozick." *The Philosophical Forum* 14, no. 1 (Fall): 43–58 [see Chapter 3, this volume].

Sabine, George H. 1958. *A History of Political Theory*. New York: Henry Holt and Company.

Samuelson, P. A. 1972. *Foundations of Economic Analysis*. New York: Atheneum.

———. 1976. *Economics*. Tenth edition. New York: McGraw-Hill.

Singer, Marcus G. 1961. *Generalization in Ethics*. New York: Knopf.

Wieser, Friedrich von. 1889. *Natural Value*. Trans. C.A. Malloch. New York: G. E. Stechert and Company [1930].

Wolff, Robert Paul, ed. 1969. *Kant: Foundations of the Metaphysics of Morals*. Indianapolis: Bobbs-Merrill.

Chapter 5

Are Marginal Products Created *Ex Nihilo*?

The Conventional Picture of Marginal Products Created *Ex Nihilo*

Marginal productivity (MP) theory has always played a larger importance in orthodox economics than could be justified by its purely analytical role. This is because MP theory is conventionally interpreted as showing that, in competitive equilibrium, "each factor gets what it is responsible for producing." The marginal unit of a factor is seen as being responsible for producing the marginal productivity of that factor, and each unit could be taken as the marginal unit. Consider the marginal product of labor MP_L. In competitive equilibrium, the value of the marginal product of labor $p \cdot MP_L$ (where p is the unit price of the output) is equal to w (the unit price of labor):

$$p \cdot MP_L = w$$

"Value of what a unit produces" = "Value received by a unit of the factor."

There are many problems in this conventional interpretation of MP theory [see, for example, Chapter 12 in Ellerman 1992]. Our purpose is to highlight an internal incoherence in the conventional treatment, to show how this difficulty can be overcome in a mathematically equivalent reformulation of MP theory, and to note how this reformulation leads to a rather different interpretation of the theory.

The problem (or internal incoherence) in the usual treatment is simply that a unit of a factor cannot produce its marginal product out of nothing. The factor must simultaneously use some of the other factors. If the marginal product of one man-year in a tractor factory is one tractor, how can a tractor be produced without using steel, rubber, energy, and so forth? But when that concurrent factor usage is taken into account ("priced out"), then the usual equations must be significantly reformulated. A new vectorial notion of the marginal product, the "marginal whole product," must be used in place of the conventional scalar "marginal product."

Before turning to the vectorial treatment of marginal products we must remove the seeming paradox in the scalar treatment. When we increase the labor in a tractor factory to produce more tractors, we will also have to increase the steel, rubber, energy, and other inputs necessary to produce tractors. That would spoil the attempt to take the increase in tractor output as the result of solely the increase in labor. But the so-called "marginal product of labor" is the result of a somewhat different hypothetical or conjectural change in production. It is assumed that factors are substitutable. To arrive at the "marginal product of labor" we must consider two changes: an increase in labor and a shift to a slightly more labor-intensive production technique so that the increased labor can be used together with exactly the same total amounts of the other factors. Since (following the hypothetical production shift) the other factors are used in the same total amounts, the extra output is then viewed as the "product" of the extra unit of labor, as if the extra product was produced *ex nihilo*.

Symmetry Restored: The Pluses and Minuses of Production

Nothing is produced *ex nihilo*. Labor cannot produce tractors without actually using other inputs. Production needs to be conceptualized in an algebraically symmetric manner. That is, there are both positive results (produced outputs) and negative results (used-up inputs), and they can be considered symmetrically.

For a nontechnical presentation, let $Q = f(K,L)$ be a production function with p, r, and w as the unit prices of the outputs Q, the capital services K, and the labor services L respectively. The outputs Q are the positive product of production but there is also a negative product, namely the used-up capital and labor services K and L. Lists or vectors with three components can be used with the outputs, capital services, and labor services listed in that order. The *positive product* would be represented as $(Q,0,0)$. The *negative product* signifying the used-up or consumed inputs could be represented as $(0,-K,-L)$. The comprehensive and algebraically symmetric notion of the product is obtained as the (component-wise) sum of the positive and negative products. It might be called the *whole product*.

$$(Q,-K,-L) = (Q,0,0) + (0,-K,-L)$$

Equation 5.1. Whole Product = Positive Product + Negative Product

The unit prices can also be arranged in a list or vector, the *Price vector* **P** = (p,r,w) [where symbols for vectors are in bold]. The product of a price vector times a quantity vector (such as the whole product vector) is the sum of the component-wise products of prices times quantities. That sum is the value of the quantity vector.

$$\mathbf{P}\cdot(Q,0,0) = (p,r,w)\cdot(Q,0,0) = pQ$$

Equation 5.2. Value of Positive Product = Revenue

$$\mathbf{P}\cdot(0,-K,-L) = (p,r,w)\cdot(0,-K,-L) = -(rK+wL)$$

Equation 5.3. Value of Negative Product = Expenses

$$\mathbf{P}\cdot(Q,-K,-L) = (p,r,w)\cdot(Q,-K,-L) = pQ - (rK+wL)$$

Equation 5.4. Value of Whole Product = Profit

Marginal Whole Products

The alternative presentation of MP theory uses the marginal version of the whole product, which we will call the "marginal whole product." The precise mathematical development is given in the Appendix. Here we develop a heuristic discrete treatment. Given the input prices and a given level of output Q_0, there are input levels K_0 and L_0 that produce Q_0 at minimum cost $C_0 = rK_0 + wL_0$.

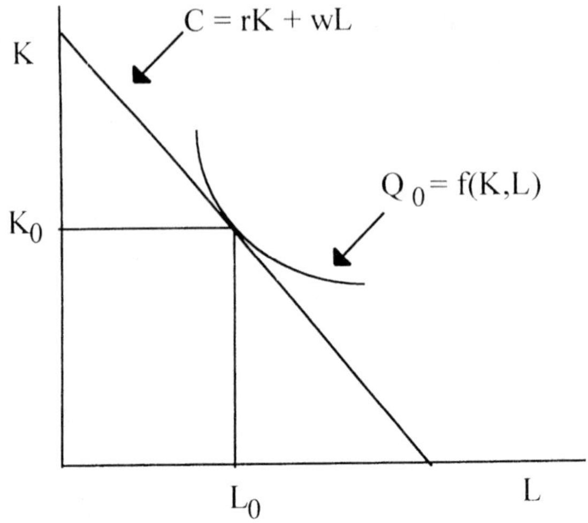

Figure 5.1. Minimum Cost to Produce Quantity Q_0

For an increase of one unit to $Q_1 = Q_0 + 1$, there will be new levels of K_1 and L_1 necessary to produce Q_1 at minimum cost.

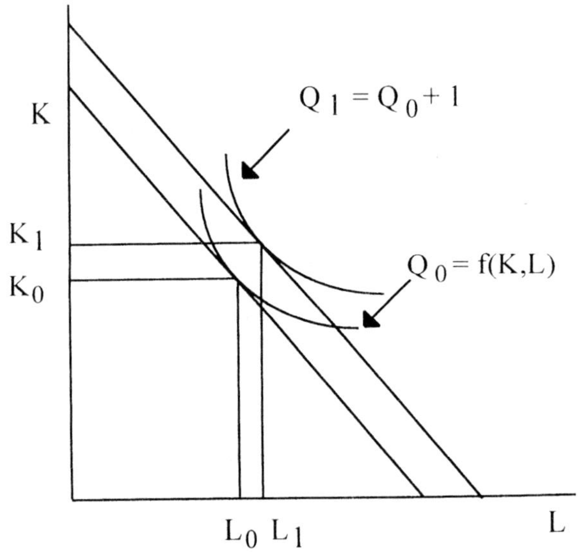

Figure 5.2. New Levels of K and L to Produce $Q_1 = Q_0 + 1$

Let $\Delta K = K_1 - K_0$ and $\Delta L = L_1 - L_0$ be the marginal increases in the amounts of capital and labor services that are necessary to produce the increase in output $\Delta Q = Q_1 - Q_0 = 1$. The minimum cost of producing Q_1 is $C_1 = rK_1 + wL_1$. Since $\Delta Q = 1$, the *marginal cost* is $MC = \Delta C/\Delta Q = \Delta C = C_1 - C_0 = rK_1 + wL_1 - (rK_0 + wL_0)$.

The marginal version of the whole product is the marginal whole product which has unit output and minus the inputs necessary to produce one more unit of output at minimum cost.

$$\mathbf{MWP} = (1, -\Delta K, -\Delta L).$$

Equation 5.5. Marginal Whole Product

The value of the marginal whole product is the marginal profit, the difference between price and marginal cost.

$$\mathbf{P} \cdot (1, -\Delta K, -\Delta L) = (p, r, w) \cdot (1, -\Delta K, -\Delta L)$$

$$= p - [(rK_1 + wL_1) - (rK_0 + wL_0)] = p - MC.$$

Equation 5.6. Value of Marginal Whole Product is Marginal Profit

If the marginal profit was positive at a given level of output, then profits could be increased by increasing the level of output. If the marginal profit was negative, then profits would increase by decreasing the level of output. Thus if profits are at a maximum, then the marginal profit must be zero. This is the usual result that $p = MC$ if profits are at a maximum.

Asymmetry Between Responsible and Non-Responsible Factors

Part of the poetic charm of the conventional presentation of MP theory was that it allowed each factor to be pictured as *active*—as being *responsible* for producing its own marginal product. But we have noted the technical absurdity of, say, labor producing tractors out of nothing else. Labor must use up steel, rubber, and other inputs to produce tractors. But if that is accepted, then it is implausible to turn around and pretend that another factor is also active—that steel uses up labor, rubber, and other factors to produce tractors.

MP theory, as an analytical economic theory, does not provide any distinction between responsible or non-responsible factors. Those notions must be imported. "Responsibility" is a legal-jurisprudential notion. Poetic license and pathetic fallacy aside, only human actions can be responsible for anything. For example, the tools of the burglary trade certainly have a causal efficacy ("productivity"), but only the burglar can be charged with responsibility for the crime. The responsibility is imputed back through the tools (as "responsibility conduits") to the human user. Thus from the viewpoint of the juridical principle of imputation ("Assign legal rights and liabilities to the de facto responsible agents"), only human actions or "labor" (including managers) should legally own and be liable respectively for the positive and negative of production, i.e., for the whole product [see Ellerman 1992].

Since MP theory does not, by itself, provide any concept of "responsible" factors, any factor or factors could be taken as the responsible factors for analytical purposes. In the mathematical appendix, the factors $x_1,\ldots,x_n$ will not be identified (as capital, labor, etc.), and we will arbitrarily take the first factor as being responsible. In our nontechnical presentation where the factors are identified, labor will be taken as the responsible factor (but the formalism would be the same, *mutatis mutandis,* for any other choice).

As the responsible factor produces the outputs (produces the positive product), it must also use up the inputs (produce the negative product). We must calculate the positive and negative product of the marginal unit of the responsible factor, labor. We will call the vector of positive and negative marginal results of labor, the "marginal whole product of labor." The marginal whole product of labor is then compared with the opportunity cost of labor (the wage w in the model).

The marginal quantities $\Delta Q = 1$, ΔK, and ΔL that appear in the marginal whole product can be used to form the ratios $\Delta Q/\Delta K$ and $\Delta Q/\Delta L$. But these ratios are **not** the marginal products. For instance, if labor is increased by this ΔL, then an additional ΔK must be used up to produce one more unit of output ($\Delta Q = 1$) in a cost-minimizing manner. The usual "marginal product" of labor is the extra product produced per extra unit of labor if the production technique is shifted so that no more extra capital is used.

In our simple model, the marginal results of labor can be calculated by dividing the marginal whole product through by ΔL to obtain $(1/\Delta L, -\Delta K/\Delta L, -1)$. Since labor also creates the marginal unit of labor $(0, 0, 1)$, the *marginal whole product of labor* is the following vector sum.

$$\mathbf{MWP_L} = (1/\Delta L, -\Delta K/\Delta L, 0)$$

$$= (1/\Delta L, -\Delta K/\Delta L, -1) + (0, 0, 1).$$

Equation 5.7. Marginal Whole Product of Labor

Multiplying through by the prices yields the corresponding value.

$$\mathbf{P{\cdot}MWP_L} = (p,r,w){\cdot}(1/\Delta L, -\Delta K/\Delta L, 0)$$

$$= (p - r\Delta K)/\Delta L = w + (p - MC)/\Delta L.$$

Equation 5.8. Value of Marginal Whole Product of Labor

If $\mathbf{P{\cdot}MWP_L}$ (the value of the fruits of the marginal unit of labor) exceeds w (the opportunity cost of the marginal unit of labor), then it is profitable to increase the use of labor to produce more output by using up more capital services. Conversely, if $\mathbf{P{\cdot}MWP_L}$ is less then w, then the use of the marginal unit of labor does not cover its opportunity cost so it would be better to reduce the level of labor. Thus for profits to be maximized, the value of the marginal whole product of labor must equal the opportunity of labor.

$$\mathbf{P{\cdot}MWP_L} = w.$$

Equation 5.9. Profit Max Implies:
Value of Marginal Whole Product of Labor = Wage

Since $\mathbf{P{\cdot}MWP_L} = w + (p - MC)/\Delta L$, the above result is equivalent to the previous $p = MC$.

Comparison of the Two Treatments of MP Theory

We have given an alternative treatment of MP theory. This treatment uses the juridical notion of the responsible factor (here taken as labor) to organize the presentation. The crux of the two presentations is in the two marginal conditions concerning labor:

Conventional labor equation:	$p{\cdot}MP_L = w$
Alternative labor equation:	$\mathbf{P{\cdot}MWP_L} = w.$

Figure 5.3. Comparison of Two Equations for Labor

When costs are minimized, both labor conditions are equivalent to the familiar profit maximization condition $p = MC$.

In the conventional labor equation, p and MP_L (as well as w) are scalars. In the alternative equation, **P** and $\mathbf{MWP_L}$ are vectors (while w remains a scalar). The conventional interpretation of MP_L pictures labor as producing marginal products without using up any inputs ("virgin birth of marginal products"). The marginal whole product of labor $\mathbf{MWP_L}$ gives the picture of the marginal effect of labor as producing outputs by using up other inputs.

Since the alternative presentation gives a more realistic treatment of marginal production, one might ask why it isn't used. One "problem" in the alternative treatment is that it introduces an asymmetry between labor and the nonhuman factors—or in more abstract terms, between the responsible and non-responsible factors. Since conventional production is based on all factors being treated symmetrically as being legally rentable or hirable, it is inconvenient to have a theory that suggests an alternative arrangement [as in Ellerman 1992].

One could, of course, take capital services as the active or responsible factor, define the marginal whole product of capital as $\mathbf{MWP_K} = (1/\Delta K, 0, -\Delta L/\Delta K)$, and then show that the following condition is also equivalent to profit maximization (when costs are minimized).

$$P \cdot \mathbf{MWP_K} = r$$

Equation 5.10. Profit Max Implies:
Value of Marginal Whole Product of Capital = Rental

But instead of restoring a peaceful symmetry, this only highlights the conflict since one cannot plausibly represent both capital as producing the product by using labor, and labor as producing the product by using capital. MP theory itself provides no grounds for choosing one of the conflicting pictures over the other—for choosing the picture of the burglar using the tools to commit the crime over the picture of the tools using the burglar to commit the crime. The distinction between the two pictures comes from jurisprudence, not from economics.

The conventional treatment of MP theory is clearly superior in terms of a "symmetrical" treatment of persons and things. The marginal unit of each factor can be presented as producing its marginal product (immaculately without using other inputs). The same picture can be used for each factor without any conflict.

Since the alternative treatment that acknowledges that marginal products cannot be produced *ex nihilo* seems superior on empirical grounds, orthodox economics would indeed seem to choose the conventional treatment of MP theory over the mathematically equivalent alternative treatment on "nonempirical" grounds.

Appendix

Standard MP Theory

Let $y = f(x_1,\ldots,x_n)$ be a smooth neoclassical production function with p as the competitive unit price of the output y and $w_1,\ldots,w_n$ as the respective competitive unit prices of the inputs $x_1,\ldots,x_n$. The cost minimization problem involves the input prices and a given level of output y_0:

$$\text{minimize:} \quad C = \sum_{i=1}^{n} w_i x_i$$

$$\text{subject to:} \quad y_0 = f(x_1,\ldots,x_n)$$

Figure 5.4. Minimize Cost to Product Given Output

Forming the lagrangian

$$L = \sum w_i x_i + \lambda[y_0 - f(x_1,\ldots,x_n)],$$

the first-order conditions

$$\partial L / \partial x_i = w_i - \lambda \, \partial f / \partial x_i = 0 \ \text{ for } \ i = 1,\ldots,n$$

$$\text{solve to: } \lambda = \frac{w_1}{\partial f / \partial x_1} = \cdots = \frac{w_n}{\partial f / \partial x_n}.$$

Equation 5.11.
First-Order Conditions for Cost Minimization

These equations together with the production function determine the n unknowns $x_1,\ldots,x_n$. Varying the input prices and level of output parametrically determines the *conditional factor demand functions:*

$$\begin{aligned} x_1 &= \varphi_1(w_1,\ldots,w_n,y) \\ &\vdots \\ x_n &= \varphi_n(w_1,\ldots,w_n,y). \end{aligned}$$

Equation 5.12. Conditional Factor Demand Functions

These functions give the optimum level of the inputs to minimize the cost to produce the given level of output at the given input prices. Taking the input prices as fixed parameters, we can write the conditional factor demand functions as $x_i = \varphi_i(y)$ for $i = 1,\ldots,n$. These functions define the cost-minimizing *expansion path* through input space parameterized by the level of output. Substituting into the sum for total costs yields the

$$C(y) = \sum w_i \varphi_i(y).$$

Equation 5.13. Cost Function

Differentiation by y yields the marginal cost function.

$$MC = \frac{dC}{dy} = \sum w_i \frac{\partial \varphi_i}{\partial y}.$$

Equation 5.14. Marginal Cost

The factor demand functions can also be substituted into the production function to obtain the identity:

$$y \equiv f(\varphi_1(y),\ldots,\varphi_n(y)).$$

Differentiating both sides with respect to y yields the useful equation:

$$1 = \sum_{i=1}^{n} \frac{\partial f}{\partial x_i} \frac{\partial \varphi_i}{\partial y}.$$

Multiplying both sides by the lagrange multiplier allows us to identify it as the marginal cost.

$$\lambda = \sum_{i=1}^{n} \left(\lambda \frac{\partial f}{\partial x_i} \right) \frac{\partial \varphi_i}{\partial y} = \sum w_i \frac{\partial \varphi_i}{\partial y} = MC.$$

Equation 5.15. Lagrange Multiplier of Min Cost Problem is Marginal Cost

Using the customary marginal product notation, $MP_i = \partial f / \partial x_i$ for $i = 1,\ldots,n$, the first order conditions for cost minimization can be written as:

$$MC = \frac{w_1}{MP_1} = \cdots = \frac{w_n}{MP_n}.$$

Equation 5.16. Cost Minimization Conditions

The marginal products should not be confused with the reciprocals of the factor demand functions:

$$\frac{\partial f}{\partial x_i} \neq 1 \Big/ \frac{\partial \varphi_i}{\partial y}.$$

The marginal product of x_i gives the marginal increase in y when there is both a marginal increase in x_i and a shift to a more x_i-intensive production technique so that exactly the same amount of the other inputs is used. No factor prices or cost minimization is involved in the definition. The reciprocal of $\partial\varphi_i/\partial y$ gives the marginal increase in y associated with a marginal increase in x_i when there is a corresponding increase in the other inputs so as to produce the new output at minimum cost.

MP Theory with Product Vectors

For the inclusive algebraically symmetric notion of the product, we will use vectors with the outputs listed first followed by components for the inputs. The *positive product* is $(y,0,\ldots,0)$, the *negative product* is $(0,-x_1,\ldots,-x_n)$, and their sum is the

$$\mathbf{WP} = (y,-x_1,\ldots,-x_n).$$

Equation 5.17. Whole Product Vector **WP**

The whole product vector is usually called the "production vector" or "net output vector" [Varian 1984, 8] in the set-theoretic presentations using production sets rather than production functions. Assuming that costs are minimized at each output level, we can restrict attention to the whole product vectors along the expansion path:

$$\mathbf{WP}(y) = \left(y,-\varphi_1(y),\ldots,-\varphi_n(y)\right).$$

The gradient of the whole product vector is the *marginal whole product* **MWP.**

$$\mathbf{MWP}(y) = \nabla\mathbf{WP}(y) = \left(1, -\frac{\partial\varphi_1}{\partial y}, \ldots, -\frac{\partial\varphi_n}{\partial y}\right)$$

Equation 5.18. Marginal Whole Product Vector **MWP**

The price vector is $\mathbf{P} = (p, w_1,\ldots,w_n)$, the value of the whole product (the dot product of the price and whole product vectors) is the profit.

$$\mathbf{P}\bullet\mathbf{WP} = py - \sum w_i x_i = py - C(y),$$

Equation 5.19. Value of Whole Product = Profit

and the value of the marginal whole product is the

$$\mathbf{P}\bullet\mathbf{MWP}(y) = \mathbf{P}\bullet\left(1, -\frac{\partial\varphi_1}{\partial y}, \ldots, -\frac{\partial\varphi_n}{\partial y}\right)$$

$$= p - \sum w_i \frac{\partial\varphi_i}{\partial y} = p - MC.$$

Equation 5.20. Value of Marginal Whole Product = Marginal Profit

The necessary condition for profit maximization is that the marginal whole product has zero net value, which yields the familiar conditions $p = MC$. Substituting p for MC in the cost minimization conditions yields the central equations in the usual presentation of MP theory:

$$p\ MP_i = w_i \text{ for } i = 1,\ldots,n$$

which are interpreted as showing that in competitive equilibrium, each unit of a factor is paid (w_i) the value of what it produces ($p\ MP_i$).

One Responsible Factor

We move now to the formulation of the same mathematics but with certain factors treated as responsible factors, i.e., the treatment of MP theory with responsible factors. At first we assume only one responsible factor that can be arbitrarily taken as the first factor, which provides the services x_1. In terms of totals, the responsible factor, by performing the services or actions x_1, is responsible for producing y and is responsible for using up the other inputs $x_2,\ldots x_n$. Since the customary notation lists x_1 along side the other inputs, we could also picture the responsible factor as both producing and using up x_1 (which thus cancels out). Thus the *whole product of the responsible factor* is:

$$\mathbf{WP_1} = (y, 0, -x_2, \ldots, -x_n) = \mathbf{WP} + (0, x_1, 0, \ldots, 0).$$

Equation 5.21. Whole Product of Responsible Factor x_1

The whole product of the responsible factor is the sum of the whole product and the services of the responsible factor.

Since we are now assuming only one responsible factor, we have the luxury of mathematically treating its actions as the independent variable. Restricting attention to the expansion path as usual and assuming $\partial\varphi_1/\partial y \neq 0$, we can invert the first factor demand function to obtain

$$y = \varphi_1^{-1}(x_1)$$

which can be substituted into the other factor demand functions to obtain the other inputs as functions of x_1:

$$x_i = \varphi_i\left(\varphi_1^{-1}(x_1)\right) \text{for } i = 2, \ldots, n.$$

The whole product of the responsible factor can then be expressed as a function of x_1:

$$\mathbf{WP_1}(x_1) = \left(\varphi_1^{-1}(x_1), 0, -\varphi_2(\varphi_1^{-1}(x_1)), \ldots, -\varphi_n(\varphi_1^{-1}(x_1))\right)$$

Equation 5.22. Whole Product of Responsible Factor x_1 as a Function of x_1

We can now present a realistic picture of the effects of a marginal increase in the responsible factor. A marginal increase in x_1 will both use up the other factors at the rate

$$\frac{\partial\varphi_i\left(\varphi_1^{-1}\right)}{\partial x_1} = \frac{\partial\varphi_i / \partial y}{\partial\varphi_1 / \partial y}$$

and will increase the output at the rate

$$\frac{\partial \varphi_1^{-1}}{\partial x_1} = \frac{1}{\partial \varphi_1 / \partial y}$$

along the expansion path. This information is given by the x_1 gradient of the whole product of the responsible factor, which is the *marginal whole product of the responsible factor:*

$$\mathbf{MWP_1} = \nabla \mathbf{WP_1}(x_1) = \left(\frac{1}{\partial \varphi_1 / \partial y}, 0, -\frac{\partial \varphi_2 / \partial y}{\partial \varphi_1 / \partial y}, \ldots, -\frac{\partial \varphi_n / \partial y}{\partial \varphi_1 / \partial y} \right).$$

Equation 5.23. Marginal Whole Product of Responsible Factor

This marginal whole product vector $\mathbf{MWP_1}$ presents what the responsible factor is marginally responsible for in quantity terms. Thus it should be compared with the marginal product MP_1 in the conventional treatment of MP theory. The marginal product MP_1 is fine as a mathematically defined partial derivative. But to interpret it in terms of production, one has to consider the purely notional shift to a more x_1-intensive productive technique so that exactly the same amount of the other factors is consumed. That is not how output changes in the cost-minimizing firm. The marginal whole product $\mathbf{MWP_1}$ presents the actual marginal changes in the output and the other factors associated with a marginal increase in x_1 along the expansion path.

The value of the marginal whole product of x_1 is the dot product:

$$\mathbf{P \bullet MWP_1} = \frac{\left[p - w_2 \, \partial \varphi_2 / \partial y - \cdots - w_n \, \partial \varphi_n / \partial y \right]}{\partial \varphi_1 / \partial y} = \frac{[p - MC]}{\partial \varphi_1 / \partial y} + w_1 .$$

Equation 5.24. Value of Marginal Whole Product of Responsible Factor

Thus we have that the necessary condition for profit maximization, $p = MC$, is equivalent to

$$\mathbf{P \cdot MWP_l} = w_l.$$

Equation 5.25. Profit Max Implies
Value of Marginal Whole Product = Factor Price

Production is carried to the point where the value of the marginal whole product of the responsible factor is equal to its opportunity cost given by w_l. Since we are assuming cost minimization, this is also equivalent to the conventional equation:

$$p\,MP_l = w_l.$$

Several Jointly Responsible Factors

The generalization to several jointly responsible factors is straightforward. The main mathematical difference is that we lose the luxury of parameterizing motion along the expansion path by "the responsible factor," since we now assume several such factors. Hence output will be used as the independent variable to represent motion along the expansion path.

The whole product vector **WP**(y) and the marginal whole product vector **MWP**(y) are the same as before. Suppose there are m jointly responsible factors, which we can take to be the first m factors. Intuitively, by performing the services or actions $x_1,\ldots,x_m$, the responsible factors use up the inputs $x_{m+1},\ldots,x_n$ and produce the outputs y. As before the *whole product of the responsible factors*, now symbolized $\mathbf{WP_r}(y)$, can be presented as the sum of the whole product and the services of the responsible factors:

$$\begin{aligned}\mathbf{WP_r}(y) &= \mathbf{WP} + \big(0,\varphi_1(y),\ldots,\varphi_m(y),0,\ldots,0\big)\\ &= \big(y,0,\ldots,0,-\varphi_{m+1}(y),\ldots,-\varphi_n(y)\big).\end{aligned}$$

Equation 5.26. Whole Product of Responsible Factors $x_1,\ldots,x_m$

The *marginal whole product of the responsible factors* (with variation parameterized by y) is the y gradient of $\mathbf{WP_r}(y)$:

$$\mathbf{MWP_r}(y) = \nabla\mathbf{WP_r}(y) = \left(1,0,\ldots0,-\frac{\partial\varphi_{m+1}}{\partial y},\ldots,-\frac{\partial\varphi_n}{\partial y}\right)$$

Equation 5.27. Marginal Whole Product of Responsible Factors $x_1,\ldots,x_m$

and its value is the dot product with the price vector.

$$\mathbf{P{\bullet}MWP_r} = p - w_{m+1}\frac{\partial\varphi_{m+1}}{\partial y} - \ldots - w_n\frac{\partial\varphi_n}{\partial y}$$

$$= [p - MC] + \sum_{j=1}^{m} w_j \frac{\partial\varphi_j}{\partial y}$$

Equation 5.28. Value of Marginal Whole Product of Responsible Factors $x_1,\ldots,x_m$

When producing the marginal increase in output by using up the marginal amounts of the other inputs, the responsible factors use up the marginal services

$$\left(0,\frac{\partial\varphi_1}{\partial y},\ldots,\frac{\partial\varphi_m}{\partial y},0,\ldots,0\right)$$

which have the opportunity cost of

$$\sum_{j=1}^{m} w_j \frac{\partial\varphi_j}{\partial y}.$$

Figure 5.5. Opportunity Cost of Marginal Responsible Services for Marginal Increase in y

Hence value is maximized when the responsible factors carry production to the point when the value of their marginal whole product is equal to their marginal opportunity cost which is clearly equivalent to the equation: $p = MC$ [see Equation 5.28].

$$\mathbf{P \bullet MWP_r} = \sum_{j=1}^{m} w_j \frac{\partial \varphi_j}{\partial y}$$

Equation 5.29. Value of Marginal Whole Product of Responsible Services = Their Opportunity Cost

Extreme Cases

It may be of some interest to take the two extreme cases when no factors or all factors are taken as being responsible.

When no factors are taken as responsible, then production is seen as a natural event rather than a human activity (on the assumption that humans are responsible factors). The product is produced and the inputs are used up—but not by anyone. No one is responsible. This is perhaps the world imagined by economists who adopt the pose of "social physicists" describing natural processes. Then we can make the identifications:

whole product of responsible factors	= whole product,
marginal whole product of responsible factors	= marginal whole product,
value of marginal whole product of responsible factors	= marginal profit,
opportunity cost of marginal responsible factors	= 0.

Figure 5.6. Extreme Case of No Responsible Factors

Thus $\mathbf{P \cdot MWP_r} = p - MC$ so when the value of the marginal whole product of the responsible factors is set equal to their marginal opportunity costs, then we simply have $p - MC = 0$.

If all the factors are taken as responsible then we are in the magical world of poets where "all the factors co-operate together to produce the product." In this world we can make the identifications:

whole product of responsible factors	= positive product,
marginal whole product of responsible factors	= (1,0,...,0)
value of marginal w.p. of responsible factors	= p,
opportunity cost of marginal responsible factors	= MC.

Figure 5.7. Extreme Case of All Responsible Factors

Thus $\mathbf{P \cdot MWP_r} = p$ so when the value of the marginal whole product of the responsible factors is set equal to their marginal opportunity costs MC, then we again have the equation $p = MC$.

Several Products

To illustrate the generalization to several products, we consider an example with two products y_1 and y_2. The production possibilities can be given in the form:

$$F(y_1,y_2,x_1,\ldots,x_n) = 0.$$

Given the output levels y_1 and y_2, the cost minimization problem is:

$$\text{minimize:} \qquad C = \sum_{i=1}^{n} w_i x_i$$

$$\text{subject to:} \qquad F(y_1,y_2,x_1,\ldots,x_n) = 0.$$

Figure 5.8. Cost Minimization Problem with Two Outputs

The lagrangian is

$$L = \sum_{i=1}^{n} w_i x_i - \lambda F(y_1,y_2,x_1,\ldots,x_n)$$

and the first-order conditions are $w_i = \lambda\partial F/\partial x_i$ for $i = 1,\ldots,n$. Determining the cost-minimizing input levels in terms of the given output levels yields the conditional factor demand functions

$$x_i = \varphi_i(y_1,y_2) \text{ for } i = 1,\ldots,n.$$

Equation 5.30. Conditional Factor Demand with Two Outputs

Substituting into the cost sum yield the cost function $C(y_1y_2)$ and the marginal costs

$$MC_j = \frac{\partial C}{\partial y_j} = \sum_{i=1}^{n} w_i \frac{\partial \varphi_i}{\partial y_j} \text{ for } j = 1,2.$$

Equation 5.31. Marginal Costs of the Two Outputs

The whole product vector (parameterized by y_1 and y_2) is

$$\mathbf{WP}(y_1,y_2) = (y_1,y_2,-\varphi_1(y_1,y_2),\ldots,-\varphi_n(y_1,y_2))$$

and the two marginal whole products with respect to y_1 and y_2 are the two gradients with respect to those variables:

$$\nabla_1 \mathbf{WP} = \left(1,0,-\frac{\partial\varphi_1}{\partial y_1},\ldots,-\frac{\partial\varphi_n}{\partial y_1}\right)$$

$$\nabla_2 \mathbf{WP} = \left(0,1,-\frac{\partial\varphi_1}{\partial y_2},\ldots,-\frac{\partial\varphi_n}{\partial y_2}\right)$$

Equation 5.32. Marginal Whole Products with Respect to the Two Outputs

With output unit prices p_1 and p_2, the value of the marginal whole products must be zero for profits to be maximized:

$$\mathbf{P}\bullet\nabla_j \mathbf{WP} = (p_1, p_2, w_1,\ldots,w_n)\bullet\nabla_j \mathbf{WP}$$
$$= p_j - MC_j = 0 \text{ for } j = 1,2.$$

Equation 5.33. Profit Maximization Conditions for Multiple Outputs

Let the first m factors be the responsible factors as before. The whole product of the responsible factors is the sum of the whole product and the services of the responsible factors:

$$\mathbf{WP_r}(y_1, y_2) = (y_1, y_2, 0,\ldots,0,-\varphi_{m+1}(y_1,y_2),\ldots,-\varphi_n(y_1,y_2))$$

Equation 5.34. Whole Product of Responsible Factors

and the marginal whole products of the responsible factors would be the two gradients with respect to y_1 and y_2. The values of those marginal whole products are:

$$\mathbf{P}\bullet\nabla_j \mathbf{WP_r} = p_j - MC_j + \sum_{i=1}^{m} w_i \frac{\partial\varphi_i}{\partial y_j} \text{ for } j = 1,2.$$

Equation 5.35. Value of Marginal Whole Products of Responsible Factors for each of the Two Outputs

To produce a marginal increase in y_1, the responsible factors must use their actions, which have the marginal opportunity cost:

$$\sum_{i=1}^{m} w_i \frac{\partial \varphi_i}{\partial y_1}$$

Figure 5.9. Marginal Opportunity Cost of Responsible Factors for Marginal Increase in y_1

and similarly for y_2. Value is maximized when the responsible factors carry production of each output to the point when the value of their respective marginal whole product is equal to their respective marginal opportunity costs:

$$\mathbf{P} \bullet \nabla_j \mathbf{WP}_r = \sum_{i=1}^{m} w_i \frac{\partial \varphi_i}{\partial y_j}$$

Equation 5.36. Profit Max Implies Value of Marginal Whole Products of Responsible Factors Is Their Opportunity Cost

which is clearly equivalent to $p_j = MC_j$ for $j = 1,2$ [see Equation 5.35]. This example with several products helps to motivate the next multi-product model where there is no substitution.

An Example Without Substitution

We have criticized the usual interpretation of MP_i as the "product of the marginal unit of x_i" on a number of grounds. For instance, a marginal increase in x_i cannot produce an increase in the output out of thin air. Other inputs will be needed. The definition of the partial derivative MP_i however assumes substitutability in the sense that there is a shift to a slightly more x_i intensive productive technique so that more output can be produced using exactly the same amount of the other factors. Yet we have shown that such an imaginary shift is not necessary to interpret marginal productivity theory. By using vectorial notions of the product, the theory can be expressed quite plausibly using marginal whole products computed along the cost-minimizing expansion path.

The luxury of the alternative treatment of MP theory becomes a necessity when there is no substitutability as in a Leontief input-output model. Hence we will give the alternative treatment of MP theory in such a model.

We will consider an example where there are n commodities $x_1,\ldots,x_n$ and labor L where the latter is taken as the services of the responsible factor. The technology is specified by the $n \times n$ matrix $\mathbf{A} = [a_{ij}]$ where a_{ij} gives the number of units of the ith good needed per unit of the jth good as output. Thus for the output column vector $\mathbf{x} = (x_1,\ldots,x_n)^T$ (the superscript "T" denotes the transpose), the vector of required commodity inputs is $\mathbf{Ax}$. The labor requirements per unit are given by the vector $\mathbf{a_0} = (a_{01},\ldots,a_{0n})$, so the total labor requirement is the scalar $L = \mathbf{a_0x}$.

Let $\mathbf{p} = (p_1,\ldots,p_n)$ be the price vector and let w be the wage rate. We assume that the outputs and inputs are separated by one time period (a "year") and that r is the annual interest rate. The competitive equilibrium condition is usually stated as the zero-profits condition with no mention of marginal productivity or the like. With labor taking its income at the end of the year, the zero-profit condition for any output vector is:

$$\mathbf{px} = (1+r)\mathbf{pAx} + w\mathbf{a_0x}.$$

Since this must hold for any $\mathbf{x}$, we can extract the following vector equation.

$$\mathbf{p} = (1+r)\mathbf{pA} + w\mathbf{a_0}$$

Equation 5.37. Competitive Equilibrium Condition

We now show how this condition can be derived using MP-style reasoning with products represented as vectors. The whole product will be a $2n+1$ component column vector since the output vector $\mathbf{x}$ is produced a year after the input vector $\mathbf{Ax}$. The following notation for the whole product is self-explanatory:

$$\mathbf{WP} = \begin{bmatrix} \mathbf{x} \\ -\mathbf{Ax} \\ -\mathbf{a_0x} \end{bmatrix}.$$

Equation 5.38. Whole Product Vector **WP**

The whole product of the responsible factor is, as always, the sum of the whole product and the services of the responsible factor (since the factor is represented as both producing and using up its own services):

$$\mathbf{WP}_L = \mathbf{WP} + \begin{bmatrix} 0 \\ \vdots \\ 0 \\ \mathbf{a}_0\mathbf{x} \end{bmatrix} = \begin{bmatrix} \mathbf{x} \\ -\mathbf{A}\mathbf{x} \\ 0 \end{bmatrix}$$

Equation 5.39. Whole Product of Labor Vector $\mathbf{WP}_L$

To consider output variations, we use the output unit vectors $\delta_j = (0,\ldots,0,1,0,\ldots,0)^T$ where the "1" is in the jth place. The marginal whole product of the responsible factor with respect to the jth output will be symbolized as:

$$\nabla_j \mathbf{WP}_L = \begin{bmatrix} \delta_j \\ -\mathbf{A}\delta_j \\ 0 \end{bmatrix}.$$

Equation 5.40. Marginal Whole Product of Labor with Respect to the jth Output

and the required labor is $\mathbf{a}_0\delta_j = a_{0j}$ with the opportunity cost of wa_{0j}. The price vector stated in year-end values is $\mathbf{P} = (\mathbf{p}, (1+r)\mathbf{p}, w)$ so the value of the marginal whole product of labor is:

$$\mathbf{P}\bullet\nabla_j \mathbf{WP}_L = p_j - (1+r)\mathbf{pA}\delta_j.$$

Equation 5.41. Value of Marginal Whole Product of Labor with Respect to the jth Output

When the value of that marginal whole product of the responsible factor with respect to the jth output is set equal to opportunity cost of the necessary labor wa_{0j} for $j = 1,\ldots,n$, then we again have the same equilibrium conditions:

$$\mathbf{p} - (1+r)\mathbf{pA} = w\mathbf{a}_0.$$

Equation 5.42. Competitive Equilibrium Condition Expressed as: Value of Marginal Whole Product of Labor with Respect to Each Output = Its Opportunity Cost.

Thus the alternative presentation of MP theory with product vectors and responsible factors can be used in models without substitution where the conventional marginal products are undefined.

References

Ellerman, David. 1992. *Property & Contract in Economics*. Cambridge, Mass.: Basil Blackwell.

Varian, Hal. 1984. *Microeconomic Analysis*. Second edition. New York: W. W. Norton.

Chapter 6

Double-Entry Bookkeeping: Mathematical Formulation and Generalization

Introduction

Double-entry bookkeeping illustrates one of the most astonishing examples of intellectual insulation between disciplines, in this case, between accounting and mathematics. Double-entry bookkeeping (DEB) was developed during the fifteenth century and was first recorded in 1494 as a system by the Italian mathematician Luca Pacioli [1494]. Double-entry bookkeeping has been used for several centuries in the accounting systems of the market economies throughout the world. Incredibly, however, the mathematical formulation for DEB is not known, at least not in the field of accounting.

The mathematical basis behind DEB (algebraic operations on ordered pairs of numbers) was developed in the nineteenth century by Sir William Rowan Hamilton as an abstract mathematical construction to deal with complex numbers and fractions [Hamilton 1837]. The particular example of the ordered pairs construction that is relevant to DEB, called the "group of differences," is the one used in undergraduate algebra courses to construct a number system with negative numbers ("additive inverses" in technical terms) by using operations on ordered pairs of positive numbers (including zero). All that is required to grasp the connection with DEB is to make the identification:

> ordered pairs of numbers in construction of positive and negative numbers = two-sided T-accounts of DEB (debits on the left side and credits on the right side).

In view of this identification, the "group of differences" will be called the *Pacioli group*.

In spite of some attention to DEB by mathematicians [e.g., DeMorgan 1869, Cayley 1894, and Kemeny et al. 1962], this connection has been little noticed in mathematics. One (perhaps solitary) exception is the following passage in a semi-popular book by D. E. Littlewood.

> The bank associates two totals with each customer's account, the total of moneys credited and the total of moneys withdrawn. The net balance is then regarded as the same if, for example, the credit amounts of £102 and the debit £100, as if the credit were £52 and the debit £50. If the debit exceeds the credit the balance is negative.
>
> This model is adopted in the definition of signed integers. Consider pairs of cardinal numbers (a, b) in which the first number corresponds to the debit, and the second to the credit. [1960, 18]

With this exception, the author has not been able to find a single mathematics book, elementary or advanced, popular or esoteric, which notes that the ordered pairs of the group of differences construction are the T-accounts used in the business world for about five centuries. And this mathematical basis for DEB is totally unknown in the "parallel universe" of accounting.

This almost complete lack of cross-fertilization between mathematics and accounting is a topic of some interest for intellectual history and the sociology of knowledge. The story is probably rather simple from the mathematics side. Double-entry bookkeeping is apparently too mundane to hold the sustained attention of mathematicians. The real question lies on the accounting side. Over the last century, how could professional accountants and accounting professors have failed to find the mathematical basis for DEB even though it was part of undergraduate algebra?

One acid test of a mathematical formulation of a theory is the question of whether or not it facilitates the generalization of the theory. Normal bookkeeping does not deal with incommensurate physical quantities; everything is expressed in the common units of money. A long-standing question is the possible generalization of DEB to deal with incommensurates with no common measure of value.

In the literature on the "mathematics of accounting" there was a proposed "solution" to this question, a system of physical accounting that was published repeatedly [see Ijiri 1965, 1966, and 1967] and was largely accepted by the accounting community. In this system, most of the structure of DEB was lost:

- there was no balance sheet equation,
- there were no equity or proprietorship accounts,
- the temporary or nominal accounts could not be closed, and
- the "trial balance" did not balance.

It is common for certain aspects of a theory to be lost in a generalization of the theory. The accounting community had apparently accepted the failure of all these features of DEB as the necessary price to be paid to generalize DEB to incommensurate physical quantities. For instance, the systems of "Double-entry multidimensional accounting" previously published in the accounting literature [see also Charnes et al. 1972, 1976, or Haseman and Whinston 1976] had acquiesced in the absence of the balance-sheet equation.

> For instance, the convenient idea of an accounting identity is lost since the dimensional and metric comparability it assumes is no longer present except under special circumstances. [Ijiri 1967, 333]

When DEB is mathematically formulated using the group of differences, then the generalization to vectors of incommensurate physical quantities is immediate and trivial. All of the normal features of DEB (such as the balance-sheet equation, the equity account, the temporary accounts, and the trial balance) are preserved in the generalization [see Ellerman 1982, 1986]. Thus the "accepted" generalized model of DEB was simply a failed attempt at generalization which had been received as a successful generalization that unfortunately had to "sacrifice" certain features of DEB.

In spite of the results that can be obtained from a simple border crossing between mathematics and accounting, the successful mathematical treatment and generalization of double-entry bookkeeping (first published over a decade ago) will take years if not decades to become known and understood in accounting.

The Pacioli Group

We will develop the Pacioli group using vectors (ordered lists of numbers) for multidimensional accounting. The usual case of scalar accounting can be identified with the special case of using one dimensional vectors. A vector $x = (x_1,\dots,x_n)$ is *non-negative* if and only if all its components x_i are non-negative (positive or zero). The ordered pairs of non-negative vectors will be called *T-accounts* and will be denoted as follows for vectors d and c.

$$[\ d\ //\ c\ ] = [\ \text{debit vector}\ //\ \text{credit vector}\ ]$$

Equation 6.1. Definition of T-Accounts

The left-hand side (LHS) vector d is the debit entry and the right-hand side (RHS) vector c is the credit entry. A fraction is also an ordered pair of whole numbers or integers where the two integers are the numerator and denominator of the fraction.

The algebraic operations on T-accounts are much like the operations on fractions except that addition is substituted for multiplication. In order to illustrate the additive-multiplicative analogy between T-accounts and fractions, the basic definitions will be developed in parallel columns.

T-accounts add together by adding debits to debits and credits to credits $[w\ //\ x] + [y\ //\ z] = [w+y\ //\ x+z]$. The identity element for addition is the zero T-account [0 // 0]. Given two T-accounts [w // x] and [y // z], the *cross-sums* are the two vectors obtained by adding the credit entry in one T-account to the debit entry in the other T-account. The equivalence relation between T-accounts is defined by setting two T-accounts *equal* if their cross-sums are equal: $[w\ //\ x] = [y\ //\ z]$ if $w+z = x+y$. The negative or additive inverse of a T-account is obtained by reversing the debit and credit entries: $-[w\ //\ x] = [x\ //\ w]$. Given two vectors $x = (x_1,\ldots,x_n)$ and $y = (y_1,\ldots,y_n)$, let max(x,y) be the vector with the maximum of x_i and y_i as its ith component, and let min(x,y) be the vector with the minimum of x_i and y_i as its ith	Fractions multiply together by multiplying numerator with numerator and denominator with denominator $(w/x)(y/z) = (wy/xz)$. The identity element for multiplication is the unit fraction 1/1. Given two fractions w/x and y/z, the *cross-multiples* are the two integers obtained by multiplying the numerator of one faction with the denominator of the other fraction. The equivalence relation between fractions is defined by setting two fractions *equal* if their cross-multiples are equal: $w/x = y/z$ if $wz = xy$. The multiplicative inverse of a fraction is obtained by reversing the numerator and denominator: $(w/x)^{-1} = x/w$. Given two integers w and x, let lcm(w,x) be the least common multiple of w and x, and let gcd(w,x) be the greatest common divisor of w and x (the largest integer dividing both).

component.
Two non-negative vectors x and y are said to be *disjoint* if min(x,y) = 0. A T-account [x //y] is in *reduced form* if x and y are disjoint. Every T-account [x //y] has a unique reduced representation
[x − min(x,y) // y − min(x,y)].

Consider the T-account
[(12, 3, 8) // (10, 5, 4)].
The minimum of the debit and credit vectors is (10, 3, 4) so the reduced form representation is
[(2, 0, 4) // (0, 2, 0)].

Two integers w and x are said to be *relatively prime* if gcd(w,x) = 1. A fraction w/x is in *lowest terms* if w and x are relatively prime. Each fraction w/x has a unique representation in lowest terms
(w/gcd(w,x))/(x/gcd(w,x)).

Consider the fraction
28/35.
The greatest common divisor of the numerator and denominator is 7 so the fraction in lowest terms is
4/5.

That completes the construction of the *Pacioli group* P^n where each element is an ordered pair [x // y] of non-negative n-dimensional vectors. The Pacioli group P^n is isomorphic with all of $\mathbf{R}^n$ (the set of all n-vectors with positive and negative components) under two isomorphisms: the debit isomorphism, which maps [w // x] to w − x, and the credit ismorphism, which maps [w // x] to x − w. In order to translate from T-accounts [x // y] to general vectors z, one only need specify whether to use the debit or credit isomorphism. This will be done by labeling the T-account as *debit balance* or *credit balance*. Thus if a T-account [x // y] is debit balance, the corresponding vector is x − y, and if it is credit balance, then the corresponding vector is y − x.

The Double-entry Method

The double-entry method of accounting is a method of using the Pacioli group to perform additive algebraic operations on equations such as the conventional balance sheet equation:

$$\text{Assets} = \text{Liabilities} + \text{Net Worth.}$$

Equation 6.2. Balance-Sheet Equation

Vector equations are first *encoded* in the Pacioli group. A T-account equal to the zero T-account [0 // 0] is called a *zero account*. Equations encode as zero-accounts. Since the vectors in a T-account must be non-negative, we must first develop a way to separate out the positive and negative components of a vector. The *positive part* of a vector x is $x^+ = \max(x,0)$, the maximum of x and the zero vector [note that "0" is used depending on the context to refer to the zero scalar or the zero vector]. The *negative part* of x is $x^- = -\min(x,0)$, the negative of the minimum of x and the zero vector. Both the positive and negative parts of a vector x are non-negative vectors. Every vector x has a "Jordan decomposition" $x = x^+ - x^-$.

Given any equation in $\mathbf{R}^n$, $w + \ldots + x = y + \ldots + z$, each left-hand side (LHS) vector w is encoded as a debit-balance T-account $[w^+ // w^-]$ and each right-hand side (RHS) vector y is encoded as a credit-balance T-account $[y^- // y^+]$. Then the original equation holds if and only the sum of the encoded T-accounts is a zero-account:

$$w + \ldots + x = y + \ldots + z$$

if and only if

$$[w^+ // w^-] + \ldots + [x^+ // x^-] + [y^- // y^+] + \ldots + [z^- // z^+]$$

is a zero-account.

Equation 6.3. Encoding an Equation as a Zero T-Account

Given the equation, the sum of the encoded T-accounts is called the *equational zero-account* of the equation. Since only plus signs can appear between the T-accounts in an equational zero-account, the plus signs can be left implicit. The listing of the T-accounts in an equational zero-account (without the plus signs) is the *ledger*.

Changes in the various terms or "accounts" in the beginning equation are recorded as *transactions*. Transactions must be recorded as valid algebraic operations which transform equations into equations. Since equations encode as zero-accounts, a valid algebraic operation would transform zero-accounts into zero-accounts. There is only one such operation in the Pacioli group: add on a zero-account. Zero plus zero equals zero. The zero-accounts representing transactions are called *transactional zero-accounts*. The listing of the transactional zero-accounts is the *journal*.

A series of valid additive operations on an equation can then be presented in the following standard scheme:

  Beginning Equational Zero-Account
+ Transactional Zero-Accounts
= Ending Equational Zero-Account

or, in more conventional terminology,

Beginning Ledger
+ Journal
= Ending Ledger.

The process of adding the transactional zero-accounts to the initial ledger to obtain the ledger at the end of the accounting period is called *posting the journal to the ledger*. The fact that a transactional zero-account is equal to [0 // 0] is traditionally expressed as the *double-entry principle* that transactions are recorded with equal debits and credits. The summing of the debit and credit sides of a computed equational zero-account to check that it is indeed a zero-account is traditionally called the *trial balance*.

It remains to decode the ending equational zero-account to obtain the equation that results from the algebraic operations represented in the transactions. The T-accounts in an equational zero-account can be arbitrarily partitioned into two sets DB (debit balance) and CB (credit balance). T-accounts [w // x] in DB are decoded as $w-x$ on the left side of the equation, and T-accounts [w // x] in CB are decoded as $x-w$ on the right side of the equation. Given a zero-account, this procedure yields an equation. In an accounting application, the T-accounts in the final equational zero-account would be partitioned into sets DB and CB according to the side of the initial equation from which they were encoded.

To illustrate encoding and decoding equations, consider the vector equation

$$(6, -3, 10) + (-2, 5, 2) = (4, 2, 8).$$

Equation 6.4. Sample Vector Equation to be Encoded

It encodes as the equational zero-account

$$[(6, 0, 10) // (0, 3, 0)] + [(0, 5, 2) // (2, 0, 0)] + [(0, 0, 0) // (4, 2, 8)].$$

Figure 6.1. Equation Encoded as a Zero T-Account

To illustrate decoding, consider another equational zero-account,

$$[(8, 1, 4) // (2, 3, 6)] + [(1, 13, 3) // (5, 4, 2)] + [(2, 1, 3) // (4, 8, 2)].$$

Figure 6.2. Sample Zero T-Account to be Decoded

Let the first two T-accounts be debit balance and the third one credit balance. Then the equational zero-account decodes as the vector equation

$$(6, -2, -2) + (-4, 9, 1) = (2, 7, -1).$$

Equation 6.5. Decoded Equation

Given the additive-multiplicative analogy between the double-entry T-accounts and the double-entry fractions, one could develop a whole system of multiplicative double-entry bookkeeping [see Ellerman 1982, 58–66 for the theory with an example].

A Simple Example of Value Accounting

Consider an example of a company with the simplified initial balance sheet equation:

Assets	=	Liabilities	+	Equity
15,000	=	10,000	+	5,000.

Equation 6.6. Beginning Scalar Balance Sheet

The balance sheet equation encodes as an equational zero-account which, by leaving out the plus signs, becomes the following initial ledger of T-accounts.

Assets	Liabilities	Equity
[15,000 // 0]	[0 // 10,000]	[0 // 5,000]

Figure 6.3. Beginning Ledger of T-Accounts

A transaction will change two or more of the accounts. The fact that a transaction changes two or more accounts has nothing to do with the "doubleness" of double-entry bookkeeping. DEB is a system of *recording* transactions that uses the *double*-sided T-accounts of positive numbers (or the double-sided fractions in the multiplicative case). Any other way of recording the transaction (e.g., using positive and negative numbers) would also have to change two or more accounts in an equation. If one item in an equation changes, then clearly one or more other items in the equation must also change in order for the equation to still be true.

Consider three transactions in a productive firm.

1. $1,200 of input inventories are used up in production.
2. $1,500 of product is produced and sold.
3. $800 principal payment is made on a loan.

Each transaction is then encoded as a transactional zero-account and added to the equational zero-account.

	Assets	Liabilities	Equity
	[15,000 // 0]	[0 // 10,000]	[0 // 5,000]
1.	[0 // 1,200]		[1,200 // 0]
2.	[1,500 // 0]		[0 // 1,500]
3.	[0 // 800]	[800 // 0]	
	=========	=========	=========
Totals	[16,500 // 2,000]	[800 // 10,000]	[1,200 // 6,500]
= (in reduced form)	[14,500 // 0]	[0 // 9,200]	[0 // 5,300].

Figure 6.4. Initial Ledger + Journal = Ending Ledger

Each T-account is decoded according to whether it was encoded as debit balance or credit balance to obtain the ending balance sheet equation.

$$\begin{array}{ccccc} \text{Assets} & = & \text{Liabilities} & + & \text{Equity} \\ 14{,}500 & = & 9{,}200 & + & 5{,}300. \end{array}$$

Equation 6.7. Ending Balance-Sheet Equation

A Simple Example of Multidimensional Property Accounting

When the scalars (single non-negative numbers) of value accounting are replaced by non-negative vectors, then the vectors can be interpreted as representing the physical amounts of different types of property. We will consider a simple model where there are only three types of property: cash, outputs, and inputs. These goods will be listed in that order in each three-dimensional vector.

Let the initial asset vector be (9000, 40, 50) so the firm has $9000 cash, 40 units of the output in inventory, and 50 units of the input in inventory. The firm also has a $10000 liability represented by the vector (10000, 0, 0) so the equity vector (Assets − Liabilities) is given by the vector (−1000, 40, 50). Thus the initial balance sheet (vector) equation is:

$$\begin{array}{lcccc} \text{Assets} & = & \text{Liabilities} & + & \text{Equity} \\ (9000, 40, 50) & = & (10000, 0, 0) & + & (-1000, 40, 50). \end{array}$$

Equation 6.8. Initial Vector Balance-Sheet Equation

This encoded as the following equational zero-account or ledger:

Assets	Liabilities	Equity
[(9000, 40, 50)//(0, 0, 0)]	[(0, 0, 0)//(10000, 0, 0)]	[(1000, 0, 0)//(0, 40, 50)].

Figure 6.5. Initial Vector T-Accounts in Ledger

The underlying production process is very simple. Two units of the inputs are combined to make one unit of the output. Hence the following physical transactions underlie the previous value transactions (where we split the production and sale of the outputs are the transactions 2a and 2b).

1. 30 units of the inputs are used up in production.
2a.15 units of the product are produced.
2b.15 units of the product are sold for $100 each.
3. $800 principal payment is made on a loan.

These transactions are then encoded as transactional zero-accounts and added to the ledger T-accounts.

	Assets	Liabilities	Equity
	[(9000, 40, 50)//(0, 0, 0)]	[(0, 0, 0)//(10000, 0, 0)]	[(1000, 0, 0)//(0, 40, 50)].
1.	[(0, 0, 0)//(0, 0, 30)]		[(0, 0, 30)//(0, 0, 0)]
2a.	[(0, 15, 0)//(0, 0, 0)]		[(0, 0, 0)//(0, 15, 0)]
2b.	[(1500, 0, 0)//(0, 15, 0)]		[(0, 15, 0)//(1500, 0, 0)]
3.	[(0, 0, 0)//(800, 0, 0)]	[(800, 0, 0)//(0, 0, 0)]	
	=================	=================	=================
	[(10500, 55, 50)//(800, 15, 30)]	[(800, 0, 0)//(10000, 0, 0)]	[(1000, 15, 30)//(1500, 55, 50)]
=	[(9700, 40, 20)//(0, 0, 0)]	[(0, 0, 0)//(9200, 0, 0)]	[(0, 0, 0)//(500, 40, 20)]

Figure 6.6. Initial Vector Ledger + Journal = Ending Vector Ledger

where the last line of ledger accounts is in reduced form. The reduced accounts are then decoded to obtain the ending balance-sheet equation:

$$\text{Assets} = \text{Liabilities} + \text{Equity}$$

$$(9700, 40, 20) = (9200, 0, 0) + (500, 40, 20).$$

Equation 6.9. Ending Vector Balance-Sheet Equation

Given a set of prices or valuation coefficients, the vectors can be evaluated so that the vector accounts of property accounting collapse to the scalar accounts of value accounting. For instance, suppose that the prices per unit are (cash, output, input) = (1, 100, 40). Multiplying the physical quantities times their price and adding up yields the balance-sheet equation of the previous example of value accounting.

$$\text{Assets} = \text{Liabilities} + \text{Equity}$$

$$14{,}500 = 9{,}200 + 5{,}300.$$

Equation 6.10. Scalar Equation = Price Vector times Vector Equation

Thus we see how property accounting can use double-entry accounting with vectors to trace out the property transactions that underlie the value transactions recorded in conventional accounting.

References

Cayley, A. 1894. *The Principles of Book-keeping by Double Entry*. Cambridge: Cambridge University Press.

Charnes, A., C. Colantoni, W. W. Cooper, and K. O. Kortanek. 1972. "Economic, Social and Enterprise Accounting and Mathematical Models." *Accounting Review* 47, no. 1 (January): 85–108.

Charnes, A., C. Colantoni, and W. W. Cooper. 1976. "A Futurological Justification for Historical Cost and Multidimensional Accounting." *Accounting, Organizations, and Society* 1, no. 4: 315–37.

DeMorgan, Augustus. 1869. "On the Main Principle of Book-Keeping." In *Elements of Arithmetic*. London: James Walton.

Ellerman, David. 1982. *Economics, Accounting, and Property Theory*. Lexington, Mass.: D.C. Heath.

———. 1985. "The Mathematics of Double Entry Bookkeeping." *Mathematics Magazine*. 58 (September): 226–33.

———. 1986. "Double Entry Multidimensional Accounting." *Omega, International Journal of Management Science* 14, no. 1: 13–22.

Hamilton, Sir William Rowan. 1837. "Theory of Conjugate Functions, or Algebraic Couples: with a Preliminary and Elementary Essay on Algebra as the Science of Pure Time." *Transactions of the Royal Irish Academy* 17: 293–422.

Haseman, W., and A. Whinston. 1976. "Design of a Multidimensional Accounting System." *Accounting Review* 51, no. 1: 65–79.

Ijiri, Y. 1965. *Management Goals and Accounting for Control*. Amsterdam: North-Holland.

———. 1966. "Physical Measures and Multi-dimensional Accounting." In *Research in Accounting Measurement*, ed. R. K. Jaedicke, Y. Ijiri, and O. Nielsen, 150–64. Sarasota Fla.: American Accounting Association.

———. 1967. *The Foundations of Accounting Measurement: A Mathematical, Economic, and Behavioural Inquiry*. Englewood Cliffs, N.J.: Prentice-Hall.

Kemeny, J., A. Schleifer, J. L. Snell, and G. Thompson. 1962. *Finite Mathematics with Business Applications*. Englewood Cliffs, N.J.: Prentice-Hall.

Littlewood, D. E. 1960 (orig. 1949). *The Skeleton Key of Mathematics*. New York: Harper Torchbooks.

Pacioli, L. 1494. "Summa de Arithmetica, Geometrica, Proporcioni et Propocionalita." Trans. J. B. Geijsbeck. In: Geijsbeck, J. 1914. *Ancient Double-Entry Bookkeeping*. Houston: Scholars Book Company.

Chapter 7

The Semantics Differentiation of Minds and Machines

Introduction

After several decades of debate, a definitive differentiation between minds and machines seems to be emerging into view. The differentiating criterion emerges from logic as well as computer science itself. Computing machines (e.g., Turing machines) carry out formal processes of symbol manipulation. Symbols are manipulated solely on the basis of their form, not their intended interpretation. Such symbol-crunching processes are usually called "syntactic" or "formal computational."

This leads to the specification of a process that could not be duplicated on a computer, that is, a process that operates on symbols not according to their syntactic form but according to their semantic meaning. Since such processes would use the meaning or intended interpretation of the symbols, they are semantic rather than syntactic in character. One simple example is the process of logical reasoning in the human mind. The best result that could be obtained with a computer is simulation (not duplication) by programming the computer to formally manipulate the symbols in a manner that is correct or appropriate in view of their intended interpretation. Hence the basic tenet of computer science that computers are formal symbol manipulators yields this "semantics differentiation" between minds and computers.

There are other roads that lead to the same principle. One is the philosophy of mind. A symbol does not have an intrinsic meaning; it is not intrinsically "about something." The semantic content or meaning of a symbol is ascribed to it by a mind. My thought of my coffee cup, however, does have an intrinsic aboutness. It is not simply interpreted as being about the coffee cup (e.g., by a third party); the thought is about the coffee cup. This intrinsic "aboutness" or "directedness" of most mental states is called "intentionality." The semantics of an intentional mental state is built-in; the semantics of a symbol must be externally imputed or ascribed to it. Intentionality cannot be duplicated by formal symbol manipulation processes alone (e.g., by computers) since those processes are, by definition, independent of the symbols' aboutness. Computers lack inherent intentionality.

When approached from the philosophy of mind, the semantics differentiation would be better called the "intentionality differentiation." It has been expounded and ably defended by John Searle [1980, 1981, 1982, 1983, 1984, . . .]. A precomputer version of the intentionality thesis was used by Franz Brentano as a mental-physical differentiation [see McAlister 1976]. The notion of intentionality itself descends from the Middle Ages [see Spiegelberg in McAlister 1976, or "Intentionality" in Edwards 1967]. The notion was also central to the thought of Edmund Husserl and the subsequent philosophy of phenomenology [Dreyfus 1982]. Searle's book [1983] seems based on the principle that intentionality is too important to be left to phenomenologists. The book presents a path-breaking treatment of intentionality, which does not require one to learn the exotic proprietary vocabulary of the phenomenological literature.

The Semantics Differentiation

My treatment of the semantics/intentionality differentiation will be based on the approach from semantics, not intentionality. The notion of "intentionality" is foreign to computer science. No new theory of intentionality will be presented here. Nor is a complete theory of intentionality needed for a differentiation of minds and machines. My point is that the rigorous notions of syntax and semantics drawn from mathematical logic, while far short of a theory of intentionality, are nevertheless sufficient to illustrate the differentiation of minds from machines.

The syntax-semantics distinction is familiar to computer scientists, mathematicians, and philosophers from modern logic: formal syntax versus truth-functional or model-theoretic semantics. A number of semantic theories have been developed for various special purposes:

Kripke semantics, functorial semantics, possible-world semantics, Montague semantics, denotational semantics, situational semantics, and so forth. The arguments for the semantics differentiation will be illustrated using the familiar and noncontroversial semantics of propositional and first-order logic.

The semantics differentiation between minds and machines is internal to computer science itself. The operations of a Turing machine are formal symbol manipulations, and all the operations of a general purpose digital computer can be characterized as Turing machine operations (subject to practical limitations such as memory and time). Computers are syntactical engines whose operations always manipulate symbols solely on the basis of their form, not their intended interpretation. A process that did operate on symbols using their intended interpretation could not be duplicated on a computer. Thus the semantics differentiation is based on the computer science characterization of "what computers do."

This semantics differentiation is not "new"; it is essentially a "folk theory" deriving from work in logic (formal syntax, recursive function theory, and model theory) that dates from the early part of this century. It doesn't need to be rediscovered; it needs to be understood. There are several systematic reasons why the semantics differentiation has been misunderstood. Much of my task is to attempt to resolve these misunderstandings.

The Semantics Differentiation is Nonfunctionalist

Semantics is not differentiated from syntax on behaviorist or functionalist grounds. There is a range of cases where semantics and syntax yield the same "behavior." Consider any consistent and complete formal theory such as an axiomatization of propositional or first-order logic. In an axiom system for first-order logic, the semantic notion of validity and the syntactic notion of theoremhood exhibit the same "behavior" in the sense that they specify the same set of first-order formulas. Under the intended interpretation of the logical symbols, the axioms are valid and the formal rules of inference preserve validity, so all the theorems are valid. By the completeness theorem, all valid formulas can be derived as theorems. Hence the semantics and the syntax of first-order logic yield the same set of formulas (i.e., the same "behavior" or "function"). Yet no one would interpret this completeness result as proving that the semantics and syntax of first-order logic are the same thing. The completeness theorem does not erase the differentiation between semantics and syntax. Indeed, without the differentiation there would have been no equivalence to prove.

It would be a simple misunderstanding to think that the completeness theorem "proves" that validity *is* a syntactic notion; it only proves that there is a functionally equivalent syntactic notion. Yet, time and time again, one finds the analogous misunderstanding in the artificial intelligence (AI) literature. If a mental (semantic) operation can be successfully programmed on a computer (by definition, a syntactic device), then it is claimed this would show that the mental operation was a "formal computable" operation, i.e., was syntactic. Nothing of the sort follows. First-order validity has been perfectly "programmed" in the formal axiomatizations of first-order logic, but that hardly proves validity is a syntactic notion. What it does show is that the differentiation between validity and theoremhood in first-order logic cannot be made on behavioral or functional grounds.

This line of argument can be applied to the warhorse of Turing machine functionalism, the Turing test itself. Suppose that human mental activities could be successfully programmed so that the program would pass the Turing test with flying colors (i.e., the programmed computer would be behaviorally indistinguishable from a person communicating over a teletype). Two points should be made. First, if a computer does pass the Turing test, it does not demonstrate that the human mental activities are solely syntactic or formal computational (for the reasons given above). Second, a successful Turing test does not disprove the semantics differentiation anymore than does the completeness theorem for first-order logic. It is not a behavioral differentiation.

Because the semantics differentiation is nonbehavioral, it places no behavioral or functional restrictions on "what computers can do." AI critics who project behavioral limitations on computers (e.g., "Computers might play good checkers, but could never play championship chess") cannot base their assertions on the semantics differentiation. The differentiation is very liberally disposed towards work in the artificial intelligence field since it places no theoretical limit on the human behavior that can be programmed (and perhaps improved upon) with a digital computer.

The Irrelevance of the Godel Incompleteness Theorem

Since the semantics differentiation was illustrated using a *completeness* theorem (for first-order logic), it should be clear that the Godel Incompleteness Theorem (for systems with the expressive power of arithmetic) is irrelevant to the argument. One does not need the Godel Incompleteness Theorem to separate semantics from syntax. It neither adds to nor subtracts from the semantics differentiation.

Applications of the Godel Theorem to the mind/machine differentiation are often plagued by an order-of-the-quantifiers misunderstanding. The theorem does not show that there is a true proposition that is formally undecidable in any given formal system of sufficient expressive power. It shows that given any formal system of sufficient power, there is a proposition, true in the intended interpretation, that is formally undecidable in that system (assuming consistency). That proposition is decidable in stronger systems (add it as an axiom), but the stronger systems will generate other undecidable propositions.

The undecidability demonstrated by the Godel Theorem is not absolute; it is relative to the given formal system. If there were an "Absolute Godel Theorem" yielding an absolutely undecidable proposition, then that would be relevant to the semantics differentiation. That would show it to be a behavioral differentiation. But there is no such "Absolute Godel Theorem" and the semantics differentiation by itself places no constraint on computer behavior.

Why Johnniac Can't Add

It is virtually impossible to use computers or even talk about them without adopting an intentionalist idiom. This manner of speaking (and mode of thought) imputes the intended interpretation of the programmer to the computer running the program.

Consider a Turing machine that computes the successor function on the natural numbers N. Given the natural number n as input, it computes $n+1$ as the output. A contiguous block of $n+1$ 1's on the Turing machine tape denotes the natural number n. The structure and the program of the Turing machine are specified by its "quintuples" [e.g., Minsky 1967, 119], which specify the behavior of the machine in terms of the symbol being read and the current internal state of the machine. The machine is programmed so that when it starts reading the leftmost 1 in the input block of 1's, it moves over to the right end of the block, prints an additional 1, and halts.

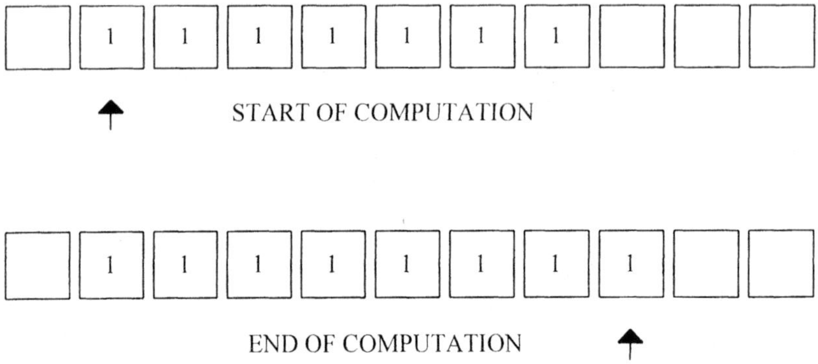

Figure 7.1. Action of Turing Machine to Compute Successor Function

Given a block of 1's representing n, the machine outputs a block of 1's representing $n+1$, i.e., it computes the successor function.

Or does it? Let $f:N \to N$ be an effectively calculable isomorphism of the natural numbers onto themselves (e.g., any finite permutation). Now interpret a block of $n+1$ ones as denoting $f(n)$ instead of n. Then given n, it is denoted by the block of $f^{-1}(n)+1$ ones. The Turing machine adds a 1 to obtain a block of $f^{-1}(n)+2$ ones that denotes the natural number $g(n) = f(f^{-1}(n)+1)$. The function g is not the successor function unless f is the identity function.

If the previous Turing machine computed the successor function, do we now have a *different* Turing machine that computes g? No. The Turing machine is exactly the same. It is specified by its "quintuples" and they are completely unchanged. The intended interpretation of the blocks of ones on the tape was never a part of the specification or operation of the Turing machine. It operates on the formal symbols on the tape in a manner independent of their interpretation.

It is only the whole system consisting of the syntactical operations (the Turing machine) plus the semantics (the interpretation of the symbols) that yields a computation of some function on the natural numbers. The Turing machine by itself does not compute the successor function or any of the infinity of other functions obtained by choosing different effectively calculable coding functions $f:N \to N$. It formally operates on the symbols in a specified way regardless of the coding function used to interpret the symbols.

We thus have the absurd-sounding result that Johnniac cannot add! The apparent absurdity of this conclusion only underscores the entrenchment of the intentionalist idiom in our everyday thought and language. We unthinkingly impute to the computer itself the intended interpretation of the program. But it is precisely in these discussions of the capacities of minds and machines that the semantic interpretation must be bracketed aside from the syntactical symbol manipulation device—no matter how much this cuts across everyday idioms.

The Intentionalist Fallacy

Animism, the imputation of aspects of human mentality to nonhuman entities, is an ancient habit of thought. Primitive tribes took an "intentional stance" [Dennett 1978, 6] toward natural events such as rainstorms. The thunder and lightning expressed the anger of the spirits. John Ruskin called the artistic imputation of emotions to natural events the "pathetic fallacy" (e.g., "The waves pounded angrily on the rocks"). Neoclassical economists picture capital goods and natural resources as "agents of production" that (who?) "cooperate" together with people to produce the products. "Together, the man and shovel can dig my cellar" or "land and labor together produce the corn harvest" [Samuelson 1976, 536-37]. A shovel is only a tool for the hands while a computer is a tool for the mind. If orthodox economists are unable to resist imputing reponsible agency to shovels and land, it is not surprising to find a widespread intentionalist manner of speaking about the most sophisticated machinery ever devised, the modern digital computer.

But our task requires peeling away the popular idiom from the unadorned facts. In our prior example, we saw that contrary to what "everyone knows," computers cannot add. Addition is an operation defined on natural numbers. Computers operate on formal symbols. There is an infinity of ways a programmer could interpret the symbols as referring to natural numbers, and the Turing machine operates independently of all such semantic interpretations.

There was nothing particular about the example. The same sort of differentiation between the syntactic computer operation and its intended semantic interpretation can be applied to any and all computer programs. Computers do not compute the "computable functions." Computers are programmed to formally manipulate symbols in an appropriate manner that can be interpreted as computing the computable functions. Computers do not process semantic information. Computers are programmed to manipulate symbols in a manner that can be interpreted as the processing of information about some subject matter. "The stars run blindly" and so do the so-called "goal-seeking mechanisms." Computers can be appropriately programmed so that by running blindly, certain goals will in fact be pursued.

The imputation of the intended interpretation of the program to the programmed computer could be called the "intentionalist fallacy." The intentionalist fallacy pervades the AI literature. The intentionalist idiom is the *lingua franca* of AI. There is no need to change the idiom. There is a need to understand it as only a manner of speaking or as an "intentional stance," not as a serious explanatory hypothesis (an hypothesis that, in any case, could be easily refuted by reference to the nonsemantic character of computers). Computers are used by humans to perform computations, to process information, and to seek goals. The syntax of the activity is programmed into the computer so that it will be correct or appropriate in light of the semantics supplied by the human user.

The Amphibious Nature of Programs

There are a number of arguments in the AI literature that attempt to show that computers can have (inherent) intentionality. By far the most common argument derives from the intentionalist fallacy.

In addition to the examples cited above, consider the idea of the "mind as program," i.e., mental processes as instantiations of programs. A program is always "amphibious" in that it has two sides: the program as a formal symbol manipulation process and the intended semantic interpretation of the program. A computer can carry out only the former, while a mind can carry out the latter.

For a simple pre-computer example of this two-sidedness, consider the logical rule of inference *modus ponens*. There is the rule itself as a semantic inference, and there is the syntactic formalization of the rule. For the semantic rule, let P and Q be propositions and let $\Rightarrow$ represent the truth-functional conditional. The semantic rule is:

$$\text{If P is true and if P} \Rightarrow \text{Q is true, then infer that Q is true.}$$

Equation 7.1. Semantic Modus Ponens

This is easily formalized as the syntactic rule:

Given the symbols "P" and "P $\Rightarrow$ Q" as inputs,

output the symbol "Q".

Equation 7.2. Syntactic Modus Ponens

The word "deduction," like the word "program," might be used ambiguously to mean either the formal syntactic operation or the underlying semantic rule. The two rules are not identical. The syntactic rule formalizes and "simulates" the semantic rule but does not duplicate it. It is the semantic rule that gives correctness to the syntactic rule under the usual interpretation of the symbols.

The dual nature of programs is used in one of the exciting methodologies that has grown out of AI, the use of programs as models in cognitive science. The semantic interpretation of the program refers to the mental operations being modeled; the syntactic character of the program allows the model to be run on a computer. These models no more show the mind to operate on formal computational principles than hydraulic or electrical models for the macro-economy (which some economists have constructed) show the economy to run on hydraulic or electrical principles.

The amphibious nature of programs (syntax and semantics) is often abused in AI arguments. When it is argued that programs have intentionality because, for example, they survey alternatives and seek goals (as in a chess-playing program), that refers to the semantic interpretation of the program. When it is said that a computer runs the program, that refers to the program's syntactic side as a formal symbol manipulation routine (independent of its semantic interpretation). Now consider the following argument.

> Programs have intentionality (e.g., they survey possibilities or seek goals).
> Computers run programs.
> Therefore, computers have intentionality.

The argument is incorrect due to the shift in the meaning of "programs" in the first and second sentences. The first occurrence of "programs" refers to the semantic interpretations while the second refers to the syntactic rules. It is one form of the intentionalist fallacy to impute the semantic interpretation of the program to the program qua symbol manipulation routine.

The Formalization of Semantics

Another line of argument against the semantics differentiation is that semantics can be programmed. This argument might be stated as follows.

> Today, the semantics differentiation has some force because present-day attempts to program semantic relations have been so limited and crude. But eventually sophisticated methods will be developed so that the semantics of thought can be programmed on a computer.

A similar argument holds that the syntax/semantics distinction is relative; the semantics of one level can be formalized in the syntax of a higher level. These arguments fail to understand the nature of the semantics differentiation. I share the optimism about programming or formalizing many of the semantic aspects of thought. The point is that what one then has is a formalization of the notion, a "syntacticalization" of the semantic notion, not the semantic notion itself.

An example can again be found in logic. There are two quite different syntactic systems which might be associated with the semantics of first-order logic. We previously considered the relationship between first-order semantics and a formal axiom system for first-order logic. In a process that might be called "syntactic ascent," the semantic interpretation of first-order syntactic formulas in first-order models can itself be modeled in a formal system of axiomatic set theory.

Proponents of "Strong AI" interpret the semantics differentiation as claiming that the semantic relationship between a symbolic structure and its environment cannot itself be modeled. They argue that a sophisticated computer system could internally represent an external state of affairs. It could then appropriately relate this internal model with the internal symbol structure so the symbols would then exhibit "aboutness." In this manner, strong AI proponents claim that intentionality can be modeled on a computer.

I agree. The semantics differentiation would agree that intentionality can (in theory) be modeled on a computer. Indeed, that modeling process is a computer version of syntactic ascent as when the semantics of first-order logic is formalized in axiomatic set theory. Suppose that the sentence P(a) in some first-order language L is satisfied in the first-order model B.

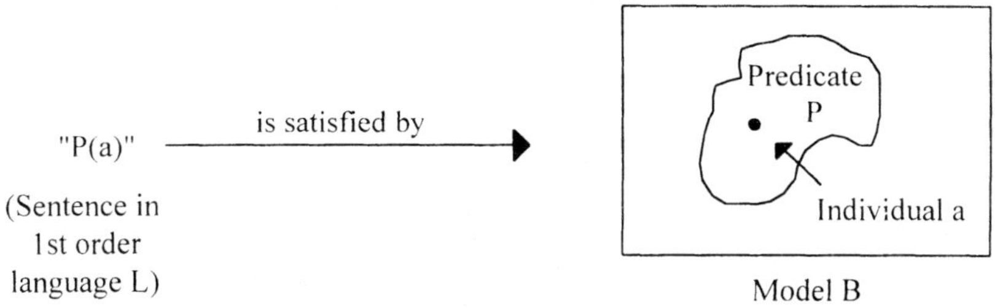

Figure 7.2. Sentence P(a) is Satisfied in Model B

The notion of being a sentence in first-order language L could be represented in a system of axiomatic set theory by, say, a formula WFF("P(a)"). The notion of being a (set theoretic) model for the first-order language could be represented by a formula M(B). The semantic notion that a sentence P(a) is satisfied by a model B could be represented by some formula S("P(a)",B).

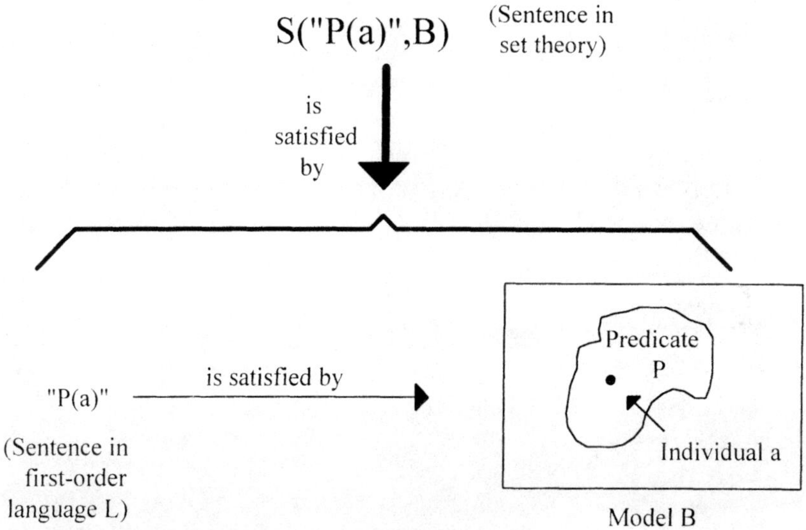

Figure 7.3. Modeling of Semantic Relationship in Set Theory

Relationships between the syntax of a first-order language and its semantic models could then be formally derived within a system of axiomatic set theory. In this manner, the semantics of first-order languages can be modeled in the syntax of axiomatic set theory.

This example of syntactic ascent is rigid and static in comparison with the potential flexible and adaptable computer modeling of the semantic relationship between a perceiving, acting agent and the environment. But both are examples of modeling semantics within syntax, and thus the clear-cut logical example suffices to illustrate the point.

What has been gained by the modeling? Certainly no one would claim that it proves that the semantic relationship between a sentence P(a) and a model B *is* a syntactic notion, only that it can be modeled in the syntax of another formal theory. This is reminiscent of Searle's distinction between duplication and simulation. First-order model-theoretic semantics can be simulated in the syntax of axiomatic set theory, but not duplicated.

The modeling produces a formalization of the semantic relationship, not the semantic relationship being modeled. The distinction between the syntactic machinery (formal set theory in this case) and the intended interpretation (e.g., the semantics of first-order theories) remains the same. The claims of strong AI would require the reproduction (duplication) of the semantic relationship, not its formalization (simulation) in some syntactic system such as a digital computer.

Computer programs can be written *about* anything: playing chess, balancing Aunt Rachel's checkbook, or modeling the semantics of linguistic representations. A program as a syntactic operation is no less formal and no less independent of its content when the intended interpretation happens to be the semantics of certain symbols and representations rather than playing chess or computing the successor function.

Syntax + Robotics = Semantics?

There is another AI argument that might be called the "syntax + robotics = semantics" thesis. Jerry Fodor [1980] gave this "Robot Reply" in his response to Searle's argument. Can intentionality be physically realized by adding physical transducers to symbol crunchers? The argument is that by adding to a digital computer the robotic capabilities to sense and manipulate the environment, the computer can understand the referents of its symbols and thus add a semantic dimension to its syntactic operations. This "Robot Reply" argument is essentially a hardware-oriented variation on the formalization-of-semantics argument considered above.

Robotic abilities certainly do add extra dimensions of power and versatility to a computer. But they do not add a semantic dimension. The computer continues to operate on formal syntactic principles as before, but the range of functions encoded in the syntax can be greatly extended.

For instance, robotic abilities might allow the replacement of certain human inputs of semantic information with purely syntactic links. Suppose a human operator makes certain measurements and then appropriately programs a numerically controlled (NC) machine. An NC machine with robotic sensors could be programmed and calibrated to take the measurements and automatically adjust its control program in an appropriate manner. The analog-to-digital interface between the robotic sensors and the computer could be designed so the relevant physical characteristics of the environment are transformed into the appropriate formal properties of the symbolic structures being manipulated by the computer. The role of the system designer and programmer is pushed back to that of structuring the whole computer-cum-robot system so that by running blindly (i.e., blind to its intended function), it in fact runs in accordance with its intended function.

In simpler terms, a physical connection between a symbol and the environment does not give the symbol an intrinsic aboutness. It does not supply the missing ingredient to transform syntax into semantics. Transducers transmit causes, not meanings. The root of the "syntax + robotics = semantics" thesis is a confusion between the *cause* of an event and the *meaning* of the event under a certain scheme of interpretation.

Fred Dretske's gas gauge example illustrates this ambiguity:

> Our humble gauge even exhibits the rudiments of intensionality (sic)—representing the amount of gas in my tank. [1983, 82]

Consider the event of the gauge showing "Empty." The meaning of this event under the usual interpretation is, of course, that the tank is empty. The cause of the event is quite distinct. The whole distinction between the mechanism functioning correctly or being "broken" hinges on the correspondence or lack of it between the intended meaning and the cause of the gauge showing "Empty." The physical transducer between the gas tank and gauge does not supply intentionality or meaning to the Empty-event; it only supplies a cause that may or may not correspond with the intended meaning.

If the cause and the meaning of an event were identical, then gas gauges could not malfunction. And the same holds for robots. The robot reply involves the same confusion between cause and meaning as the ascription of intentionality to the gas gauge. The physical transducers of a robotic system will supply a whole new range of causes to affect the symbol-crunching events in the computer. But, as in the case of the humble gas gauge, the causal connection is quite distinct from the intended interpretation or meaning of the symbolic events [for a more information-theoretic treatment of the robot reply, see Ellerman 1986].

Massive Parallelism and All That

Yet another argument holds that advances in hardware and software, such as massive parallelism, will eventually lead to digital computers that have intentionality. Minsky uses this argument in addressing Searle's presentation of the intentionality differentiation.

> I just can't see why Searle is so opposed to the idea that a really big pile of junk might have feelings like ours. He proposes no evidence whatever against it, he merely tries to portray it as absurd to imagine machines, with minds like ours—intentions and all—made from stones and paper instead of electrons and atoms. [Minsky 1980, p. 440].

Regardless of one's intuitions about intentionality, it is easy to answer this argument using the semantics approach to the mind/machine differentiation. A Turing machine does not cease being a formal symbol manipulation device as one keeps adding quintuples until it becomes "really big." Adding more and more axioms to a formal syntactic system does not suddenly yield a semantic system. Since a semantic system operates on different principles (i.e., using the meaning of the symbols), it cannot be obtained as a "really big" syntactic system. This is not a question of "evidence"; it follows from the definition of Turing machines or other symbol manipulation systems. Thus the size and sophistication of the computers and programs are quite irrelevant to the semantics differentiation.

Conclusion

Minds crunch symbols according to their intended interpretation. Digital computers crunch symbols solely on the basis of their form.

Minds program computers to formally crunch symbols in a manner that is appropriate in view of the intended interpretation of the symbols.

Computers can only carry out formal syntactic processes. The human mind can carry out semantic processes. Thus minds and machines may be differentiated on the basis of two fundamentally different ways of operating on symbols:

1. semantically according to their meaning, and
2. syntactically in a manner independent of their meaning.

In the author's opinion, many AI researchers are "only" trying to obtain what we have agreed is possible, the functional modeling or simulation of human intentionality on a digital computer. That is the success they seek, and they are quite impatient with "philosophical" arguments over whether that is simulation or duplication. While the simulation/duplication distinction does have philosophical import, it is not "philosophical" in the pejorative sense of being vague since it can be illustrated by examples from logic such as the relationship between first-order semantics and axiomatic set theory. An AI researcher might grant the "theoretical" distinction but consider it "unimportant" because it is nonbehavioral. Indeed, computers are so useful in human society precisely because for behavioral purposes, the semantics differentiation between minds and machines is not relevant.

References

Dennett, Daniel. 1978. *Brainstorms*. Cambridge, Mass.: MIT Press.

Dretske, F. 1983. Precis of "Knowledge and the Flow of Information." *Behavioral and Brain Sciences* 6:55–90.

Dreyfus, Hubert, ed. 1982. *Husserl, Intentionality, and Cognitive Science*. Cambridge, Mass.: MIT Press.

Edwards, Paul, ed. 1967. *The Encyclopedia of Philosophy*. New York: Macmillan/Free Press.

Ellerman, David. 1986. "Intentionality and Information Theory." *The Behavioral and Brain Sciences* 9:1 (March): 143–44.

Fodor, Jerry A. 1980. "Searle On What Only Brains Can Do." *The Behavioral and Brain Sciences* 3:431–32.

Haugeland, John, ed. 1981. *Mind Design*. Cambridge, Mass.: MIT Press.

McAlister, Linda, ed. 1976. *The Philosophy of Brentano*. Atlantic Highlands, N.J.: Humanities Press.

Minsky, Martin. 1967. *Computation: Finite and Infinite Machines*. Englewood Cliffs, N.J.: Prentice-Hall.

Minsky, Martin. 1980. "Decentralized Minds." *The Behavioral and Brain Sciences* 3:439–40.

Samuelson, Paul. 1976. *Economics*. Tenth edition. New York: McGraw-Hill.

Searle, John R. 1980. "Minds, Brains and Programs" and "Intrinsic Intentionality." *Behavioral and Brain Sciences* 3:417–24 and 450–56.

———. 1981. "Analytic Philosophy and Mental Phenomena." *Midwest Studies in Philosophy* 6:405–23.

———. 1982. "The Myth of the Computer." *New York Review of Books* 29, no. 7:3–6.

———. 1983. *Intentionality*. New York: Cambridge University Press.

———. 1984. *Minds, Brains and Science*. London: British Broadcasting Corporation.

Chapter 8

Category Theory as the Theory of Concrete Universals

Introduction: "Bad Platonic Metaphysics"

Consider the following examples of "bad metaphysics."

> Given all the entities that have a certain property, there is one entity among them that exemplifies the property in an absolutely perfect and universal way. It is called the "concrete universal." There is a relationship of "participation" or "resemblance" so that all the other entities that have the property "participate in" or "resemble" that perfect example, the concrete universal. And conversely, every entity that participates in or resembles the universal also has the property. The concrete universal represents the "essence" of the property. All the other instances of the property have "imperfections." There is a process of removing imperfections so that by removing all the imperfections, one arrives at the essence of the property, the concrete universal. For instance, if the property is "whiteness," then the concrete universal (if it existed) would be something that was "perfectly white" and so that anything else would be white if and only if it resembled (in terms of color) that perfect example of whiteness.

To the modern ear, all this sounds like the worst sort of "bad Platonic metaphysics." Yet there is a mathematical theory developed within the last fifty years, category theory, that provides precisely that treatment of concrete universals within mathematics.

A simple example using sets will illustrate the points. Given two sets A and B, consider the property of sets: $F(X) \equiv$ "X is contained in A and is contained in B." In other words, the property is the property of being both a subset of A and a subset of B. In this example, the *participation* relation is the subset relation. There is a set, namely the intersection or meet of A and B, denoted $A \cap B$, that has the property (so it is a "concrete" instance of the property), and it is universal in the sense that any other set has the property if and only if it participates in the universal example:

concreteness:	$F(A \cap B)$, i.e., $A \cap B$ is a subset of both A and B, and
universality:	X participates in $A \cap B$ if and only if $F(X)$, i.e., X is a subset of $A \cap B$ if and only if X is contained in both A and B.

Given a set X with the property of "being a subset of both A and B," an *imperfection* of X is another set X′ with the property but which is not contained in X. If sets X and Y both have the property, and X is contained in Y then Y is said to be *more essential* (in the sense of being "equally or more of the essence") than X. If Y is more essential than X then any imperfection of Y is an imperfection of X, and X may have a few other imperfections of its own. In this case, the process of eliminating or filtering out imperfections and becoming "more essential" is the process of taking the union of sets. If X and Y have the property, then their union $X \cup Y$ is more essential than both X and Y. Hence if we take the union of all the instances of the property (the union of all the subsets of both A and B), then we will arrive at the "essence" of the property without any imperfections, namely the intersection $A \cap B$.

This example of a concrete universal is quite simple, but all this "bad metaphysical talk" has highly developed and precise models in category theory. This interpretation of category theory as the theory of concrete universals is the main point of our paper. But we will briefly mention two other controversies in philosophy related to concrete universals: the Third Man Argument and the set theoretical paradoxes.

The Third Man Argument against self-predication in Platonic scholarship is that if "whiteness itself" is white along side all other white objects then there must be a "One over the Many" (a super whiteness) by virtue of which they are all white, and so on in an infinite regress. But with the rigorous modeling of concrete universals in category theory, we see that the flaw in the Third Man Argument is the assumption that the "One over the Many" is distinct from the "Many." In the example cited above, the process of forming the "One over the Many" was the process of taking the union of all the sets with the property (of being a subset of both A and B). But the "One" which was the result of taking this union, namely A∩B, was also one of the "Many" (one of the subsets of both A and B taken in the union).

In the first half of this century, set theory was shaken by the discovery of the set theoretical paradoxes such as Russell's Paradox. The original idea of set theory was to be a general theory of universals where a universal for any given property was an entity such that all objects would have the property if and only if they had a certain relation to that special universal representing the property. The candidate for this universal entity was the set of all objects with the property so that an object would have the property if and only if it was a member of that set. But this broad definition of "set" allowed the fatal paradoxes. Moreover, the paradoxes all followed because of the possibility in naive set theory of self-predication. For instance, Russell's Paradox resulted from considering the set R of all sets that are not members of themselves. The question of self-predication, "Is R a member of itself or not?", leads to the paradox.

Set theory was reconstructed to eliminate the paradoxes using the iterative notion of a set where the set representing a property was forced to be more "abstract" than all the entities with the property. Hence the universals in reformed set theory were always "abstract universals" that were incapable of self-predication. The paradoxes of naive set theory resulted from the hubris of trying to be a general theory of universals that could be both abstract and concrete at the same time. Once set theory was reconstructed as the theory of abstract universals, the question arises "Is there also a mathematical theory of concrete unviersals?" We answer "Yes"; that theory is category theory.

Thus the interpretation of category theory as the theory of concrete universals allows one to make a little more sense out of set theory being forced—on pain of paradox—to eschew self-predication. Abstract and concrete universals require rather different mathematical treatments. The paradoxes resulted from trying to use one theory for both types of universals.

The interpretation of category theory as the theory of concrete universals again raises the question of category theory's relation to the foundation of mathematics. Lawvere and Tierney's theory of topoi is an elegant category-theoretic generalization of set theory so it generalizes the set-theoretic foundations of mathematics in many new directions. We argue that category theory is also relevant to foundations in a different way, as the theory of concrete universals. Category theory provides the framework to identify the concrete universals in mathematics, the concrete instances of a mathematical property that exemplify the property in such a perfect and paradigmatic way that all other instances have the property by virtue of participating in the concrete universal.

Theories of Universals

In Plato's Theory of Ideas of Forms (ειδη), a property F has an entity associated with it, the *universal* u_F, which uniquely represents the property. An object x has the property F, i.e., F(x), if and only if (iff) the object x *participates* in the universal u_F. Let μ (from μεθεξιζ or methexis) represent the participation relation so

$$\text{``}x\ \mu\ u_F\text{''} \text{ reads as ``x participates in } u_F\text{''}.$$

Given a relation μ, an entity u_F is said to be *a universal for the property F* (with respect to μ) if it satisfies the following *universality condition:*

$$\text{for any } x,\ x\ \mu\ u_F \text{ if and only if } F(x).$$

A universal representing a property should be in some sense unique. Hence there should be an equivalence relation ($\approx$) so that universals satisfy a *uniqueness condition:*

$$\text{if } u_F \text{ and } u_F' \text{ are universals for the same F, then } u_F \approx u_F'.$$

A mathematical theory is said to be a *theory of universals* if it contains a binary relation μ and an equivalence relation $\approx$ so that with certain properties F there are associated entities u_F satisfying the following conditions:

(I) *Universality:* for any x, x μ u_F iff F(x), and
(II) *Uniqueness:* if u_F and u_F' are universals for the same F [i.e., satisfy (I) above], then $u_F \approx u_F'$.

A universal u_F is said to be *abstract* if it does not participate in itself, i.e., $\neg(u_F\ \mu\ u_F)$. Alternatively, a universal u_F is *concrete* if it is self-participating, i.e., $u_F\ \mu\ u_F$.

Set Theory as the Theory of Abstract Universals

There is a modern mathematical theory that readily qualifies as a theory of universals, namely set theory. The universal representing a property F is the set of all elements with the property:

$$u_F = \{ x \mid F(x) \}.$$

The participation relation is the set membership relation usually represented by $\in$. The universality condition in set theory is the equivalence called a (naive) *comprehension axiom:* there is a set y such that for any x, $x \in y$ iff F(x). Set theory also has an *extensionality axiom,* which states that two sets with the same members are identical:

$$\text{for all } x, (x \in y \text{ iff } x \in y') \text{ implies } y = y'.$$

Thus if y and y′ both satisfy the comprehension axiom scheme for the same F then y and y′ have the same members so y = y′. Hence in set theory the uniqueness condition on universals is satisfied with the equivalence relation ($\approx$) as equality (=) between sets. Thus naive set theory qualifies as a theory of universals.

The hope that naive set theory would provide a *general* theory of universals proved to be unfounded. The naive comprehension axiom lead to inconsistency for such properties as

$$F(x) \equiv \text{``x is not a member of x''} \equiv x \notin x$$

If R is the universal for that property, i.e., R is the set of all sets which are not members of themselves, the naive comprehension axiom yields a contradiction.

$$R \in R \text{ iff } R \notin R.$$

Equation 8.1. Russell's Paradox

The characteristic feature of Russell's Paradox and the other set theoretical paradoxes is the self-reference wherein the universal is allowed to qualify for the property represented by the universal, e.g., the Russell set R is allowed to be one of the x's in the universality relation: $x \in R$ iff $x \notin x$.

There are several ways to restrict the naive comprehension axiom to defeat the set theoretical paradoxes, e.g., as in Russell's type theory, Zermelo-Fraenkel set theory, or von Neumann-Bernays set theory. The various restrictions are based on an iterative concept of set [Boolos 1971] which forces a set y to be more "abstract", e.g., of higher type or rank, than the elements $x \in y$. Thus the universals provided by the various set theories are "abstract" universals in the intuitive sense that they are more abstract than the objects having the property represented by the universal. Sets may not be members of themselves.[1]

With the modifications to avoid the paradoxes, a set theory still qualifies as a theory of universals. The membership relation is the participation relation so that for suitably restricted predicates, there exists a set satisfying the universality condition. Set equality serves as the equivalence relation in the uniqueness conditions. But set theory cannot qualify as a *general* theory of universals. The paradox-induced modifications turn the various set theories into theories of *abstract* (i.e., non-self-participating) universals since they prohibit the self-membership of sets.

Concrete Universals

Philosophy contemplates another type of universal, a *concrete universal*. The intuitive idea of a concrete universal for a property is that it is an object that has the property and has it in such a universal sense that all other objects with the property resemble or participate in that paradigmatic or archetypal instance. The concrete universal u_F for a property F is *concrete* in the sense that it has the property itself, i.e., $F(u_F)$. It is *universal* in the intuitive sense that it represents F-ness is such a perfect and exemplary manner that any object resembles or participates in the universal u_F if and only if it has the property F.

The intuitive notion of a concrete universal occurs in ordinary language (the "all-American boy"), in theology ("the Word made flesh"), in the arts and literature (the old idea that great art uses a concrete instance to universally exemplify certain human conditions), and in philosophy (the perfect example of F-ness with no imperfections, only those attributes necessary for F-ness).

The notion of a concrete universal occurred in Plato's Theory of Forms [Malcolm 1991]. Plato's forms are often considered to be abstract or non-self-participating universals quite distinct and "above" the concrete instances. In the words of one Plato scholar, "not even

God can scratch Doghood behind the Ears" [Allen 1960]. But Plato did give examples of self-participation or self-predication, e.g., that Justice is just [Protagoras 330]. Moreover, Plato often used expressions that indicated self-predication of universals.

> But Plato also used language which suggests not only that the Forms exist separately (χωριστα) from all the particulars, but also that each Form is a peculiarly accurate or good particular of its own kind, i.e., the standard particular of the kind in question or the model (παραδειγμα) to which other particulars approximate. [Kneale and Kneale 1962, 19]

But many scholars regard the notion of a Form as *paradeigma* or concrete universal as an error.

> For general characters are not characterized by themselves: humanity is not human. The mistake is encouraged by the fact that in Greek the same phrase may signify both the concrete and the abstract, e.g. το λευκον (literally "the white") both "the white thing" and "whiteness", so that it is doubtful whether αυτο το λευκον (literally "the white itself") means "the superlatively white thing" or "whiteness in abstraction". [Kneale and Kneale 1962, 19–20]

Thus some Platonic language is ambivalent between interpreting a form as a concrete universal ("the superlatively white thing") and an abstract universal ("whiteness in abstraction").

The literature on Plato has reached no resolution on the question of self-predication. Scholarship has left Plato on both sides of the fence; many universals are not self-participating but some are. It is fitting that Plato should exhibit this ambivalence since the self-predication issue has only come to a head in this century with the set theoretical antinomies. Set theory had to be reconstructed as a theory of universals that were rigidly non-self-participating.

The reconstruction of set theory as the theory of abstract universals cleared the ground for a separate theory of universals that are always self-participating. Such a theory of concrete universals would realize the self-predicative strand of Plato's Theory of Forms.

A theory of concrete universals would have an appropriate participation relation μ so that for certain properties F, there are entities u_F satisfying the universality condition: for any x, x μ u_F if and only if F(x). The universality condition and $F(u_F)$ imply that u_F is a *concrete* universal in the previously defined sense of being self-participating, u_F μ u_F. A theory of concrete universals would also have to have an equivalence relation so the concrete universals for the same property would be unique up to that equivalence relation.

Is there a precise mathematical theory of concrete universals? Is there a theory that is to concrete universals as set theory is to abstract universals? Our claim is that category theory is precisely that theory.

To keep matters simple, all our examples will use one of the simplest examples of categories, namely partially ordered sets [for less trivial examples with more of a category-theoretic flavor, see Ellerman 1988]. Consider the universe of subsets P(U) of a set U with the inclusion relation $\subseteq$ as the partial ordering relation. Given sets a and b, consider the property

$$F(x) \equiv x \subseteq a \;\&\; x \subseteq b.$$

The participation relation is set inclusion $\subseteq$ and the intersection $a \cap b$ is the universal u_F for this property F(x). The universality relation states that the intersection is the greatest lower bound of a and b in the inclusion ordering:

$$\text{for any } x,\ x \subseteq a \cap b \text{ iff } x \subseteq a \;\&\; x \subseteq b.$$

The universal has the property it represents, i.e., $a \cap b \subseteq a \;\&\; a \cap b \subseteq b$, so it is a self-participating or concrete universal. Two concrete universals for the same property must participate in each other. In partially ordered sets, the antisymmetry condition, $y \subseteq y' \;\&\; y' \subseteq y$ implies $y = y'$, means that equality can serve as the equivalence relation in the uniqueness condition for universals in a partial order.

Category Theory as the Theory of Concrete Universals

For the concrete universals of category theory,[2] the *participation relation* is the *uniquely-factors-through* relation. It can always be formulated in a suitable category as:

"$x \mu u$" means "there exists a unique arrow $x \to u$".

Then x is said to *uniquely factor through* u, and the arrow $x \to u$ is the unique factor or participation morphism. In the universality condition,

$$\text{for any } x,\ x \mu u \text{ if and only if } F(x),$$

the existence of the identity arrow 1_u:u→u is the self-participation of the concrete universal that corresponds with F(u), the application of the property to u. In category theory, the equivalence relation used in the uniqueness condition is the isomorphism (≅).[3]

It is sometimes convenient to "turn the arrows around" and use the dual definition where "x μ u" means "there exists a unique arrow u→x" that can also be viewed as the original definition stated in the dual or opposite category.

Category theory qualifies as a theory of universals with participation defined as "uniquely factors through" and the equivalence relation taken as isomorphism. The universals of category theory are self-participating or concrete; a universal u uniquely factors through itself by the identity morphism.

Category theory as the theory of concrete universals has quite a different flavor from set theory, the theory of abstract universals. Given the collection of all the elements with a property, set theory can postulate a more abstract entity, the set of those elements, to be the universal. But category theory cannot postulate its universals because those universals are concrete. Category theory must find its universals, if at all, among the entities with the property.

Universals as Essences

The concrete universal for a property represents the essential characteristics of the property without any imperfections (to use some language of an Aristotelian stamp). All the objects in category theory with universal mapping properties such as limits and colimits [viz. Schubert 1972, Chaps. 7–8] are concrete universals for universal properties. Thus the universals of category theory can typically be presented as the limit (or colimit) of a process of filtering out or eliminating imperfections to arrive at the pure essence of the property.

Consider the previous example of the intersection a∩b of sets a and b as the concrete universal for the property F of being contained in a and in b. Given a set x with the property of "being a subset of both a and b," an *imperfection* of x is another set x′ with the property but which is not contained in x.

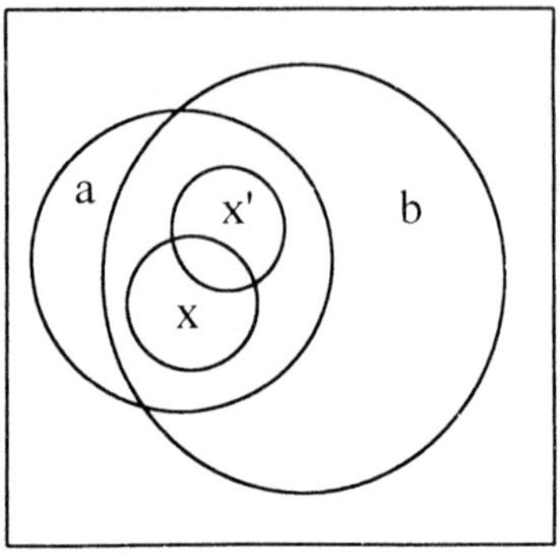

Figure 8.1. The set x′ is an *imperfection* of the set x (relative to the property of being a subset of both a and b).

If sets x and y both have the property, and x is contained in y then y is said to be *more essential* (in the sense of being "equally or more of the essence") than x.

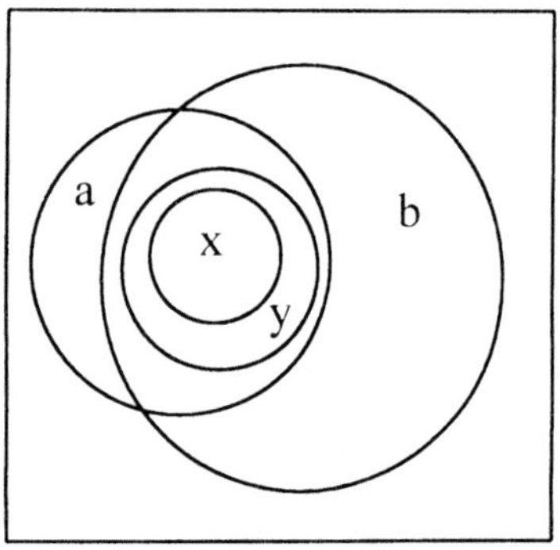

Figure 8.2. The set y is *more essential* than x (with respect to the property of being a subset of both a and b).

If y is more essential than x then any imperfection of y is an imperfection of x, and x may have a few other imperfections of its own. In this case, the process of eliminating or filtering out imperfections and becoming "more essential" is the process of taking the union of sets. If we remove all the imperfections, i.e., add to x all the other elements common to a and b, then we arrive at the "essence" of the property, the concrete universal a∩b for the property.

The property $F(x) \equiv x \subseteq a \ \& \ x \subseteq b$ is preserved under arbitrary unions:

$$\text{if } F(x_\beta) \text{ for any } x_\beta \text{ in } \{x_\beta | \beta \in B\}, \text{ then } F(\cup_\beta x_\beta).$$

Hence given any collection of instances $\{x_\beta | \beta \in B\}$ of the property F, their union is more essentially F than the instances. None of the sets in the collection are imperfections of the union. Thus the limit of this process, the "essence of F-ness," can be obtained as the union of *all* the instances of F:

$$\cup\{x \mid x \subseteq a \ \& \ x \subseteq b\} = a \cap b.$$

Equation 8.2. The Essence of being a Subset of Set a and a Subset of Set b is Obtained by Filtering Out All Imperfections.

It has *no* imperfections relative to the property F so it is the concrete universal. Moreover, since the universal is concrete, the set $a \cap b$ is among the sets x involved in the union and it contains all the other such sets x. Thus the union is "taken on," i.e., is equal to one of the sets in the union.

All the category theory examples can be dualized by "reversing the arrows." Reversing the inclusion relation in the definition of F yields the property:

$$G(x) \equiv a \subseteq x \ \& \ b \subseteq x.$$

The participation relation μ for G is the reverse of inclusion $\supseteq$ and the union of a and b is the concrete universal. The universality condition is:

$$\text{for all } x, \ x \supseteq a \cup b \text{ iff } a \subseteq x \ \& \ b \subseteq x.$$

If x has the property G but is not the universal, then x has certain imperfections. An imperfection of x (relative to the G property) would be given by another set x′ containing both a and b but not containing x. A set of instances of G could be purified of some imperfections by taking the intersection of the set. G-ness is preserved under arbitrary intersections. The intersection of a collection of sets with the property G is (equally or) more essential than the sets in the collection. None of the sets in the collection are imperfections of the intersection. Thus the universal or essence of G-ness can be obtained as the intersection of *all* the sets with the property G:

$$\cap\{x \mid a \subseteq x \ \&\ b \subseteq x\} = a \cup b.$$

The union of a and b has no imperfections relative to the property G.

Entailment as Participation Between Concrete Universals

In Plato's Theory of Forms, a logical inference is valid because it follows the necessary connections between universals. Threeness entails oddness because the universal for threeness "brings on" [επιφερει or epipherei, viz. Vlastos 1981, 102; or Sayre 1969, Part IV] or "shares in" the universal for oddness. In a mathematical theory of universals, the "entailment" relation between universals is defined as follows: given universals u_F and u_G,

u_F *entails* u_G if for any x, if $x \ \mu \ u_F$ then $x \ \mu \ u_G$.

In set theory, the participation relation μ is the membership relation $\in$ so the entailment relation between sets as abstract universals is the *inclusion* relation. Thus in set theory as the theory of abstract universals, the entailment relation (inclusion) between universals is not the same as the participation relation (membership). Considerable effort was expended in the history of logic to clearly understand the difference between inclusion and membership, e.g., between the copulas in "All roses are beautiful" and "The rose is beautiful."

In category theory, the participation relation μ is the uniquely-factors-through relation and the universals are self-participating. If u_G entails u_F, then $x \ \mu \ u_G$ implies $x \ \mu \ u_F$. Since $u_G \ \mu \ u_G$ (a relationship that does not hold for abstract universals), it follows that $u_G \ \mu \ u_F$. In short, for the concrete universals of category theory,

Entailment relation = Participation relation restricted to concrete universals.

To speak in a philosophical mode for illustrative purposes, let "The Rose" and "The Beautiful" be the concrete universals for the respective properties. In the theory of concrete universals, the general statement "All roses are beautiful" and the singular statement "The Rose is beautiful" are *equivalent*. Both express the proposition that "The Rose participates in The Beautiful," and that proposition is distinct from the statement "The rose is beautiful" (about a rather imperfect plant in one's backyard).

For an example of entailment, let us first consider another universal in the partial order of subsets of some given universe set. Given sets a and b, the *complement of a relative to b* is the concrete universal for the property

$$G(x) \equiv a \cap x \subseteq b.$$

Let the concrete universal by symbolized as a⇒b so by concreteness and universality we have:

$$a \cap (a \Rightarrow b) \subseteq b, \text{ and}$$
$$\text{for all } x,\ x \subseteq a \Rightarrow b \text{ iff } a \cap x \subseteq b.$$

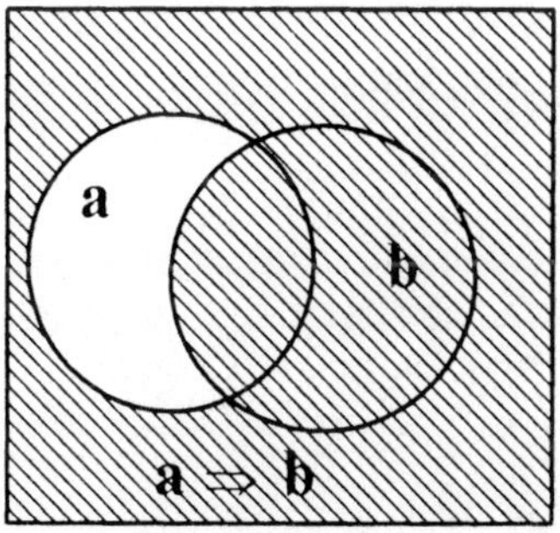

Figure 8.3. Relative complement a⇒b is the union of b with the complement of a.

The property $F(x) \equiv x \subseteq a \;\&\; x \subseteq b$ entails the property $G(x) \equiv a \cap x \subseteq b$. The entailment between the properties is realized concretely by the participation relationship between the two concrete universals for the respective properties:

$$a \cap b \subseteq a \Rightarrow b.$$

Equation 8.3. Universal for F Participates in Universal for G

We can now pair together the statements in our intuitive example and the corresponding rigorous statements in the set theoretical example (using the correlation "The Rose" ↔ (a∩b) and "The Beautiful" ↔ a⇒b). The three statements in each column of the table are equivalent.

Intuitive Example	Corresponding Rigorous Statement in Set Example
All roses are beautiful.	For all subsets x, $x \subseteq a$ & $x \subseteq b$ implies $a \cap x \subseteq b$.
The Rose is beautiful.	$a \cap (a \cap b) \subseteq b$.
The Rose participates in The Beautiful.	$a \cap b \subseteq a \Rightarrow b$.

Adjoint Functors

One of the most important and beautiful notions in category theory is the notion of a pair of adjoint functors. We will try to illustrate how adjoint functors relate to our theme of concrete universals while staying within the methodological restriction of using examples from partial orders (where adjoint functors are called "Galois connections").

We have been working within the inclusion partial order on the set of subsets P(U) of a universe set U. Consider the set of all ordered pairs of subsets $<a,b>$ from the Cartesian product $P(U) \times P(U)$ where the partial order (using the same symbol $\subseteq$) is defined by pairwise inclusion. That is, given the two ordered pairs $<a',b'>$ and $<a,b>$, we define

$$<a',b'> \subseteq <a,b> \text{ if } a' \subseteq a \text{ and } b' \subseteq b.$$

Order-preserving maps can be defined each way between these two partial orders. From P(U) to $P(U) \times P(U)$, there is the diagonal map $\Delta(x) = <x,x>$, and from $P(U) \times P(U)$ to P(U), there is the meet map $\cap(<a,b>) = a \cap b$. Consider now the following "*adjointness relation*" between the two partial orders:

$$c \subseteq \cap(<a,b>) \text{ iff } \Delta(c) \subseteq <a,b>$$

Equation 8.4. Adjointness Relationship

for sets a, b, and c in P(U). It has a certain symmetry that can be exploited. If we fix $<a,b>$, then we have the previous universality condition for the meet of a and b:

$$\text{for any c in } P(U),\ c \subseteq \cap(\langle a,b\rangle) \text{ iff } \Delta(c) \subseteq \langle a,b\rangle.$$

Equation 8.5. Universality Condition for Meet of Sets a and b

The defining property on elements c of P(U) is that $\Delta(c) \subseteq \langle a,b\rangle$ (just a fancy way of saying that c is a subset of both a and b). But using the symmetry, we could fix c and have another universality condition using the reverse inclusion in $P(U) \times P(U)$ as the participation relation:

$$\text{for any } \langle a,b\rangle \text{ in } P(U)\times P(U),$$

$$\langle a,b\rangle \supseteq \Delta(c) \text{ iff } c \subseteq \cap(\langle a,b\rangle).$$

Equation 8.6. Universality Condition for $\Delta(c)$

Here the defining property on elements $\langle a,b\rangle$ of $P(U) \times P(U)$ is that the meet of a and b is a superset of the given set c. The concrete universal for that property is the image of c under the diagonal map $\Delta(c) = \langle c,c\rangle$, just as the concrete universal for the other property defined given $\langle a,b\rangle$ was the image of $\langle a,b\rangle$ under the meet map $\cap(\langle a,b\rangle) = a \cap b$.

Thus in this adjoint situation between the two categories P(U) and $P(U) \times P(U)$, we have a pair of maps ("adjoint functors") going each way between the categories such that each element in a category defines a certain property in the other category and the map carries the element to the concrete universal for that property.

$$P(U) \underset{\cap}{\overset{\Delta}{\rightleftarrows}} P(U) \times P(U)$$

Figure 8.4. Example of Adjoint Functors Between Partial Orders

The notion of a pair of adjoint functors is ubiquitous; it is one of the main tools that highlights concrete universals throughout modern mathematics.

The Third Man Argument in Plato

Much of the modern Platonic literature on self-participation and self-predication [e.g., Malcolm 1991] stems from the work of Vlastos on the Third Man argument [1981]. The name derives from Aristotle, but the argument occurs in the dialogues.

> But now take largeness itself and the other things which are large. Suppose you look at all these in the same way in your mind's eye, will not yet another unity make its appearance—by virtue of which they all appear large?
>
> So it would seem.
>
> If so, a second form of largeness will present itself, over and above largeness itself and the things that share in it, and again, covering all these, yet another, which will make all of them large. So each of your forms will no longer be one, but an indefinite number. [Parmenides, 132]

If a form is self-predicative, the participation relation can be interpreted as "resemblance." An instance has the property F because it resembles the paradigmatic example of F-ness. But then, the Third Man argument contends, the common property shared by Largeness and other large things gives rise to a "One over the many," a form Largeness* such that Largeness and the large things share the common property by virtue of resembling Largeness.* And the argument repeats itself giving rise to an infinite regress of forms. A key part of the Third Man argument is what Vlastos calls the *Non-Identity thesis:*

> NI If anything has a given character by participating in a Form, it is not identical with that Form. [Vlastos 1981, 351]

It implies that Largeness* is not identical with Largeness.

P. T. Geach [1956] has developed a self-predicative interpretation of Forms as standards or norms, an idea he attributes to Wittgenstein. A stick is a yard long because it resembles, lengthwise, the standard yard measure. Geach avoids the Third Man regress with the exceptionalist device of holding the Form "separate" from the many so they could not be grouped together to give rise to a new "One over the many." Geach aptly notes the analogy with Frege's ad hoc and unsuccessful attempt to avoid the Russell-type paradoxes by allowing a set of all and only the sets which are not members of themselves—except for that set itself [viz. Quine 1955a, Geach 1980].

Category theory provides a mathematical model for the Third Man argument, and it shows how to avoid the regress. The category-theoretic model shows that the flaw in the Third Man argument lies not in self-predication but in the Non-Identity thesis [viz. Vlastos 1954, 326–329]. "The One" is not necessarily "over the many"; it can be (isomorphic to) one among the many. In mathematical terms, a colimit or limit can "take on" one of the elements in the diagram. In the special case of sets ordered by inclusion, the union or intersection of a collection of sets is not necessarily distinct from the sets in the collection; it could be one among the many.

For example, let $A = \cup \{A_\beta\}$ be the One formed as the union of a collection of many sets $\{A_\beta\}$. Then add A to the collection and form the new One* as

$$A^* = \cup \{A_\beta\} \cup A.$$

This operation leads to no Third Man regress since $A^* = A$.

Whitehead described European philosophy as a series of footnotes to Plato, and the Theory of Forms was central to Plato's thought. We have seen a number of ways in which the interpretation of category theory as the theory of concrete universals provides a rigorous self-predicative mathematical model for Plato's theory of Forms and for the intuitive notion of a concrete universal elsewhere in philosophy.

Category Theory and Foundations

What is the relevance of category theory to the foundations of mathematics? Today, this question might be answered by pointing to Lawvere and Tierney's *theory of topoi* [e.g., Lawvere 1972, Lawvere et al. 1975, or Hatcher 1982]. Topos theory can be viewed as a categorically formulated generalization of set theory to abstract sheaf theory. A set can be viewed as a sheaf of sets on the one-point space, and much of the machinery of set theory can be generalized to sheaves (e.g., the author's 1971 dissertation [1974] generalizing the ultraproduct construction to sheaves on a topological space). Since much of mathematics can be formulated in set theory, it can be reconstructed with many variations in topoi.

The concept of category theory as the logic of concrete universals presents quite a different picture of the foundational relevance of category theory. Topos theory is important in its own right as a generalization of set theory, but it does not exclusively capture category theory's foundational relevance. Concrete universals do not "generalize" abstract universals, so as the theory of concrete universals, category theory does not try to generalize set theory, the theory of abstract universals. Category theory presents the theory of the other type of universals, the self-participating or concrete universals.

Logic becomes concrete in category theory as the theory of concrete universals. Facts become things. Properties F can be realized concretely as universals u_F. The fact that x is an F-instance is realized concretely by the unique participation $x \rightarrow u_F$. A universal implication "for all x, F(x) implies G(x) is realized concretely by the unique participation morphism $u_F \rightarrow u_G$ wherein one universal "brings on" or entails another universal.

Category theory is relevant to foundations in a different way than set theory. As the theory of concrete universals, category theory does not attempt to derive all of mathematics from a single theory. Instead, category theory's foundational relevance is that it provides universality concepts to characterize the important structures or forms throughout mathematics.

The Working mathematician knows that the importance of category theory is that it provides a criterion of importance in mathematics. Category theory provides the concepts to isolate the universal instance from among all the instances of a property. The Concrete Universal is the most important instance of a property beause it represents the property in a paradigmatic way. It shows the essence of the property without any imperfections. All other instances have the property by virtue of participating in the Concrete Universal.

Notes

1. Quine's system ML [1955b] allows "V ∈ V" for the universal class V, but no standard model of ML has ever been found where "⊂" is interpreted as set membership [viz. Hatcher 1982, Chapter 7]. We are concerned with theories that are "set theories" in the sense that "∈" can be interpreted as set membership.

2. To help establish notation, a category may be defined as follows [e.g., MacLane and Birkhoff 1967 or MacLane 1971]:

A *category* C consists of

(a) a set of *objects* a, b, c, ...,
(b) for each pair of objects <a,b>, a set $\hom_C(a,b) = C(a,b)$ whose elements are represented as *arrows* or *morphsims* f: a → b,
(c) for any $f \in \hom_C(a,b)$ and $g \in \hom_C(b,c)$, there is the *composition* gf: a→b→c in $\hom_C(a,c)$,
(d) composition of arrows is an associative operation, and
(e) for each object a, there is an arrow $1_a \in \hom_C(a,a)$, called the *identity* of a, such that for any f: a→b and g:c→a, $f1_a = f$ and $1_a g = g$.

An arrow f:a→b is an *isomorphism* if there is an arrow g:b→a such that fg = 1_b and gf = 1_a.

3. Thus it must be verified that two concrete universals for the same property are isomorphic. By the universality condition, two concrete universals u and u′ for the same property must participate in each other. Let f:u′→u and g:u→u′ be the unique arrows given by the mutual participation. Then by composition gf:u′→u′ is the unique arrow u′→u′ but $1_{u'}$ is another such arrow so by uniqueness, gf = $1_{u'}$. Similarly, fg:u→u is the unique self-participation arrow for u so fg = 1_u. Thus mutual participation of u and u′ implies u ≅ u′.

References

Allen, R. E. 1960. "Participation and Predication in Plato's Middle Dialogues." *The Philosophical Review* 64:147–64.

Boolos, George. 1971. "The Iterative Conception of Set." *The Journal of Philosophy* 68 (April 22):215–31.

Eilenberg, S., and MacLane, S. 1945. "General Theory of Natural Equivalences." *Transactions of the American Mathematical Society* 58:231–94.

Ellerman, David P. 1974. "Sheaves of Structures and Generalized Ultraproducts." *Annals of Mathematical Logic* 7 (December): 163–95.

———. 1988. "Category Theory and Concrete Universals." *Erkenntnis* 28: 409–29.

Geach, P. T. 1956. "The Third Man Again." *The Philosophical Review* 65: 72–82.

———. 1980. *Logic Matters*. Berkeley: University of California Press.

Hatcher, William. 1982. *The Logical Foundations of Mathematics*. Oxford: Pergamon Press.

Kneale, William, and Martha Kneale. 1962. *The Development of Logic*. Oxford: Oxford University Press.

Lawvere, W., ed. 1972. *Springer Lecture Notes in Mathematics 274: Toposes, Algebraic Geometry and Logic*. Berlin: Springer-Verlag.

Lawvere, W., C. Maurer, and G. C. Wraith. 1975. *Springer Lecture Notes in Mathematics 445: Model Theory and Topoi*. Berlin: Springer-Verlag.

MacLane, Saunders. 1971. *Categories for the Working Mathematician*. New York: Springer-Verlag.

MacLane, Saunders, and Garrett Birkhoff. 1967. *Algebra*. New York: MacMillan.

Malcolm, John. 1991. *Plato on the Self-Predication of Forms*. Oxford: Clarendon Press.

Quine, W.V.O. 1955a. On Frege's Way Out. *Mind*. 64: 145–59.

Quine, W.V.O. 1955b. *Mathematical Logic*. Cambridge, Mass.: Harvard University Press.

Sayre, Kenneth. 1969. *Plato's Analytic Method*. Chicago: University of Chicago Press.

Schubert, Horst. 1972. *Categories*. Trans. Eva Gray. New York: Springer-Verlag.

Vlastos, Gregory. 1981. *Platonic Studies*. Princeton: Princeton University Press.

Vlastos, Gregory, ed. 1978. *Plato: A Collection of Critical Essays I: Metaphysics and Epistemology*. Notre Dame: University of Notre Dame Press.

Chapter 9

Keiretsu, Proportional Representation, and Input-Output Theory

Introduction

In view of the modern economic success of Japan, more and more attention is turning to Japanese models of corporate ownership and management. Many of the large, world-famous Japanese corporations are part of ownership groups called *keiretsu*. There is cross ownership between the companies in the group as well as some ownership outside the group that is traded on the stock market. In spite of the partial outside ownership, the *keiretsu* often behave as "self-owning" groups.

What is the meaning of the circular cross-ownership relations? The answer depends on the assumptions made about the companies acting as "transmission belts" (for votes and dividends) between their shares and the shares they hold in other companies. The realistic assumption is that the companies do not act as transmission belts. Then majority cross ownership within a *keiretsu* results in a form of group ownership controlled by the senior managers and bankers in the group. Analysis of this Japanese form of group ownership and comparisons with employee ownership in the West are topics worthy of consideration.

The realistic assumption, however, is often not the one that leads to a mathematically interesting theory (a very common occurrence in mathematical economics). We develop the technically interesting theory that the companies in a cross-owning group serve as vote-and-dividend transmission belts between their shares and the shares they own. Since the ownership pattern is circular, the effects of passing through the votes and dividends lead to an infinite series. The appropriate mathematical framework is input-output theory where the infinite series is the series expansion of the Leontief inverse matrix [see Ellerman 1991]. Even though input-output theory is over forty years old, this application to circular ownership patterns seems to be new.

There is an "unexpected" connection between this analysis of ownership structures and the controversy surrounding proportional representation (PR) in voting systems. This connection allows one to examine PR in a new light and to see why it may not be appropriate in complex political systems.

The Primal Theory of Own and Gross Values

The Cross-Ownership Matrix

There are n firms in the ownership federation or *keiretsu*, and a_{ij} is the proportion of firm j directly owned by firm i.

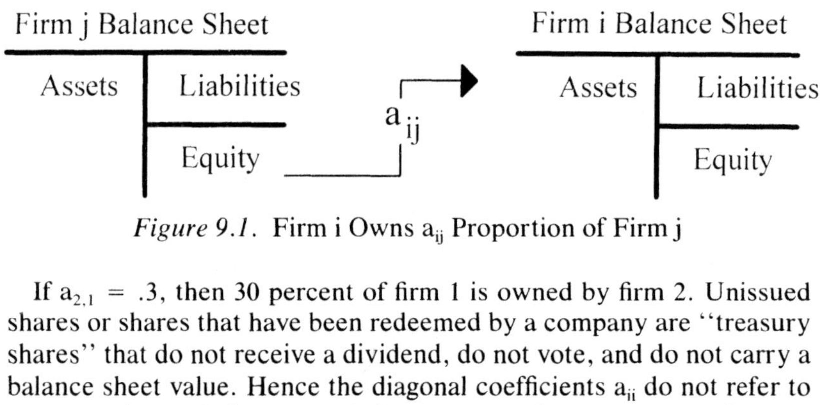

Figure 9.1. Firm i Owns a_{ij} Proportion of Firm j

If $a_{2,1} = .3$, then 30 percent of firm 1 is owned by firm 2. Unissued shares or shares that have been redeemed by a company are "treasury shares" that do not receive a dividend, do not vote, and do not carry a balance sheet value. Hence the diagonal coefficients a_{ii} do not refer to treasury shares. It is assumed that a corporation cannot own its own shares as assets on the balance sheet so $a_{ii} = 0$ (which corresponds to "netting out" the self-transactions of an industry in the usual interindustry analysis).

Let $A = [a_{ij}]$ for $i, j = 1,\ldots,n$ be the (non-negative) *cross-ownership matrix*. Let $\mathbf{1} = (1,\ldots,1)$ be the row vector of n ones so $\mathbf{1}A$ is the row vector of column sums, which is denoted $c = (c_1,\ldots,c_n) = \mathbf{1}A$. The sum c_j of the jth column gives the proportion of the jth company that is owned by the other companies in the group so $1 - c_j$ gives the proportion of the jth company that is "external" in the sense of being owned by legal parties other than the remaining $n-1$ firms in the group. It is assumed that each company has some external ownership so $c_j < 1$. Under that assumption, the Leontief inverse $[I-A]^{-1}$ exists and is non-negative [see Hadley 1961, 118–19].

Own Values and Gross Values

Given a corporation in the ownership federation, we must distinguish between its own shares called "own shares" and the shares it owns in other companies called "owned shares." The direction of causality is different for dividends and votes. The primal input-output theory is concerned with dividends and other income flows that we assume are transmitted by the company from owned shares to own shares. The dual theory is applied to votes that we assume the board of directors passes on from own shares (i.e., the shareholders) to owned shares.

Consider, for example, the flows of dividends. Each company has two types of dividends on its shares: its own dividends (the dividends from its own operations) and the dividends received on owned shares (which we assumed are passed through to the company's own shares). Let $d = (d_1,\ldots,d_n)'$ (the apostrophe indicates transpose) be the column vector of *own dividends* for each company due to its own operations, and let $x = (x_1,\ldots,x_n)'$ be the column vector of *gross or total dividends* declared by the companies. Then Ax is the column vector of dividends received by the companies on the owned shares, and the total dividends are the sum of the *received dividends* (which are passed through by assumption) and the own dividends.

$$x = Ax + d$$

Equation 9.1. Gross Dividends x = Received Dividends Ax + Own Dividends d

The usual Leontief inverse computes the gross dividends from the own dividends: $x = [I-A]^{-1}d$.

The cross-ownership relations do not create any new dividends but they do change the distribution. The dividends $(1-c_j)x_j$ received by the external shareholders of firm j are, in general, different from the own dividends d_j of firm j. But since the dividends received by each firm on its owned shares were simply passed through, the total of the dividends accruing to external shareholders must equal the total of the own dividends **1**d:

$$\sum_{j=1}^{n}(1-c_j)x_j = \mathbf{1}(I-A)x = \mathbf{1}d$$

Equation 9.2. Total External Dividends = Total Own Dividends

The application is not unique to dividends. Any corporate stock/flow value that is transmitted by the a_{ij} coefficients can also be used. For instance, let d_j be the stock quantity that is the net asset value (assets minus liabilities) at a point in time of the jth firm without counting the net asset value of the owned shares. Let x_j be the total net asset value of the jth firm. The total net asset values x are given as the net asset values Ax of the owned shares plus the net asset values of the firms independent of their owned shares. The total net asset values $x = [I-A]^{-1}d$ are "inflated" above the "real" values d, but the sum of the net asset values belonging to external shareholders, $\mathbf{1}(I-A)x = (\mathbf{1}-c)x$, equals the sum of the real values **1**d.

It is useful to construct a general interpretation that includes the special cases. Let d_j be a (stock or flow) *own value* held or generated by the jth firm independently of the cross ownership relations. Let x_j be the corresponding *gross value* associated with the jth firm. Gross values are "transmitted" between companies by the a_{ij} coefficients. The *received values* Ax of the owned shares "pass through" each company and add to the own values d to yield the gross values x.

$$x = Ax + d$$

Equation 9.3. Gross Values x = Received Values Ax + Own Values d

The gross value x can be computed as the Leontief inverse times the own values d, that is, $x = [I-A]^{-1}d$. By the representation of the Leontief inverse as the sum of a matrix series,

$$[I-A]^{-1} = I + A + A^2 + \cdots,$$

Equation 9.4. Leontief Inverse Matrix as an Infinite Series

the gross value x is the direct own values d plus the first stage received values Ad plus the second stage received values A^2d and so forth: $x = d + Ad + A^2d + \cdots$.

Let $B = [b_{ij}] = [I-A]^{-1}$ be the Leontief inverse. The general interpretation of the Leontief inverse is that it gives the "ultimate" direct and indirect cross-ownership relations between the corporations—where each firm is represented as having 100 percent direct self-ownership.

> The ij-element b_{ij} of the **Leontief inverse** is the total direct and indirect proportion of the jth firm owned by the ith firm for $i \neq j$,
>
> and
>
> $b_{ii} = 1 +$ total indirect self-ownership of ith firm.

Let $I-C$ be the $n \times n$ diagonal matrix with the diagonal entries $1-c_j$ for $j = 1,\ldots,n$. The matrix $D = (I-C)[I-A]^{-1}$ will be called the *external ownership matrix.*

> The D_{ij} element of the **external ownership matrix** D gives the proportion of total (direct and indirect) ownership of jth firm by the external shareholders of ith firm.

The column sums of the non-negative matrix A are less than one since they represent the proportion of each firm directly owned by the other firms. Hence $I-C$ is non-negative and thus $D = (I-C)[I-A]^{-1}$ is also non-negative. Moreover the columns of D sum to one since

$$\mathbf{1}D = \mathbf{1}(I-C)[I-A]^{-1} = (1-c)[I-A]^{-1} = \mathbf{1}[I-A][I-A]^{-1} = \mathbf{1}I = \mathbf{1} = (1,\ldots,1).$$

Let $y = (y_1,\ldots,y_n)' = ((1-c_1)x_1,\ldots,(1-c_n)x_n)'$ be the column vector of *external values* accruing to the external shareholder(s) of the firms. The external values y can be computed directly from the own values d by the external ownership matrix:

$$y = Dd.$$

Equation 9.5. External Values y = External Ownership D × Own Values d

The ith external value y_i is not necessarily equal to the ith own value d_i, but the sum of the external values, $\mathbf{1}y = \mathbf{1}Dd = \mathbf{1}d$, is equal to the sum of the own values.

The Dual Theory of Ownership and Control

Premature Majoritization versus Proportional Representation

In traditional input-output theory, the direction of determination reverses itself between the primal and dual theories. In the primal theory, the levels of the outputs determine the level of the inputs, while in the dual price theory, the value of the primary inputs determines the value of the outputs. In a corporation, control flows in the opposite direction to value. Value flows from the corporation to the shareholders (in dividends and capital gains) while control and ownership rights go (in theory) from the shareholders to the corporation. Since what we have taken as the primal theory is concerned with the flow of value from corporations to the external shareholders, we will take the dual theory as being concerned with the flow of control and ownership rights in the opposite direction from the external shareholders to the firms.

When there is cross ownership of corporations, control questions are no less subtle and intertwined than valuation questions. To understand the complexities, we must first consider how majority voting outcomes can be manipulated through majoritization at the level of subgroups or districts. Each decision is a yes-or-no question that can be represented by a "1" or a "0." A yes-or-no question put to any company in the group will eventually be put to every other company in the group that is directly or indirectly an owner of the given company. We assume that the boards vote as directed by the shareholders, so the question will ultimately be decided by the external shareholders of the companies in the group.

Given the votes of the shareholders (external and other companies in the group), there are two ways that the board can vote on the owned shares. The board could majoritize and vote all the owned shares as a block according to the majority outcome, or the board could simply pass through the percentages for and against on the owned shares. For instance, if the shareholders vote 60 percent in favor and 40 percent against, the majoritizing board would vote all the owned shares in favor, while the pass-through board would vote 60 percent of the owned shares in favor and 40 percent against.

The pass-through board is the corporate version of proportional representation (PR), while the majoritizing board corresponds to the system of districts with single representatives representing a majority of the voters in the district. It is easy to see how the system of majoritizing districts can lead to violations of majority rule. Suppose there are nine voters with four in favor and five against a proposal.

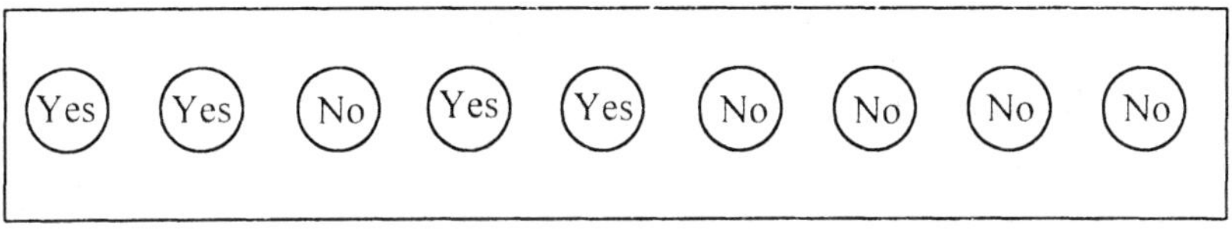

Figure 9.2. Majority Votes No

By majority rule, the proposal would fail. But now suppose the electorate is divided into equal sized districts (as is the goal in the U.S. House of Representatives), and that two of the three districts each have two of the yes votes.

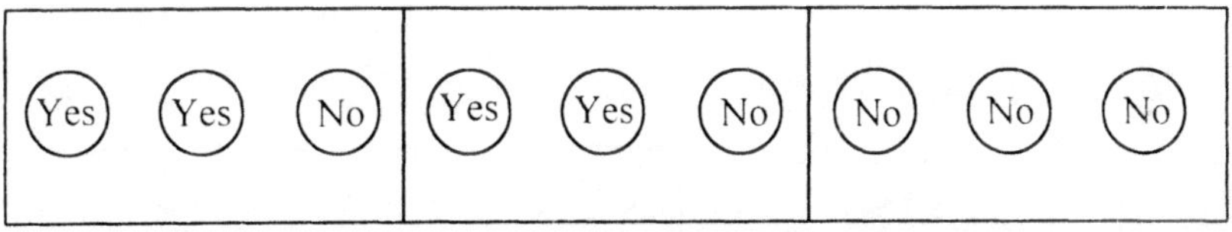

Figure 9.3. Majority of Representatives Vote Yes

Then by majority voting at the district level, two out of the three districts would vote in favor of the proposal so it would pass (in violation of majority rule by the ultimate voters). If the districts did not majoritize but only passed through the proportions for and against the proposal, then the result would be the same as in the direct referendum without districts. Thus the pass-through system gives a correct representation of the electorate, while "premature majoritization" at the district level can allow manipulation of the results. The PR system with large districts and many party representatives for each district to roughly represent the voters' party preferences is an attempt to reproduce the pass-through system in a system of party representatives.

Majoritization in each district and majority voting by districts can thus give a result in opposition to the majority of the primary voters. This has occurred, for example, in the American Electoral College. The unit rule of casting all of a state's electoral votes according to the majority vote in the state resulted in Benjamin Harrison defeating Grover Cleveland in the 1888 presidential election even though Cleveland had 5,540,050 popular votes to Harrison's 5,444,337.

The problems generated by premature majoritization (e.g., with majority-elected single representative districts) are the subject of a large literature in political science on proportional representation (PR) [see the bibliography in Dummett 1984]. John Stuart Mill gave the classic case for PR in his *Considerations on Representative Government* [1861] and Walter Bagehot [1867] gave a classic critique of PR in the context of multiparty systems. In this century, Hoag and Hallett [1969, orig. 1926] reviewed the arguments for PR, while Hermens [1972, orig. 1941] reviewed the case against PR in multiparty politics.

Pyramidal holding company schemes are the corporate versions of the premature majoritization. To adapt the previous example, suppose we have a corporation with $400 paid in by shareholder A and $500 paid in by shareholder B. Clearly B is the majority shareholder.

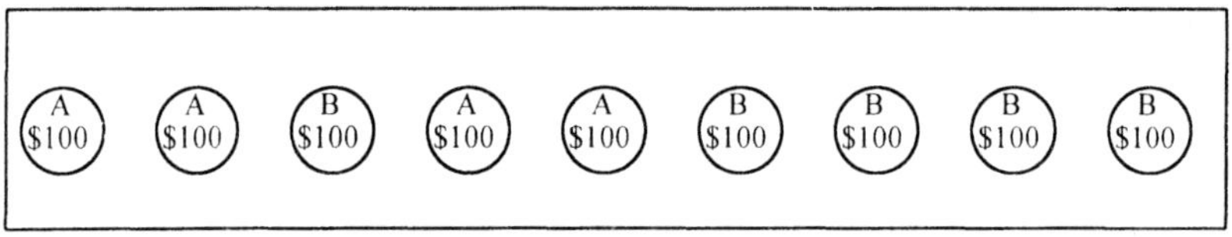

Figure 9.4. Investor B is Majority Shareholder in Company

Now suppose that instead of putting money directly into the company, two other "parent" companies are formed, AABAAB Inc. and BBB Inc. The investors put their money into these parent companies, and then the money is invested into the daughter company in return for its shares.

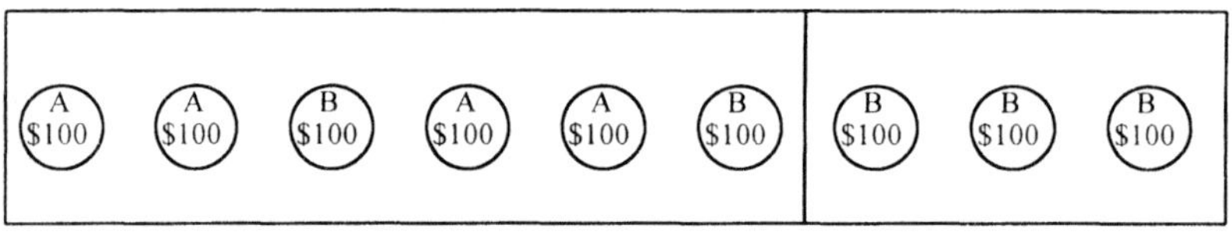

Figure 9.5. Investor A Controls Company Through Pyramidal Holding Company

Investor A owns two-thirds of AABAAB Inc., which in turn owns two-thirds of the daughter company. Thus if the corporate boards majoritize decisions, then investor A controls AABAAB, and it, in turn, controls the daughter company. Therefore, the holding company structure allows investor A to control the daughter company with only a minority of the ultimate capital. If the corporate boards (e.g., in

AABAAB) only pass through the shareholder votes, then investor B would have control of the daughter company as in the structure without the parent companies.

If the daughter company has to make a decision, then it, of course, has to majoritize the votes of its shareholders to a yes-or-no decision. But when that question is put to the AABAAB company as a shareholder in the daughter company, there is no reason for it to vote all its shares as a block ("premature majoritization"). When AABAAB polls its shareholders, suppose that A votes in favor with B against. Then AABAAB Inc. could pass through the votes to its shares in the daughter as two-thirds in favor and one-third against the proposition. Shareholder B's vote would have $(1/3) \times (2/3) = 2/9$ weight through the AABAAB company and 3/9 weight through the BBB company, so its 5/9 weight overall would give B majority control of the daughter company.

The situation is considerably more complicated in the circular ownership federation—particularly with the pass-through voting assumption. Under that assumption, the Leontief inverse is needed to compute the proportions voted by the company boards in terms of the external shareholder votes. We construct an example of an ownership federation with five companies. Using premature majoritization, the external majority shareholder of one of the companies can control the other four companies through a pyramidal structure. But with pass-through voting, that majority shareholder in one firm controls only that firm and the other four firms are controlled by their own direct external shareholders.

Suppose JPM (as in J. P. Morgan) is the 51 percent external owner of Firm 1. Firm 1 owns 51 percent of Firm 2. Firm 1 and Firm 2 each own 25.5 percent of Firm 3 for a total of 51 percent. Firms 1, 2, and 3 each own 17 percent of Firm 4 for a total of 51 percent. And Firms 1, 2, 3, and 4 each own 12.75 percent of Firm 5 for a total of 51 percent. Thus it appears that JPM "controls" (i.e., has 51 percent control of) Firm 1 and through it, Firm 2 as well. But Firm 1 and Firm 2 together control Firm 3 and so forth. Thus JPM seems to control all five firms through the pyramid structure. If we split the other 49 percent of Firm 1 equally between Firms 2 through 5, then that would not appear to change matters since JPM already controls Firms 2 through 5. The following table gives the cross-ownership matrix A (in the bordered area) with the a_{ij} expressed in percentage form, i.e., a_{ij} is the percent of ownership of Firm j by Firm i.

	Firm 1	Firm 2	Firm 3	Firm 4	Firm 5
Firm 1	0.00%	51.00%	25.50%	17.00%	12.75%
Firm 2	12.25%	0.00%	25.50%	17.00%	12.75%
Firm 3	12.25%	0.00%	0.00%	17.00%	12.75%
Firm 4	12.25%	0.00%	0.00%	0.00%	12.75%
Firm 5	12.25%	0.00%	0.00%	0.00%	0.00%
Ext.Control	51.00%	49.00%	49.00%	49.00%	49.00%
Total	100.00%	100.00%	100.00%	100.00%	100.00%

Figure 9.6. Cross-Ownership Matrix A for Pyramidal Holding Structure

Each firm decides a question by majority voting, where "majority" means more than 50 percent of the ownership. In the pyramidal structure, JPM owns 51 percent of Firm 1 so he can always control Firm 1's decisions. The question is about the other firms. JPM is, in effect, using the firms as multilevel districts to inflate the effect of his vote. JPM's actual indirect ownership of Firm 2 is 51 percent of 51 percent or about 26 percent, assuming we ignore the circular feedback effects of each of the other firms' 12.25 percent ownership stakes in Firm 1. Taking the circular effects into account, we will see that JPM's total indirect ownership of Firm 2 is about 31.86 percent. But by using Firm 1 as a district for "premature majoritization," JPM in effect is disenfranchising the 12.25 percent stakes of the other firms and their external shareholders. Thus he gains control of Firm 2, and the process repeats itself for the other firms.

The cure for the manipulation, as noted above, is not to majoritize prematurely. Each "district" vote should be passed along in its true proportions—as is the intent of the various schemes of electoral reform using proportional representation. Since the cross-ownership structure is, in general, circular, adding up the final votes means summing an infinite series, namely the series expansion of the Leontief inverse matrix. With this introductory motivation, we may turn to the theoretical development of the dual theory.

Direct and Indirect Ownership and Control

The external shareholder(s) of each of the n firms votes as a unit to determine the zero-or-one variables $w_1, w_2, \ldots, w_n$. Let $w = (w_1, w_2, \ldots, w_n)$ be the row vector of external shareholder votes. As before, let $c = (c_1, \ldots, c_n) = (1, \ldots, 1)A = \mathbf{1}A$ be the column sums of A that represent proportions of the firms owned by the other firms, so $\mathbf{1}-c=(1-c_1,\ldots,1-c_n)$ is the row vector representing the proportions of the firms owned by the external shareholders. Let $I-C$ be the $n \times n$ diagonal matrix with the $1-c_i$ entries on the diagonal. Hence $w(I-C)=(w_1(1-c_1),\ldots,w_n(1-c_n))$ is the row vector of external shareholder votes weighted by their proportion of ownership in the firms.

The final decisions of the n firms are to be determined by majoritizing the n variables $p_1, p_2,\ldots, p_n$ which represent the final sums of the w_i votes tallied using the ownership relations represented by the cross-ownership matrix A. For a variable p with $0 \leq p \leq 1$, the *majoritization* of p, maj(p), is defined by:

$$\text{maj}(p) = \begin{cases} 0 \text{ if } 0 \leq p \leq .5 \\ 1 \text{ if } .5 < p \leq 1 \end{cases}.$$

Equation 9.6. Majoritization Function

The decision variables p are obtained as the sum of the decisions pA passed on from the other firms plus the external shareholders' decisions $w(I-C)$: $p=pA+w(I-C)$. The variables p to be majoritized to obtain each firm's decision are thus computed as:

$$p = w(I-C)[I-A]^{-1}.$$

Equation 9.7. Firms' Decision Variables p in terms of External Shareholder Votes w

Let $D=(I-C)[I-A]^{-1}$be the external ownership matrix. The equation $p=wD$ expresses the decision variables as the "ultimate" (direct and indirect) ownership-weighted sum of the external votes w. Hence each p_j is the weighted sum of the w_i's where the non-negative weights in the jth column of D sum to one. Since each vote w_i is zero or one, $1 \leq p_j \leq 0$ for all j. Majoritization of the final tally p_j means that Firm j's decision is affirmative if $p_j > .50$ and negative otherwise.

The ultimate ownership of all the n firms is in the hands of the external shareholders who cast the votes $w_1,\ldots,w_n$. But due to the cross-ownership relations expressed in the matrix A, the external shareholders have more than just their direct ownership of their companies. The D_{ij} entry in the D matrix gives the proportion of ultimate (direct and indirect) ownership of Firm j by the external shareholders of Firm i.

$$p = wD = w(I-C)[I-A]^{-1} = w(I-C)[I+A+A^2+\cdots]$$

Equation 9.8. Circular Ownership Gives Infinite Summation of Votes

The calculation of the decision variables results from passing the true proportions of the ultimate w_i votes through the "districts" or firms, and summing all the stages in the series expansion of the Leontief inverse.

Consider the previous example of five firms with a "pyramidal" holding company structure with JPM owning 51 percent of Firm 1 as the top of the pyramid. The external ownership matrix D is expressed in percentages in the bordered area of the following table.

	Firm 1	Firm 2	Firm 3	Firm 4	Firm 5
Ext. Shareholders of Firm 1	62.48%	31.86%	24.06%	20.13%	17.66%
Ext. Shareholders of Firm 2	12.17%	55.21%	17.18%	14.38%	12.62%
Ext. Shareholders of Firm 3	9.70%	4.95%	52.74%	11.46%	10.05%
Ext. Shareholders of Firm 4	8.29%	4.23%	3.19%	51.67%	8.59%
Ext. Shareholders of Firm 5	7.35%	3.75%	2.83%	2.37%	51.08%
Column Sums	100.00%	100.00%	100.00%	100.00%	100.00%

Figure 9.7. External Ownership Matrix $D=(I-C)[I-A]^{-1}$ in Pyramidal Example

We see that when the "district" vote manipulations are prevented by passing through the true proportions of the votes, then—far from JPM controlling all five firms—JPM controls only Firm 1. The other diagonal entries are all larger than 50 percent so the other external shareholders would each have control of their companies. They own 49 percent directly, and their indirect ownership through the cross ownership relations puts each over 50 percent.

For instance, the third column of D expresses p_3 as a weighted sum of the w_i votes:

$$p_3 = .2406w_i + .1718w_2 + .5274w_3 + .0319w_4 + .0283w_5.$$

Since the coefficient of w_3 is greater than .50, the external shareholder of Firm 3 has a controlling interest of 52.74 percent in Firm 3 (in spite of only having 49 percent direct ownership). If w_3 is one, then p_3 majoritizes to one, and if w_3 is zero, then p_3 rounds down to zero.

Thus $maj(p_3) = w_3$ regardless of the other w_i votes (recall the w_i's are here taken as zero-or-one variables). Without using the "district" structure to disenfranchise minority shareholders by premature majoritization, JPM only has 24.06 percent of the ultimate ownership of Firm 3 (as shown by the $D_{1,3}$ entry).

The Primal and Dual Theories

The ownership-weights matrix D permits a concise statement of the primal and dual theories (note that it is somewhat arbitrary which theory is called "primal" and which "dual"). Consider the column vector d of own values for the firms and the row vector w of external shareholder votes.

$$y = Dd$$

Equation 9.9. Primal Theory: External Values = External Ownership × Own Values

$$p = wD$$

Equation 9.10. Dual Theory: Firm Votes = External Votes × External Ownership

A more general interpretation can be constructed. A "primal" variable is a value variable where the direction of determination runs from the firms to the shareholders (i.e., the firms give value to the shares, not vice versa). A "dual" variable is a control/ownership variable where the direction of determination runs from the shareholders to the firms.

Given primal values d for the firms prior to considering cross-ownership relations, $y = Dd$ gives the corresponding values for the external shareholders after taking the cross-ownership relations into account.

Given dual values w for the external shareholders prior to considering cross-ownership relations, $p = wD$ gives the corresponding values for the firms after considering the cross-ownership relations.

For another example of a dual variable, let w_i be the proportion of the external shareholding of Firm i that is directly held by a given legal party, say, JPM. Take d to be the column vector of own dividends for the firm. Then the dividends accruing to JPM can be computed in two ways.

$$wy = w(Dd) = (wD)d = pd$$

Equation 9.11. Direct Ownership × External Dividends = Total Ownership × Own Dividends

Since y = Dd gives the dividends accruing to the external shareholders, wy gives the dividends accruing to JPM. Alternatively, p = wD gives the proportions of each firm directly and indirectly owned by JPM so pd is JPM's dividends.

A New Look at Proportional Representation

What new light does this comparison with pyramidal holding structures throw on the debate about PR? First, we have focused on premature majoritization as the crucial difference between PR and non-PR systems. We have seen that the "solution" to the "problem" of premature majoritization is pass-through voting. All the elaborate theories about PR and systems of voting so as not to waste votes in premature majoritization [see Dummett 1984] have been something of a distraction. They can be seen as ways to approximate pass-through voting. Instead of debating the intricacies of the various PR systems, we can thus focus on the basic question: "Is pass-through voting (no matter how obtained) what is desired?"

If the answer is "Yes" then the House of Representatives and the Senate (and the various chambers in other representative systems) are merely anachronisms that can be replaced by direct electronic polling of the citizens (as seems to be advocated by some partisans of "electronic democracy"). Are representatives supposed to exercise intelligence in debating and deciding an issue, or are they simply supposed to "represent" their constituents without any independent decision making?

Some representative systems exist in which the delegates are not supposed to deliberate; they should merely pass through the votes of their constituents. The Electoral College in the American presidential elections is one example. Yet the "unit rule" means that there is premature majoritization at the state level so that the result can end up being elected with a minority of the popular votes cast in a two-way race (as in Harrison's victory over Cleveland in 1888). There seems to be little reason why the Electoral College should not be eliminated. There is no need to replace it with a representative system using pass-through voting since there is no need for representatives at all in collecting the votes of a presidential election. A direct vote count will suffice.

Another situation where pass-through voting may be appropriate are trusts such as the Employee Stock Ownership Plan or ESOPs. Corporate shares owned by the employees of a company are held in a special tax-favored trust. The trustees (unlike the directors of the company) have a rather formal role and are not usually selected for their wisdom or expertise. The trustee might even be the trust department of a bank. When casting votes to elect the board of directors, the trustees can pass through the proportions of the votes of the employee shareholders. There is no need for any elaborate PR voting system. If the ESOP trustees do majoritize, then it is not because the trustees are supposed to be a deliberative body. It is because the majority of the employee-owners in the ESOP want to inflate their voting strength (relative to the non-ESOP shareholders) by using block voting.

We shall assume (without arguing the point here) that the chambers of representative bodies such as the House of Representatives and the Senate are intended to be deliberative bodies. They are not supposed to just count the noses (or telegrams) of their constituents. They are supposed to be the sort of individuals who can bring some wisdom and experience to bear on the questions, who can engage in adversarial debates to sharpen the issues, and who can arrive at the end of the decision-making process at a better and wiser decision than could be obtained by taking a referendum of the undeveloped and uninformed opinions of the constituents. Or the point could be put the other way around. The sort of questions of social decision making that could be best answered after deliberation, research, and debate are the sort of questions that should be put to a deliberative body as opposed to a referendum.

In the past, referenda were quite costly and difficult to administer. But with modern electronics, widespread referenda are now quite feasible. Electronic demagogues, who want social questions put directly to the public in electronic referenda, miss the whole deliberative side of social choice. Social choice theory as represented, for example, in Arrow's Impossibility Theorem also misses that deliberative dimension [see Arrow 1951]. That theory sees social decisions as being based on nose counting, but then worries about what rule to use to convert the nose counts into decisions. For instance, Arrow generalized the parlor paradox of majority voting by showing that any general rule that satisfied a number of seemingly reasonable requirements would lead to similar paradoxes. The subsequent development of "social choice theory" has been a perfect example where rather trite questions dominated the theory because those questions could be treated mathematically, and the substantive questions that were not formally tractable were passed over in silence (e.g., in a world of rather asymmetric information and bounded rationality, should social choice just be a matter of nose counting?).

To conclude, we have noted that some representative bodies are intended as deliberative bodies while others are best seen as "transmission belts" to pass along the votes of the constituents. When a representative body is properly deliberative, then majoritization at that level of decision making is not "premature." It would seem that many proponents of proportional representation have confused deliberative representation and pass-through representation, and have thus tried to "reform" the legislative bodies of government into better transmission belts of "public opinion."

References

Arrow, K. J. 1951 (rev. 1963). *Social Choice and Individual Values*. New York: John Wiley & Sons.

Bagehot, W. 1966. [1867]. *The English Constitution*. Ithaca: Cornell University Press.

Dummett, Michael. 1984. *Voting Procedures*. Oxford: Clarendon Press.

Ellerman, David. 1991. "Cross Ownership of Corporations: A New Application of Input-Output Theory." *Metroeconomica* 42, no. 1: 33–46.

Hadley, G. 1961. *Linear Algebra*. Reading, Mass.: Addison-Wesley.

Hermens, F. A. 1972 [1941]. *Democracy or Anarchy: A Study of Proportional Representation*. New York: Johnson Reprint Company.

Hoag, Clarence G., and George H. Hallett. 1969 [1926]. *Proportional Representation*. New York: Johnson Reprint Company.

Mill, John Stuart. 1958 [1861]. *Considerations on Representative Government*. Indianapolis: Bobbs-Merrill.

Chapter 10

Finding the Markets in the Math: Arbitrage and Optimization Theory

Introduction: Finding the Markets in the Math

One of the fundamental insights of mainstream neoclassical economics is the connection between competitive market prices and the Lagrange multipliers of optimization theory in mathematics. Yet this insight has not been well developed. In the standard theory of markets, competitive prices result from the equilibrium of supply and demand. But in a constrained optimization problem, there seems to be no mathematical version of supply and demand functions so that the Lagrange multipliers could be seen as equilibrium prices. How can one "Find the markets in the math" so that Lagrange multipliers will emerge as equilibrium market prices?

We argue that the solution to the "Finding the markets in the math" problem is to reconceptualize equilibrium as the absence of profitable arbitrage instead of the equating of supply and demand. With each proposed solution to a classical constrained optimization problem, there is an associated market. The maximand is one commodity, and each constraint provides another commodity on this market. Given a marginal variation in one commodity, one can define the marginal change in any other given commodity so the market has a set of exchange rates between the commodities. The usual necessary conditions for the proposed solution to solve the maximization problem are the same as the conditions for this mathematically defined "market" to be arbitrage-free. The prices that emerge from the arbitrage-free system of exchange rates (normalized with the maximand as numeraire) are precisely the Lagrange multipliers. We also show that the cofactors of a matrix describing the marginal variations can be taken as the prices (before being normalized) so the Lagrange multipliers can always be presented as ratios of cofactors.

Starting with any square m × m matrix (with rank $\geq$ m − 1), a market can also be defined and the cofactors given a price interpretation so that an economic interpretation can be constructed for the inverse matrix and for Cramer's Rule.

The relevant mathematical result, which dates back to Augustin Cournot in 1838, is that:

> there exists a system of prices for the commodities such that the given exchange rates are the price ratios if and only if the exchange rates are arbitrage-free (in the sense that they multiply to one around any circle).

This simple graph-theoretic theorem is known in its additive version as Kirchhoff's Voltage Law (KVL):

> there exists a system of potentials at the nodes of a circuit such that the voltages on the wires between the nodes are the potential differences if and only if the voltages sum to zero around any cycle.

Kirchhoff's work was published in 1847, so it might be called "the Cournot-Kirchhoff law."

There is also an additive version of the additive KVL. If two commodities are swapped, one unit for one unit, then usually some additional "boot" must be paid for the higher valued commodity. For each pair of goods i and j, suppose we are given an amount boot(i,j) that is the additional cash boot that needs to be paid along with one unit of good i in order to receive one unit of good j. Then KVL takes the form:

> Given a system of boots for commodity swaps, there exists a set of unit prices for the goods such that the boot necessary for an exchange of units is the price difference if and only if the system of boots is arbitrage-free in the sense of summing to zero around any circle.

We show that this Cournot-Kirchhoff law has many applications outside of electrical circuit theory and economics. For instance, the second law of thermodynamics can be formulated as the impossibility of a certain form of "heat arbitrage" between temperature reservoirs, and the "prices" that emerge in this case are the Kelvin absolute temperatures of the reservoirs. Yet another application of the arbitrage framework is in probability theory. Profitable arbitrage in the market for contingent commodities is called "making book." A person's subjective probability judgments satisfy the laws of probability if they are "coherent" in the sense of not allowing book to be made against the person. Thus arbitrage on the market for contingent commodities enforces the laws of probability.

Arbitrage-related concepts have been applied successfully in financial economics. Merton H. Miller and Franco Modigliani used impressive arbitrage arguments in proving their famous irrelevance theorem [1958]. Stephen A. Ross [Ross 1976a, 1976b] and his colleagues have developed Arbitrage Pricing Theory so that it is now recognized as a fundamental principle in finance theory [Varian 1987]. Our purpose here is not to use arbitrage concepts to study financial markets, but to find the mathematically defined "markets" and the related arbitrage concepts in the mathematics of all classical constrained optimization problems.

Arbitrage in Graph Theory

A *directed graph* $G = (G_0,G_1,t,h)$ is given by a set G_0 of *nodes* (numbered 0, 1,...,m), a set G_1 of *arcs* (numbered 1,2,...,b), and *head* and *tail functions* $h,t:G_1 \rightarrow G_0$, which indicate that arc j is directed from its tail, the t(j) node, to its head, the h(j) node.

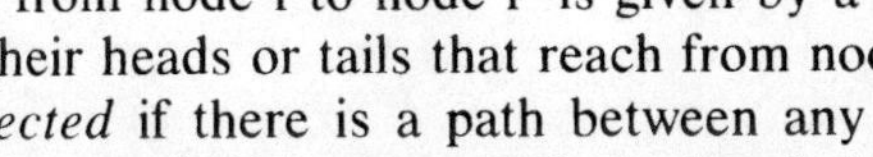

Figure 10.1. Arc j from Tail t(j) to Head h(j)

It is assumed that there are no loops at a node, i.e., $h(j) \neq t(j)$ for all arcs j. A *path* from node i to node i′ is given by a sequence of arcs connected at their heads or tails that reach from node i to node i′. A graph is *connected* if there is a path between any two nodes. It is assumed that the graph G is connected. A closed circular path where no arc occurs more than once is a *cycle* [for more graph theory, see any text such as Berge and Ghouila-Houri 1965].

Let T be any group (not necessarily commutative) written multiplicatively (i.e., a set with a binary product operation defined on it, with an identity element 1 and with every element having a multiplicative inverse or reciprocal). For most of our purposes, T can be taken as R*, the multiplicative group of nonzero reals. In the motivating economic interpretation, a different commodity is associated with each node, and the arcs represent channels of exchange or transformation between the commodities at the nodes. A function $r{:}G_1 \rightarrow T$ is a *rate system* giving exchange or transformation rates. Given an arc j, one unit of the t(j) commodity can be transformed into $r(j) = r_j$ units of the h(j) commodity.

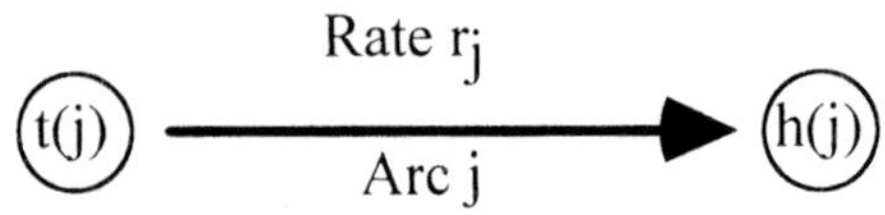

Figure 10.2. Transformation Rate r_j on Arc j

A graph (G,r) with a rate system r represents a market, so it will be called a *market graph.* These group-labeled graphs are also called "voltage graphs" [Gross 1974] or "group graphs" [Harary et al. 1982].

All transformations are reversible. If arc j is traversed against the arrow, the transformation rate is the reciprocal $1/r_j$. Given a path c from node i to i′, the *composite rate* r[c] is the product of the rates along the path using the reciprocal rate for any arc traversed against the direction of the arrow. A function $P{:}G_0 \rightarrow T$ labeling the nodes is a *price system* (or absolute price system). A rate system $Q(P){:}\ G_1 \rightarrow T$ can be *derived* from a price system by taking the price ratios

$$Q(P)(j) = P(h(j))^{-1}P(t(j)).$$

Equation 10.1. Derived Rate on arc j = Price at Tail Divided by Price at Head

Derived rate systems have certain special properties:

1. for any path c from i to i′, $Q(P)[c] = P(i')^{-1}P(i)$,
2. for any two paths c and c′ from i to i′, $Q(P)[c] = Q(P)[c']$, and
3. for any cycle c, $Q(P)[c] = 1$.

Given a market graph (G,r), the rate system r is said to be *path-independent* if for any two paths c and c′ between the same nodes, $r[c] = r[c']$. The rate system is said to be *arbitrage-free* if for any cycle c, $r[c] = 1$ ["arbitrage-free" = "balanced" in much of the graph-theoretic literature following Harary 1953].

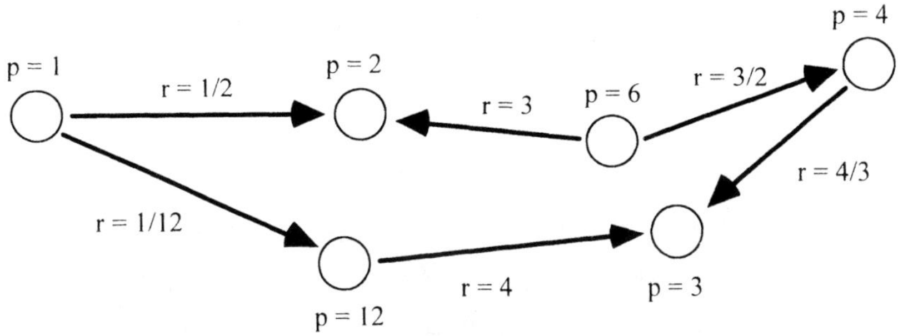

r[c] =(1/2)(1/3)(3/2)(4/3)(1/4)(12) = 1

Figure 10.3 An Arbitrage-Free Market Graph

In an idealized international currency exchange market with no transaction costs, if the product of the exchange rates around a circle is greater than one, profitable arbitrage is possible. If the product is less than one, then exchange around the circle in the opposite direction would be profitable arbitrage. Hence the market is arbitrage-free if the product of exchange rates around the circle is one.

A rate system derived from a price system has both the properties of being path-independent and arbitrage-free, and, in fact, the three properties are equivalent. That equivalence theorem is the finite multiplicative version of the calculus theorem about the equivalence of the conditions:

1. a vector field is the gradient of a potential function,
2. a line integral of the vector field between two points is path-independent, and
3. a line integral of the vector field around any closed path is zero.

Cournot-Kirchhoff Arbitrage Theorem: Let (G,r) be a market graph with $r:G_1 \to T$ taking values in any group T. The following conditions are equivalent:

1. there exists a price system P such that Q(P) = r,
2. the rate system r is path-independent, and
3. the rate system r is arbitrage-free.

For a proof of this straightforward noncommutative generalization of Kirchhoff's Voltage Law (1847) and Cournot's earlier (1838) arbitrage-free condition, see Ellerman [1984, 1990].

Examples of Arbitrage-Free Conditions

Kirchhoff's Voltage Law

The original "arbitrage-free" condition in electrical circuit theory is Kirchhoff's voltage law (KVL). It is the additive version of the multiplicative arbitrage principle. In economics, the commodity with the price of 1 is the numeraire. In circuit theory, the node with a potential of 0 is the "ground" or "datum" node. A real-valued function on the nodes of a graph is a "potential." The additive version of the quotient operator Q( ) is the difference operator, which assigns to each arrow the difference between the potentials at the tail and head of the arrow. If an assignment of reals to the arrows of the graph comes from a potential on the nodes by taking these differences, then the assignment to the arrows is called a "potential difference" or "tension." Reals assigned to the arrows can be added up around any cycle (taking care to take the negative of the number if the arrow is traversed backwards). The Arbitrage Theorem then yields:

KVL: An assignment to the arrows is a potential difference if and only if it adds to zero around any cycle.

Assemblies of Gears or Wheels

A train of gears (or wheels) that went around in a circle would be perfectly useless, but it provides an amusing example of an arbitrage-free condition. Gear ratios multiply along a gear train so this example uses the arbitrage theorem in its multiplicative form. Angular velocities on the shafts play the role of the commodity prices. If angular velocities can be assigned to the shafts so that their quotients are the gear ratios, then the whole gear assembly can move. Otherwise it would be rigid. Thus a gear assembly has a motion if and only if the product of gear ratios around any circular gear train is one.

By placing two or more gears on the same shaft, a circular gear train need not have all the gears in the same plane. But if all the gears are in the same plane (e.g., if they are all lying on a table), then the product of gear ratios around any circle will always be plus one (even number of gears in the circle) or minus one (odd number of gears in the circle). Thus a circular gear train with all the gears in the same plane can move if and only if it has an even number of gears. Graphic artists sometimes draw a simple picture of three gears meshing in a circle, and some organizations have even used such an image as their logo. But such a gear train is a perfect example of gridlock since it cannot move.

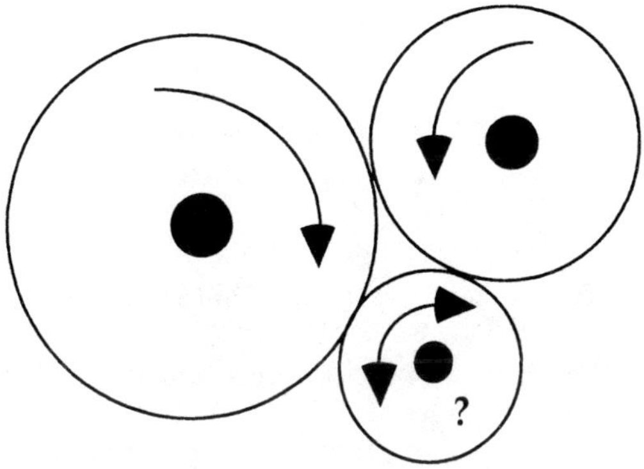

Figure 10.4. A Rigid Circular Wheel Assembly

Clique Formation in Social Groups

The arbitrage condition applied to "likes" and "dislikes" in social groups might give some insight into the ethnic mentality where likes and dislikes are based largely on being inside or outside of the clique, clan, or tribe. Each node in the graph is a person and each arrow has + 1 or − 1 according to whether the person at the tail of the arrow likes or dislikes the person at the head of the arrow. Then a graph is said to be "balanced" if it is arbitrage-free in the sense of the likes and dislikes multiplying to + 1 around any circle [e.g., Harary 1953, Harary, Norman and Cartwright 1965]. The classic "mother-in-law triangle" is an example of an unbalanced graph.

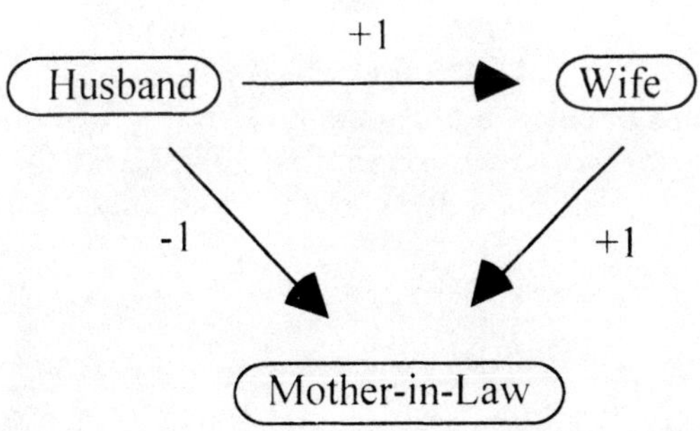

Figure 10.5. An "Unbalanced" Social Group

A "price system" marks each node or person with + 1 or − 1, and a given pattern of likes and dislikes is derived from such a marking if each person likes others with the same marking and dislikes those with a different marking. Then the arbitrage theorem gives the following result.

> A social group with a given pattern of likes and dislikes can be partitioned into two clans such that all likes are intraclan and all dislikes are between clans if and only if the pattern of likes and dislikes is balanced (arbitrage-free).

Thus there is no way to group the three people in the mother-in-law triangle into two families to account for the likes and dislikes. The husband and mother-in-law (wife's mother) have to be in different families to account for their dislike, but then the wife has an identity crisis. When arbitrage is possible then, in effect, a commodity has two prices (so one can buy low and sell high). In the previous example, a wheel had to rotate in two directions at once in order for the wheel assembly to move. In this example, the pattern of likes and dislikes in the mother-in-law triangle puts the wife in the position of having two conflicting family identities.

Heat Arbitrage in Thermodynamics

The Carnot engine approach to the second law of thermodynamics (simplified for a finite number of temperatures) gives an application of the arbitrage theorem in physics. Each node is a heat reservoir with a different temperature (including for calibration purposes the freezing and boiling points of water). Each arrow is a Carnot engine that can reversibly withdraw the heat dQ_c from the low-temperature reservoir by performing the work dW, and dump the heat dQ_h into the hotter reservoir where $dQ_h = dW + dQ_c$ by the first law of thermodynamics (conservation of energy). The ratio $r = dQ_c/dQ_h$ is called the *efficiency debit* and is the positive real number assigned to the arrow. When Carnot engines are hooked in series, the composite efficiency debit is the product of the efficiency debits of the individual engines.

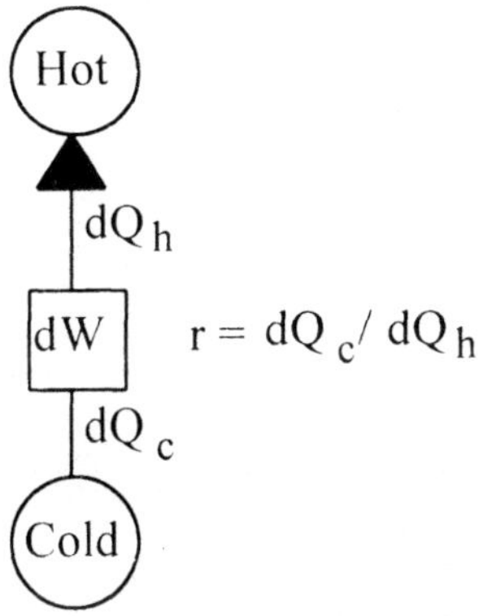

Figure 10.6. A Carnot Engine

One formulation of the second law of thermodynamics is that between any two temperatures, there is path independence in the sense that the various connecting paths must have the same efficiency debit [e.g., Morse 1964, 50]. Otherwise one could perform a type of "heat arbitrage" (move heat from the cold to hot reservoir with no net expenditure of energy) and have a "perpetual motion machine of the second kind" [e.g., Castellan 1964, Chapter 8]. By the arbitrage theorem, the second law implies that there exists a thermodynamic "price" T at each node or reservoir such that the efficiency debit of each Carnot engine is the "price ratio" T_{cold}/T_{hot}. If we normalize the freezing point of water to 0 and the boiling point to 100, then the "prices" are the Kelvin absolute temperatures of the reservoirs.

Arbitrage in Probability Theory

"Making book" means making a series of bets so that one has positive net earnings no matter what happens. That is equivalent to performing profitable arbitrage on the market for contingent commodities. A contingent commodity is a commodity conditioned on the occurrence of an event, e.g., $1000 if your number comes up in a lottery. A person subjectively assigns a probability p(E) to an event E if the person is just willing to pay p(E)S in order to receive the stake S if the event E occurs. Thus p(E) is the price the person is willing to pay for the contingent commodity "$1 if E." Suppose that a bettor places two bets with a bookie: the bettor pays $1 to get $2 if it is raining at noon, and pays $1.05 to get $2 if it is not raining at noon. By taking both bets, the bookie "makes book." No matter what happens, the bookie gives up \$2 and receives \$2.05 (= 1.00 + 1.05) for a net profit of \$.05. The bettor's probability assignments are said to be *coherent* if book cannot be made against the bettor (unlike the example). Ramsey [1960 (orig. 1926)] and de Finetti [1964 (orig. 1937)] showed that the laws of probability theory, such as p(E) + p(not-E) = 1, could be derived from the requirement of coherence. Arbitrage on the market for contingent commodities enforces the laws of probability. Even if each person has coherent probability judgments, bookies can still make their living off the combined incoherence of different people's probability judgments.

Arbitrage and Optimization Theory

A simple example of an optimization problem will now be used to illustrate our main topic, the interpretation of the necessary conditions for optimization as an arbitrage-free condition. Suppose that the problem is to find the proportions for a rectangular fenced field of maximum area for a given cost when one length of the field requires a form of fencing costing four times the fencing used on the other three sides.

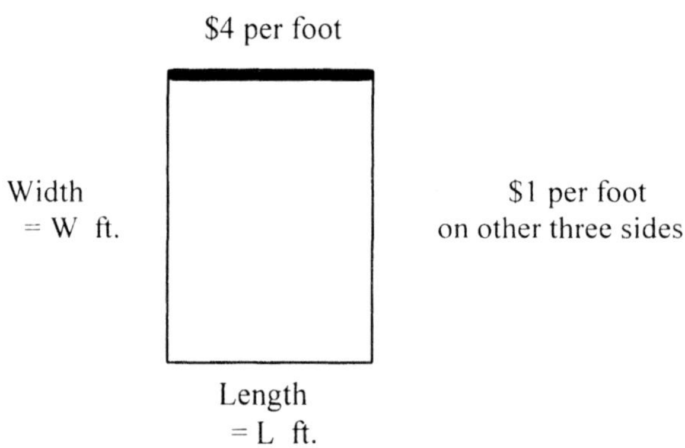

Figure 10.7. Maximize Rectangular Area with Given Cost

There are two commodities on the market, cost dollars and square feet of area. There are two ways to transform an extra dollar into area: spend the dollar to increase the width of the field or to increase the length of the field. If the dollar is spent on the width, then it buys an extra half foot on the width (the extra foot needs to be split between the two widths to keep the rectangular shape) so the area goes from WL to (W + 1/2)L. Hence the extra area is L/2. If the dollar is spent on the length, then only one-fifth of a foot can be added to the length ($.80 for one-fifth foot on the expensive side and $.20 for one-fifth foot on the cheap side). Thus the area is increased from WL to W(L + 1/5) and the extra area is W/5. Hence the two exchange rates from the cost dollars to the square feet of area are L/2 and W/5. This "market" can be pictured in an "arbitrage diagram."

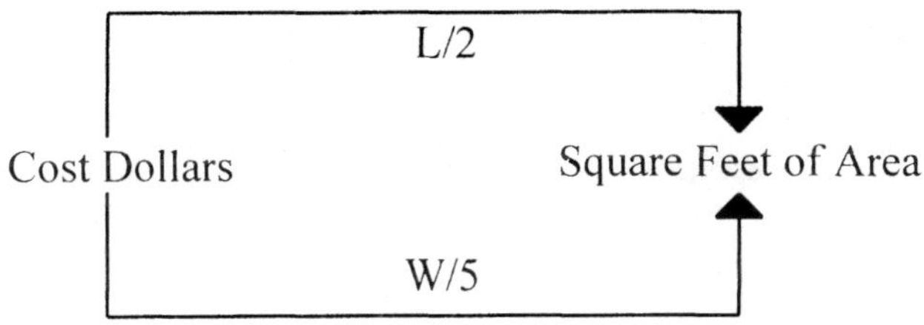

Figure 10.8. Arbitrage Diagram for Maximum Area Problem

This market is arbitrage-free if and only if the two exchange rates between the commodities are equal: L/2 = W/5. Hence the maximum area field is obtained when the length is two-fifths or 40 percent of the width. When formulated as a constrained maximization problem (maximize area subject to a fixed cost), that common rate L/2 = W/5 is the Lagrange multiplier for the problem.

Arbitrage-Free Conditions on Market Graphs

The value group T will now be specialized to R*, the multiplicative group of nonzero real numbers. But price systems P will now be *extended* by allowing zero values in the reals R, i.e.,

$$P{:}G_0 \rightarrow R.$$

An extended price system P and a rate system r are *associated* if for any arc j,

$$P(h(j))r_j - P(t(j)) = 0.$$

If the price system has all nonzero values, this is the same as the rate system being derived from the price system.

The zero-price system (all zero prices) is trivially associated with any rate system. If a rate system is not arbitrage-free, then the zero-price system is the only associated price system. With that fixed-rate system, profitable arbitrage means "getting something for nothing," so all commodities become free goods and have zero prices.

It is useful to reformulate some of the graph-theoretic notions using incidence matrices. Given (G,r), the *node-arc incidence matrix* S = $[S_{ij}]$ is the $(m+1) \times b$ matrix where:

$$S_{ij} = \begin{cases} +r_j \text{ if } \xrightarrow{\text{Arc j}} \langle \text{Node i} \rangle \\ -1 \text{ if } \xleftarrow{\text{Arc j}} \langle \text{Node i} \rangle \\ 0 \text{ Otherwise} \end{cases}$$

Equation 10.2. Node-Arc Incidence Matrix

The jth column of S has a minus one (-1) and a rate r_j, which are the results of transforming one unit of the t(j) good into r_j units of the h(j) good. Any linear combination of the columns would represent a possible market-exchange vector using the rate system r. The negative components represent the goods given up in exchange for the goods represented by the positive components. Thus the vector space of all linear combinations of columns of S, the *column space* Col(S), will be called the *exchange space* of the market graph (G,r).

Let S_0, called the *reduced incidence matrix,* be the $m \times b$ matrix obtained from S by deleting the top row, the row corresponding to node 0. If G is a connected graph (a path between any two nodes), then the reduced incidence matrix S_0 has linearly independent rows, i.e., S_0 has full row rank. Let $P^* = (P_1,\ldots,P_m)$ be a row vector such that $P^*S_0 = 0$. Some node i was connected to the "deleted" node 0 by some arc j. In order for P* to be zero the jth column of S_0, P_i must be zero. If arc j is from node i to i′ both in the node set {i,…,m}, then $P^*S_0 = 0$ implies $P_{i'}r_j - P_i = 0$ so $P_{i'}$ and P_i are both zero or both nonzero. Thus each node connected to node i must have a zero price. Since G is connected, all prices must be zero, i.e., $P^* = 0$, so the rows of S_0 are linearly independent.

Adding back the top row, the row rank of S is either m or m + 1, so the column rank, i.e., the dimension of Col(S), is also either m or

$m+1$. A subspace of R^{m+1} of dimension m (one less than the dimension of the full space) is a *hyperplane* through the origin. Thus the exchange space is either a hyperplane in R^{m+1} or is the full space.

The *left nullspace* LeftNull(S) of any matrix S is the space of vectors P such that $PS = 0$. If S is the incidence matrix of a market graph (G,r) and $P = (P_0,P_1,\ldots,P_m)$ is in LeftNull(S), i.e., $PS = 0$, then for all arcs j

$$P_{h(j)}r_j - P_{t(j)} = 0$$

so P is a price system associated with the rate system r. Hence LeftNull(S) is called the *price space* associated with the exchange space Col(S) and the elements P are called *price vectors*. The exchange space Col(S) and the price space LeftNull(S) are *orthogonal complements* of one another, i.e.,

a. X is an exchange if and only if for any price vector P, $PX = 0$, and
b. P is a price vector if and only if for any exchange X, $PX = 0$.

Since they are orthogonal complements, dim [Col(S)] + dim[LeftNull(S)] = $m+1$. Since the exchange space is of dimension m or $m+1$ (G is assumed connected), the dimension of the price space is either one or zero. A price vector with any nonzero components must have all nonzero components. Any two nonzero price vectors must be scalar multiples on one another. The two cases of a one or zero dimensional price space correspond to the cases of (G,r) being arbitrage-free or allowing profitable arbitrage. If profitable arbitrage is possible, then the fixed nonzero exchange rates r would allow one to generate any quantities of the goods so all commodities are free goods, i.e., $P = 0$ is the only price vector. These results and some easy consequences are collected together in the following theorem.

Arbitrage Theorem for Market Graphs: Let (G,r) be a market graph where G is connected and $r:G_1 \rightarrow R^*$. The following conditions are equivalent:

1. there exists a price system $P:G_0 \rightarrow R^*$ such that $Q(P) = r$,
2. the rate system r is path-independent,
3. the rate system r is arbitrage-free,
4. the price space LeftNull(S) is one-dimensional,

5. the exchange space Col(S) is a hyperplane (with a nonzero price vector as a normal vector),
6. the top row of S, s_0, can be expressed as a linear combination of the bottom m rows S_0 of S, i.e., there exist $\mu = (\mu_1,\ldots,\mu_m)$ such that $s_0 + \mu S_0 = 0$, and
7. if an exchange vector $b = Sx$ has $b_1 = \ldots = b_m = 0$, then $b_0 = 0$.

The incidence-matrix treatment of market graphs suggests a generalization of the economic interpretation to a more general matrix context. The rows represent commodities. The columns specify exchange or production possibilities. Negative entries represent goods given up in exchange or inputs to production, while positive components stand for goods received or the outputs. Any scalar multiple, positive or negative, of a column also represents a possible exchange or transformation so the column space is the space of possible exchanges or transformations. The orthogonally complementary left nullspace is the set of price vectors such that all the exchanges can be obtained as trades at those prices [for more linear algebra, see any text such as Strang 1980].

An Economic Interpretation of Cofactors, Determinants, and Cramer's Rule

Let A be a square $(m+1) \times (m+1)$ of reals, and let A(k) be the $(m+1) \times m$ matrix obtained by deleting column k for $k = 0,1,\ldots,m$. The column space Col(A(k)) is the space of exchanges spanned by the remaining m columns. Let

$$P(k) = (P_0(k),P_1(k),\ldots,P_m(k))$$

be the cofactors of the deleted column k. By the property of "expansion by alien cofactors," $P(k)A(k) = 0$ so P(k) is a "price vector" in LeftNull (A(k)). The cofactors in P(k) will be called the *k-prices*. The cofactors of any column of A are prices so that the exchanges defined by the remaining columns can be obtained at those market prices.

Now introduce the exchange (or productive) possibilities given by the deleted column k into the market. Its value at the reigning prices P(k) is the determinant $|A|$ obtained by the cofactor expansion of column k. If $|A| \neq 0$ then any vector b can be obtained as an exchange vector $Ax = b$. As in a market that allows profitable arbitrage at fixed exchange rates, any exchange is allowed and the only price vector is the zero vector.

It is therefore desirable to alter temporarily the interpretation of the columns of A. Previously the columns represented exchange or production possibilities with all commodities involved as inputs or outputs listed as components. We now interpret each column as representing the reversible input-output vector of a machine operating at unit level. But the machine's services are not represented in the input-output vector, so the value of the vector can now be interpreted as the competitive rent imputed to a unit of the machine services.

The vector of cofactor k-prices $P(k) = (P_0(k),P_1(k),\ldots,P_m(k))$ can now be interpreted as a set of commodity prices that impute zero rents to all the other m machines (excluding the kth machine). The *determinant* $|A|$ is the competitive rent (or subsidy, if negative) imputed to the unit services of machine k at those k-prices. Dividing by the determinant-as-rent, the *normalized k-prices* are the k-prices expressed in terms of the units of machine k services as numeraire.

$$P^*(k) = \frac{P(k)}{|A|}$$

Equation 10.3. Prices to Give Unit Rent to Machine k, Zero Rent to Other Machines

At the normalized k-prices P*(k), all machines have zero imputed rent—save machine k, which has an imputed rent of unity. This yields an economic interpretation of the *inverse matrix* A^{-1} as the *normalized price matrix* obtained as the column of row vectors P*(k) for k = 0,1,...,m.

$$P^* = \begin{bmatrix} P^*(0) \\ P^*(1) \\ \vdots \\ P^*(m) \end{bmatrix} = A^{-1}$$

Equation 10.4. Inverse Matrix as Matrix of Normalized Price Vectors

Suppose the machines are operated at the levels $x = (x_0,x_1,\ldots,x_m)^T$ so the net product vector is $Ax = b$. In *competitive equilibrium*, the competitive rents due on the machines must equal the value of the net product vector leaving no pure profits for arbitrageurs. Given a commodity price vector $P = (P_0,P_1,\ldots,P_m)$, the unit machine rents $R = (R_0,R_1,\ldots,R_m)$ must be such that the total rent Rx equals the value Pb of any net product b = Ax, i.e.,

$$Rx = Pb = PAx \text{ for any } x.$$

Equation 10.5. Machine Rent = Value of Net Product in Competitive Equilibrium

Thus competitive equilibrium requires the competitive rents R = PA in terms of P.

Now consider the specific price vector P*(k). The competitive rents R = P*(k)A impute a rent only to machine k, and that rent is unity. Hence the total rent $Rx = x_k = P^*(k)Ax = P^*(k)b$ is the level of operation x_k of machine k so we have derived Cramer's Rule.

$$\text{Competitive Machine Rent} = x_k$$

$$= P^*(k)b = \text{Value of Net Product.}$$

Equation 10.6. Cramer's Rule as a Competitive Equilibrium Condition

Arbitrage-Free Market Matrices

We now return to the "full-disclosure" interpretation of the columns of A. All commodities and services involved in the exchange or productive transformation are exposed as components of the column vectors.

When is a matrix like a market? One answer is when it is like the node-arc incidence matrix of a market graph. Let A be a rectangular $(m+1) \times n$ matrix with $m+1 \leq n$. Any matrix or its transpose has that form. Such a matrix A is a *market matrix* if rank $(A) \geq m$. A market matrix has a rank of m or $m+1$. A market matrix A is said to be *arbitrage-free* if rank (A) = m. The node-arc incidence matrix of a connected market graph is a market matrix. The market graph is arbitrage-free (as a graph) if and only if its incidence matrix is arbitrage-free (as a matrix).

A market matrix has m linearly independent rows that, for notational convenience, we may take to be the bottom m rows numbered $i = 1,\ldots,m$ (the top row is row 0). Every set of m columns from the $(m+1)$

$\times$ n matrix A determine a $(m+1) \times m$ submatrix A* (taking the columns in the same order as in A). As a visual aid, we can consider a $(m+1) \times 1$ "dummy" column vector $[?,?,\ldots,?]^T$ appended to the left of A* to form a m+1 square matrix. The cofactors $P_0, P_1, \ldots, P_m$ of the dummy column are the *local cofactor prices* determined by the m columns of A*. The binomial coefficient $C(n,m) = n!/(m!(n-m)!)$ gives the number of ways of choosing m columns from among n columns, so there are C(n,m) vectors of local cofactor prices (not necessarily all distinct).

At least one vector of local cofactor prices is nonzero since rank (A) $\geq$ m. The rows have been arranged so the bottom m rows are linearly independent. Let A* be a submatrix of m linearly independent columns so it has a vector of local cofactor prices $P^* = (P_0^*, P_1^*, \ldots, P_m^*)$ such that $P_0^* \neq 0$. These cofactor prices may be normalized by taking commodity 0 as the numeraire to obtain the relative prices:

$$(1, \mu_1, \ldots, \mu_m) = (1, P_1^*/P_0^*, \ldots, P_m^*/P_0^*).$$

Equation 10.7. Normalized Cofactor Prices

To complete the development of a "market" in the market matrix A, we need to define transformation rates between commodities. The important rates are the transformation rates r_i of good i into good 0 for $i = 1,\ldots,m$, which can be defined using any m linearly independent columns A*. The m activities are to be run at levels so that exactly one unit of good i is used up and zero units of good j are produced or used up for $j \neq i,0$. Then the number of units of good 0 produced gives the transformation rate r_i so that the 1 unit of good i used up is transformed into r_i units of good 0.

In matrix notation, let A_0^* be the bottom m rows of a $(m+1) \times m$ matrix A* of m linearly independent columns of A so that

$$|A_0^*| = P_0^* \neq 0.$$

Let a_0^* be the top row of A*. The activity vector x that uses up exactly one unit of good i is the x such that

$$A_0^* x = (0,\ldots,0-1,0,\ldots,0)^T = -I_i$$

where I_i is the ith column of the $m \times m$ identity matrix I so $x = (A_0^*)^{-1} I_i$. Let

$$r_i = -a_0{}^*(A_0{}^*)^{-1}I_i$$

Equation 10.8. Transformation Rate of ith Good into Numeraire 0th Good

so the vector $r = (r_1,\ldots,r_m)$ of the transformation rates defined by A* is $r = -a_0{}^*(A_0{}^*)^{-1}$.

Cofactor Price Theorem: Given any $(m+1) \times m$ submatrix A* of linearly independent columns, the transformation rates r determined by A* are equal to the normalized cofactor prices:

$$(r_1,\ldots,r_m) = (P_1{}^*/P_0,\ldots,P_m{}^*/P_0{}^*) = (\mu_1,\ldots,\mu_m).$$

Proof: For notational simplicity, we take the m columns of A* to be the first m columns of A. The transformation rates r solve the linear equations:

$$(r_1,\ldots,r_m)\begin{bmatrix} a_{11} & \cdots & a_{1m} \\ \cdots & \cdots & \cdots \\ a_{m1} & \cdots & a_{mm} \end{bmatrix} = rA_0^* = -a_0^* = -(a_{01},\ldots,a_{0m}).$$

The local cofactor prices determined by A* are the cofactors of the dummy column in the matrix:

$$\begin{bmatrix} ? & a_{01} & \cdots & a_{0m} \\ ? & a_{11} & \cdots & a_{1m} \\ \cdots & \cdots & \cdots & \cdots \\ ? & a_{m1} & \cdots & a_{mm} \end{bmatrix}$$

Using the row form of Cramer's Rule to solve for r_1 yields:

$$r_1 = \frac{\begin{vmatrix} -a_{01} \cdots -a_{0m} \\ a_{21} \cdots a_{2m} \\ \cdots \ \cdots \ \cdots \\ a_{m1} \cdots a_{mm} \end{vmatrix}}{\begin{vmatrix} a_{11} \cdots a_{1m} \\ a_{21} \cdots a_{2m} \\ \cdots \ \cdots \ \cdots \\ a_{m1} \cdots a_{mm} \end{vmatrix}} = \frac{(-1)^{2+1} \begin{vmatrix} a_{01} \cdots a_{0m} \\ a_{21} \cdots a_{2m} \\ \cdots \ \cdots \ \cdots \\ a_{m1} \cdots a_{mm} \end{vmatrix}}{P_0^*} = \frac{P_1^*}{P_0^*}.$$

To compute r_i, the right-hand side constants $-a_0{}^*$ are substituted for the ith row of $A_0{}^*$ (in the numerator of the row form of Cramer's Rule). Then $i-1$ row swaps are required to bring the $-a_0{}^*$ row up to the top. Factoring out the -1 leaves a $(-1)^i$ sign on the minor

$$\begin{vmatrix} a_{01} & \cdots & a_{0m} \\ a_{11} & \cdots & a_{1m} \\ \cdots & \cdots & \cdots \\ a_{i-1,1} & \cdots & a_{i-1,m} \\ a_{1+1,1} & \cdots & a_{i+1,m} \\ \cdots & \cdots & \cdots \\ a_{m1} & \cdots & a_{mm} \end{vmatrix}$$

but $P_i{}^*(-1)^{(i+1)+1} = (-1)^i$ times the same minor so $r_i = P_i{}^*/P_0$.

The next theorem states a number of conditions equivalent to the market matrix A being arbitrage-free. An arbitrage-free market has unique relative prices so the C(n,m) local cofactor prices must mesh or fit together in the sense of being scalar multiples of the nonzero price vector P* which was normalized to $(1,\mu_1,\ldots,\mu_m)$. The space spanned by the C(n,m) cofactor price vectors is the one-dimensional space LeftNull(A). In the application to classical optimization, the μ_i's are the Lagrange multipliers of m constraints, which are thus interpreted as the unique prices of m resources in terms of the maximand as numeraire.

Arbitrage Theorem for Market Matrices: Let A be any $(m+1) \times n$ market matrix where we assume the rows 1 through m are linearly independent. Let a_0 be the top row, and let A_0 be the bottom m rows of A. The following conditions are equivalent:

1. A is arbitrage-free,
2. the price space LeftNull (A) is one-dimensional,
3. the exchange space Col(A) is a hyperplane (with a cofactor price vector as a normal vector),
4. there exists $\mu = (\mu_1,\ldots,\mu_m)$ such that $a_0 + \mu A_0 = 0$, and
5. if an exchange vector $b = Ax$ has $b_1 = \ldots = b_m = 0$, then $b_0 = 0$. [See Ellerman 1990 for the proof.]

First-Order Necessary Conditions as Arbitrage-Free Conditions

The intuitive arbitrage reasoning as well as the formal results for arbitrage-free market matrices can be applied to yield the first-order necessary conditions for regular constrained optimization problems with equality constraints.

Consider the one-constraint problem:

$$\text{Maximize } y = f(x_1,\ldots,x_n)$$
$$\text{Subject to: } g(x_1,\ldots,x_n) = b$$

where all functions are continuously twice differentiable. There are two commodities, the resource b and the maximand y. There are n "instruments" with the levels of operation $x_1,\ldots,x_n$. At the levels $x_1,\ldots,x_n$, the amount of the resource used up is $g(x_1,\ldots,x_n)$, and $f(x_1,\ldots,x_n)$ is the amount of the maximand produced.

Let $x^o = (x_1{}^o,\ldots,x_n{}^o)$ be levels of the instruments that use up all of the available resource, i.e., $g(x_1{}^o,\ldots,x_n{}^o) = b$. Moreover, we assume that x^o is "regular" in the sense that not all the partials $\partial g(x^o)/\partial x_i = g_i$ are zero. We consider an intuitive "marginal market" defined by the possible marginal transformations of b into y. In an international currency market (without transaction costs), there might be n banks or exchange houses that to prevent arbitrage would have to offer the same rate of exchange between any two currencies. In our market, the n instrument variables offer n ways to transform the resource b into the maximand y. A marginal variation Δx_i uses up $g_i \Delta x_i$ units of b and produces $f_i \Delta x_i$ units of y so the rate of transformation is

$$\frac{f_i \Delta x_i}{g_i \Delta x_i} = \frac{f_i}{g_i}$$

Equation 10.9. Rate of Transformation of Resource into Maximand

The market is arbitrage-free if and only if the n transformation rates f_i/g_i provided by the n instruments are equal where the common rate of transformation is the Lagrange multiplier μ.

$$\frac{f_1}{g_1} = \frac{f_2}{g_2} = \cdots = \frac{f_n}{g_n} = \mu$$

Equation 10.10. Arbitrage-Free Condition

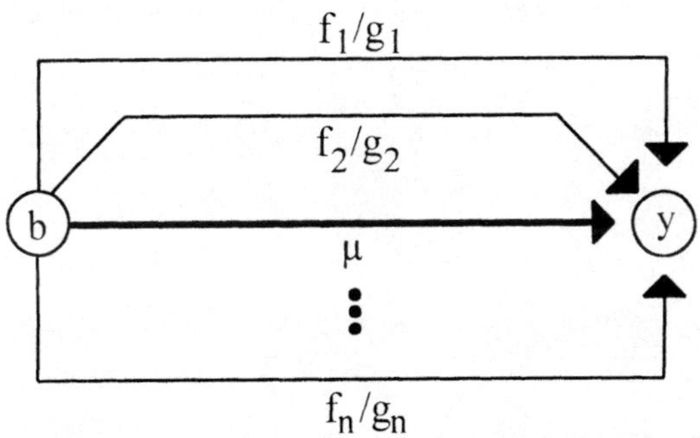

Figure 10.9. Arbitrage Diagram for the Marginal Market

Thus the first-order necessary conditions for x^o to be a constrained maximum are equivalent to the intuitive market being arbitrage-free.

To use the machinery of market matrices, let

$$A = \begin{bmatrix} f_1 & f_2 & \cdots & f_n \\ -g_1 & -g_2 & \cdots & -g_n \end{bmatrix}$$

where $-g_i$ is used instead of $+g_i$ since $g(x_1,\ldots,x_n)$ represents the amount of the resource used up. Consider any column of this market matrix coupled with the dummy column to form a square matrix:

$$\begin{bmatrix} ? & f_i \\ ? & -g_i \end{bmatrix}.$$

The cofactors of the dummy column are the local prices $P_y = -g_i$ and $P_b = -f_i$, so (assuming $g_i \neq 0$) the cofactor price ratio is the transformation rate defined by the marginal variations in the instrument x_i.

$$P_b/P_y = f_i/g_i$$

Equation 10.11 Transformation as Cofactor Price Ratio

Since $m = 1$, there are $C(n,1) = n$ sets of cofactor prices. The market matrix is arbitrage-free if and only if the n cofactor price vectors define the same price of b in terms of y (i.e., the condition of Equation 10.10).

For the previous example of maximizing the area of the rectangular field using different types of fencing, the mathematically formulated problem is:

$$\text{Maximize } y = x_1x_2$$
$$\text{Subject to: } 2x_1 = 5x_2 = b.$$

The market matrix is:

$$A = \begin{bmatrix} f_1 & f_2 \\ -g_1 & -g_2 \end{bmatrix} = \begin{bmatrix} x_2 & x_1 \\ -2 & -5 \end{bmatrix}$$

and the cofactor price ratios are given by the cofactors of the dummy columns in the matrices:

$$\begin{bmatrix} ? & x_1 \\ ? & -5 \end{bmatrix} \text{ or } \begin{bmatrix} ? & x_2 \\ ? & -2 \end{bmatrix}.$$

The mathematically defined "market" is arbitrage-free if all the cofactor price ratios are the same:

$$\frac{P_b}{P_y} = \frac{-x_1}{-5} = \frac{-x_2}{-2}$$

which gives the previous necessary conditions that the length x_2 must be two-fifths or 40 percent of the width x_1.

Consider a problem with m = 2 constraints:

$$\begin{aligned} &\text{Maximize } y = f(x_1,\ldots,x_n) \\ &\text{Subject to: } g^1(x_1,\ldots,x_n) = b_1 \\ &\qquad\qquad\quad g^2(x_1,\ldots,x_n) = b_2 \end{aligned}$$

where n > m = 2. Let G be the matrix of partials of the constraints evaluated at x^0:

$$G = \begin{bmatrix} g_1^1 & g_2^1 & \cdots & g_n^1 \\ g_1^2 & g_2^2 & \cdots & g_n^2 \end{bmatrix}.$$

The candidate point x^0 is assumed to be *regular* in the sense that G is of full row rank.

There are three commodities in the intuitive market for the problem: the maximand y and the two resources b_1 and b_2. To define a transformation rate from b_1 into y, one cannot just vary one instrument x_1 because that may also vary b_2. One must consider variations in (m) two variables x_i and x_j which leave b_2 constant and yield variations $-db_1$ and dy to define a transformation rate $r_1 = dy/db_1$ from b_1 into y. The rate for transforming b_2 into y can be similarly defined. Using the cofactor price theorem, these rates can be obtained as ratios of local cofactor prices.

Since G is of full row rank, there are m = 2 instruments x_i and x_j such that

$$G^* = \begin{bmatrix} g_i^1 & g_j^1 \\ g_i^2 & g_j^2 \end{bmatrix}$$

is nonsingular. Given the matrix (with the unknown dummy column)

$$\begin{bmatrix} ? & f_i & f_j \\ ? & -g_i^1 & -g_j^1 \\ ? & -g_i^2 & -g_j^2 \end{bmatrix}$$

the cofactors of the dummy column yield the prices:

$$P_y = g_i^1 g_j^2 - g_i^2 g_j^1$$
$$P_{b_1} = f_i g_j^2 - f_j g_i^2$$
$$P_{b_2} = f_j g_i^1 - f_i g_j^1$$

Equation 10.12. Cofactor Prices

where $P_y \neq 0$ by the choice of i and j. By the cofactor price theorem, the cofactor price ratios yield the transformation rates from the resources into the maximand. For instance, if x_i and x_j are varied to hold b_2 constant, the relative cofactor price of b_1 in terms of y, $P_{b1}/P_y = \mu_1$, gives the rate of transformation of b_1 into y defined by the variation in x_i and x_j.

For the intuitive market to be arbitrage-free, all the local cofactor prices (P_y', P_{b1}', P_{b2}') defined by any set of m = 2 instruments must be scalar multiples of the nonzero price vector (P_y, P_{b1}, P_{b2}). In formal terms, the market matrix defined by the problem is

$$A = \begin{bmatrix} \nabla f \\ -G \end{bmatrix}.$$

The first-order necessary conditions for the candidate point to be a constrained maximum are then expressed by the market matrix A being arbitrage-free and by the other equivalent conditions given in the Arbitrage Theorem for Market Matrices.

All these results for m = 2 extend to the general problem with m constraints and n variables (n > m):

$$\begin{aligned}&\text{Maximize } y = f(x_1,\ldots,x_n)\\&\text{Subject to: } g^1(x_1,\ldots,x_n) = b_1\\&\qquad\qquad\ldots\\&\qquad\qquad g^m(x_1,\ldots,x_n) = b_m.\end{aligned}$$

The candidate point x^0 satisfies the constraints and is *regular* in the sense that the $m \times n$ matrix $G = [g^j_i]$ is of full row rank. Thus there are m columns forming a nonsingular submatrix G^*. If f^* is the vector of the corresponding m partials of f, then consider the $(m+1) \times (m+1)$ matrix:

$$\left[\begin{array}{c|c} ? & f^* \\ \hline ? & -G^* \end{array}\right].$$

The cofactors of the dummy column form the local cofactor prices $P_y, P_{b1},\ldots,P_{bm}$ determined by the m chosen instruments. The intuitive market is arbitrage-free if all the C(m,n) vectors of local cofactor prices are scalar multiples of this nonzero vector. In formal terms, the first-order necessary condition for the candidate point x^0 to be a constrained maximum is equivalent to the condition that the market matrix of the problem

$$A = \begin{bmatrix} \nabla f \\ -G \end{bmatrix}$$

is arbitrage-free, which in turn is equivalent to the other conditions stated in the Arbitrage Theorem for Market Matrices.

These results point to a research program that could be developed in several directions. One direction is to show how the second-order sufficient conditions for optimality could be interpreted economically as the conditions for arbitrage to eliminate its own possibility. Preliminary results in this direction are outlined in the appendix. Another direction of development is to extend the arbitrage interpretation to other areas of optimization theory such as optimization with inequality constraints and optimal control theory.

References

Berge, Claude, and A. Ghouila-Houri, 1965. *Programming, Games and Transportation Networks*. John New York: Wiley and Sons.

Castellan, Gilbert. 1964. *Physical Chemistry*. New York: Addison-Wesley.

Cournot, Augustin. 1897 (orig. 1838). *Mathematical Principles of the Theory of Wealth*. Trans. Nathaniel Bloom. New York: Macmillan.

de Finetti, Bruno. 1964 (orig. 1937). *"Foresight: Its Logical Laws, Its Subjective Sources*. In *Studies in Subjective Probability*, ed. H. Kyburg and H. Smokler, 93–158. New York: John Wiley.

Ellerman, David P. 1984. "Arbitrage Theory: A Mathematical Introduction." *SIAM Review*. 26: 241–61.

———. 1990. "An Arbitrage Interpretation of Classical Optimization." *Metroeconomica* 41, no. 3:259–76.

Gross, Jonathan. 1974. "Voltage Graphs." *Discrete Math* 9:239–46.

Harary, Frank. 1953. "On the Notion of Balance of a Signed Graph." *Michigan Math. J.* 2:143–46.

Harary, Frank, R. Z. Norman, and D. Cartwright. 1965. *Structural Models*. New York: John Wiley.

Harary, Frank, B. Lindstrom, and H. Zetterstrom. 1982. "On Balance in Group Graphs." *Networks* 12:317–21.

Kirchhoff, G. 1847. "Über die Auflosung der Gleichungen, auf welche man dei der Untersuchung der linearen Verteilung galvanischer Strome gufuhrt wird." *Annalen der Physik und Chemie* 72:497–508.

Modigliani, Franco, and Merton H. Miller. 1958. "The Cost of Capital, Corporation Finance, and the Theory of Investment." *American Economic Review* 48:261–97.

Morse, Philip. 1964. *Thermal Physics*. New York: W. A. Benjamin.

Ramsey, Frank Plumpton. 1960 (orig. 1926). *Truth and Probability*. In *The Foundations of Mathematics*, ed. R. B. Braithwaite. Paterson, N.J.: Littlefield, Adams & Company.

Ross, Stephen A. 1976. "The Arbitrage Theory of Capital Asset Pricing." *J. Econ. Theory* 13: 341–60.

Ross, Stephen A. 1976. "Return, Risk and Arbitrage." In *Risk and Return in Finance*, ed. Irwin Friend and James L. Bicksler. Cambridge, Mass.: Ballinger.

Strang, Gilbert. 1980. *Linear Albegra and its Applications*. Second edition. New York: Academic Press.

Varian, Hal R. 1987. "The Arbitrage Principle in Financial Economics." *The Journal of Economic Perspectives* 1, no. 2:5–72.

Appendix: Second-Order Conditions as Arbitrage-Stability Conditions

The arbitrage interpretation extends to the second-order sufficient conditions. There is a natural stability notion based on arbitrage.

Stability requires that arbitrage eliminate its own possibility. The exchange of A for B tends to reduce the rate of exchange of A into B. Thus "transformation lowers the rate of transformation" is a Marshallian concept of "arbitrage stability." When applied to the market in the mathematics of classical optimization, arbitrage stability is equivalent to the second-order sufficient conditions.

Given the demand price $P_D(q)$ and supply price $P_S(q)$ as functions of quantity, Marshallian stability requires that

$$d[P_D(q) - P_S(q)]/dq = P_D' - P_S' < 0.$$

Marshallian stability is closely related to the stability notion of arbitrage eliminating its own possibility. If $P_D(q) > P_S(q)$, an arbitrageur could buy low at $P_S(q)$ and sell high at $P_D(q)$.

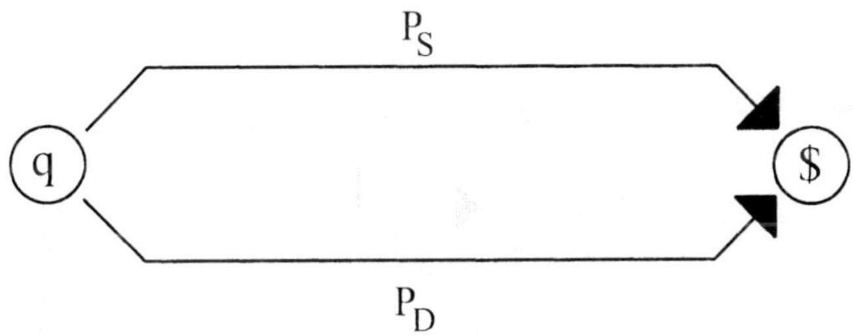

Figure 10.10. Circular Transformation Using Supply and Demand Prices

In a circular transformation of money into the commodity and back into money, the arbitrageur nets the amount $P_D(q) - P_S(q)$. Thus arbitrage will tend to eliminate its own possibility if there is Marshallian stability, $P_D' - P_S' < 0$.

Consider a simple two-variable constrained maximization problem:

$$\text{Maximize } y = f(x_1,x_2)$$
$$\text{Subject to: } g(x_1,x_2) = b.$$

All derivatives are evaluated at x^0, which satisfies the first-order necessary conditions. Hence the market

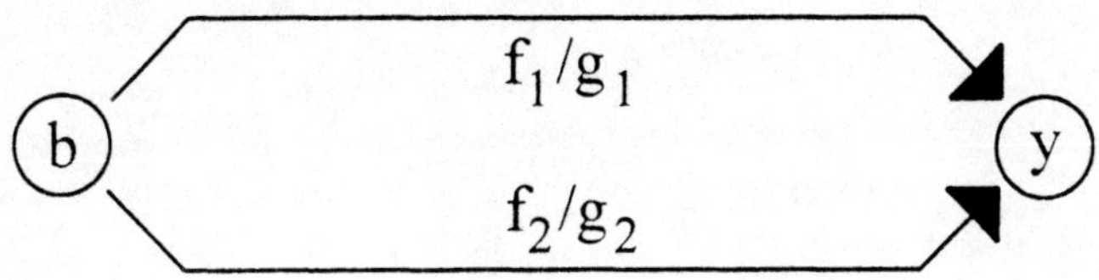

is arbitrage-free, i.e., $f_1/g_1 = f_2/g_2 = \mu$.

Consider any differentiable parameterization $x(t) = (x_1(t),x_2(t))$ defined in a neighborhood of $x(0) = x^0$ that holds b constant, i.e.,

$$dg/dt = g_1x_1' + g_2x_2' = 0$$

(where the prime denotes differentiation). This variation in the x instruments can be thought of as a circular transformation of y into b and back into y. For instance, if $g_2x_2' = -g_1x_1' > 0$, then $|f_1x_1'|$ units of y are used up and transformed into $-(g_1/f_1)f_1x_1' = -g_1x_1' = g_2x_2'$ units of b, which in turn are transformed into $(f_2/g_2)g_2x_2' = f_2x_2'$ units of y. The net change in y is

$$dy/dt = f_1x_1' + f_2x_2'.$$

For this circular transformation, f_1/g_1 is the "supply price" and f_2/g_2 is the "demand price" of b in terms of the numeraire y.

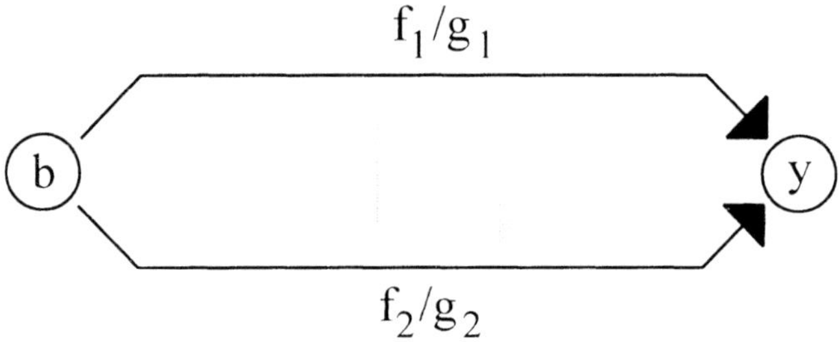

Figure 10.11. Circular Transformation in Resource-Maximand Market

Thus "Marshallian stability" applied in this context requires that

$$d[f_2/g_2 - f_1/g_1]/dt < 0.$$

Evaluating the derivative, $d[f_2/g_2 - f_1/g_1]/dt =$

$$[g_2(f_{21}x_1' + f_{22}x_2') - f_2(g_{21}x_1' + g_{22}x_2')]/g_2^2 - [g_1(f_{11}x_1' + f_{12}x_2') - f_1(g_{11}x_1' + g_{12}x_2')]/g_1^2.$$

Multiplying through by the positive $\Delta b = g_2x_2' = -g_1x_1' > 0$ and using the first-order conditions, $f_1/g_1 = f_2/g_2 = \mu$, yields

$$\Delta b\, d[f_2/g_2 - f_1/g_1]/dt =$$

$$(f_{21} - \mu g_{21})x_1'x_2' + (f_{22} - \mu g_{22})x_2'^2 + (f_{11} - \mu g_{11})x_1'^2 + (f_{12} - \mu g_{12})x_1'x_2' =$$

$$\begin{pmatrix} x_1' & x_2' \end{pmatrix} \begin{bmatrix} L_{11} & L_{12} \\ L_{21} & L_{22} \end{bmatrix} \begin{pmatrix} x_1' \\ x_2' \end{pmatrix} < 0$$

for any (x_1',x_2') such that $g_1x_1' + g_2x_2' = 0$, where L is the Lagrangian function

$$L(x_1,x_2,\mu) = f(x_1,x_2) + \mu[b - g(x_1,x_2)].$$

Thus the "Marshallian stability" conditions adapted to this arbitrage context yield the usual second-order sufficient conditions for a maximum.

The problem with Marshallian stability conditions is the generalization to multiple markets. This problem has a simple solution when reconceptualized in the arbitrage context. Instead of viewing $f_2/g_2 - f_1/g_1$ as the difference between the "demand price" and "supply price," view it as the net change in y when F_1g_1 units of y are transformed into $(f_1g_1)(g_1/f_1) = 1$ unit of b, which in turn is transformed into $1(f_2g_2)$ units of y for the net change of $\Delta y = f_2/g_2 - f_1/g_1$.

In the circular transformation previously described, $|f_1x_1'|$ units of y were transformed back into f_2x_2' units for the net change $dy/dt = f_1x_1' + f_2x_2'$. A *circular transformation* is described by any variation $x(t)$ which leaves b constant, i.e., $g_1x_1' + g_2x_2' = 0$. A circular transformation defined in a neighborhood of a critical point x^o yields no net change in y, i.e., $\Sigma f_ix_i' = 0$. Arbitrage eliminates its own possibility if the rate of change of that net amount is negative. Thus, a critical point x^0 is said to have *arbitrage stability* if for any circular transformation defined in a neighborhood of x^0, $d[\Sigma f_ix_i']/dt < 0$.

The notion of arbitrage stability extends to the "multiple markets" context of the general optimization problem:

$$\begin{aligned} &\text{Maximize } y = f(x_1,\ldots,x_n) \\ &\text{Subject to: } g_1(x_1,\ldots,x_n) = b_1 \\ &\qquad\qquad \ldots \\ &\qquad\qquad g^m(x_1,\ldots,x_n) = b_m. \end{aligned}$$

A circular transformation $x(t)$ defined in a neighborhood of a critical point $x(0) = x^0$ leaves all the b_j constant $\Sigma g_i^jx_i' = 0$ for $j = 1,\ldots,m$.

Since the "market" is arbitrage-free, the circular transformation yields no net change in y, i.e., $\Sigma f_i x_i' = 0$. The critical point x^0 has *arbitrage stability* in this more general context if any circular transformation tends to reduce the net change in y, i.e., for any circular transformation x(t),

$$\frac{d\left[\sum f_i x_i'\right]}{dt} < 0.$$

Equation 10.13. Arbitrage-Stability Condition

This arbitrage-stability condition is simply a reformulation of the usual second-order sufficient condition for a maximum, so we have an arbitrage interpretation for the sufficiency conditions.

Chapter 11

Valuation Rings: A Better Algebraic Treatment of Boolean Algebras

Introduction

A Boolean "algebra" is not an ordinary plus-and-times algebra: it is only an algebra in the sense of "universal algebra." In order to construe a Boolean algebra as a plus-and-times algebra, it can be interpreted as a Boolean ring. But there are two ways to interpret a Boolean algebra as a Boolean ring, and the second interpretation appears as little more than an oddity. Boolean duality is expressed in ad hoc nonalgebraic terms since complementation is not a ring homomorphism in the Boolean ring. Boolean duality is thought to be dependent on the "zero-one nature" of Boolean rings.

Certain rings, called "valuation rings," have been defined by Gian-Carlo Rota for the purpose of generalizing inclusion-exclusion calculations in combinatorial theory [Rota 1971]. These rings turn out to be a natural setting to formulate and to generalize the properties of Boolean algebras using ordinary plus-and-times algebras. One key to this development is that the minimal element z of the Boolean algebra is not the zero of the valuation ring constructed from the Boolean algebra. Boolean duality is captured in two multiplications on the ring (a meet-multiplication and a join-multiplication). The complementation is a ring isomorphism that carries one multiplication into the other. This generalization of Boolean duality holds when the ring of coefficients is an arbitrary commutative ring with unity (while the classical Boolean duality takes the ring to be $\mathbf{Z}_2$). When the ring of coefficients is $\mathbf{Z}_2$, then the two Boolean rings associated with the Boolean algebra are obtained as quotients of the valuation ring. The valuation ring also linearizes the Boolean algebra in the sense that the meet, join, and complementation all become linear (or bilinear) transformations.

Propositional logic deals with the special case of free Boolean algebras. The main characterization theorem shows that the valuation rings of free Boolean algebras can be constructed as special types of polynomial rings. Thus the generalized Boolean duality can be applied to these polynomials so that each polynomial has a dual polynomial. The theorems of propositional logic such as the completeness theorem can be proven and generalized using elementary reasoning with polynomials.

Rota's Valuation Rings

Let L be a distributive lattice with maximal element u and minimal element z, and let A be a ring (always commutative with unity 1). Let F(L,A) be the free A-module on the elements of L, which consists of all the finite formal sums

$$\Sigma a_i x_i \text{ for } a_i \in A,\ x_i \in L.$$

A ring structure is established on F(L,A) by defining multiplication as $x \cdot y = x \wedge y$ for lattice elements $x, y \in L$ and then extending by linearity to all the elements of F(L,A). Let J be the submodule generated by all the elements of the form

$$x \vee y + x \wedge y - x - y \text{ for } x, y \in L.$$

LEMMA: J is an ideal.

Proof: Since J is a submodule, it is sufficient to check that J is closed under multiplication by lattice elements w. Now

$$w(x \vee y + x \wedge y - x - y) = w \wedge (x \vee y) + w \wedge (x \wedge y) - w \wedge x - w \wedge y.$$

Since L is a distributive lattice, w distributes across the join and meet to yield:

$$w(x \vee y + x \wedge y - x - y) =$$
$$(w \wedge x) \vee (w \wedge y) + (w \wedge x) \wedge (w \wedge y) - w \wedge x - w \wedge y$$

which is a generator of J.

The *valuation ring* of L with values in A is defined as:

$$V(L,A) = F(L,A)/J.$$

A *valuation* on L with values in an abelian group G is a function ν:L→ G such that

$$\nu(x \vee y) + \nu(x \wedge y) = \nu(x) + \nu(y) \text{ for all x and y in L.}$$

Equation 11.1 Valuation on a Lattice

The injection L→ V(L,A) is a valuation and it is universal for valuations on L with values in an A-module.

THEOREM 1: Let M be an A-module and let ν:L→M be a valuation. Then there exists a unique linear transformation (i.e., an A-module homomorphism) ν^*:V(L,A)→M such that the following diagram commutes.

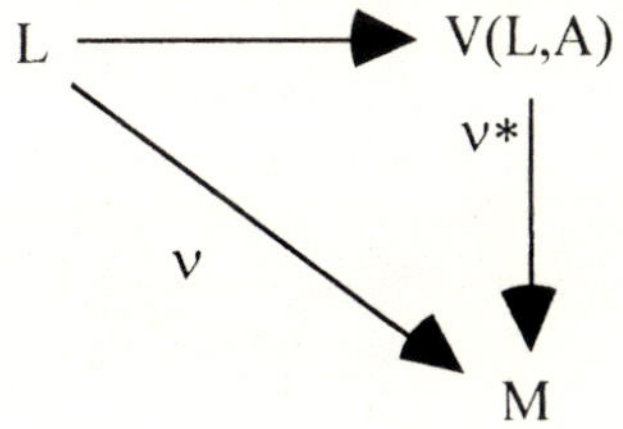

Figure 11.1. L→V(L,A) as the Universal Valuation on L

Proof: By the universality property of the free module F(L,A), there is a unique linear transformation γ:F(L,A)→M such that the left-hand triangle in the following diagram commutes.

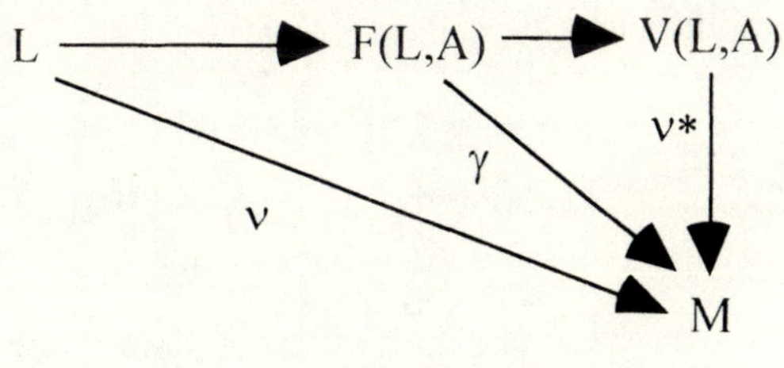

Figure 11.2. Proof of Theorem 1

Since ν is a valuation, the kernel of γ contains J, so γ extends to a unique linear transformation $\nu^*:V(L,A)\rightarrowtail M$ as desired.

For any x in L, $u\cdot x = u\wedge x = x$ so the maximal element u of L serves as the unity of the valuation ring V(L,A) (although the minimal element z is not the zero of the ring). In the situation of Theorem 1, if the A-module M is also an A-algebra and if the multiplicative condition $\nu(x\wedge y) = \nu(x)\cdot\nu(y)$ holds for all x and y in L, then the factor map ν^* is an A-algebra homomorphism. The map L→A that carries each lattice element to 1 is a valuation satisfying the multiplicative condition, so there is an A-algebra homomorphism ε: $V(L,A)\rightarrowtail A$ that takes $\Sigma a_i x_i$ to Σa_i. Hence V(L,A) is an augmented algebra with the augmentation ε. Since $z\cdot\Sigma a_i x_i = z\cdot\Sigma a_i$, the minimal element z of the lattice functions as the "integral" of the augmented valuation ring that computes the augmentation $\varepsilon(\Sigma a_i x_i) = \Sigma a_i$ of any ring element.

As in any augmented algebra, there is another natural multiplication that can be put on the A-module structure of V(L,A) in order to obtain a ring:

$$f\vee g = \varepsilon(f)g + \varepsilon(g)f - fg \text{ for all f and g in } V(L,A).$$

Equation 11.2. Dual Join-Multiplication on V(L,A)

The join notation for this dual multiplication is appropriate since if f and g are lattice elements, then $\varepsilon(f)g + \varepsilon(g)f - fg = g + f - f\wedge g = f\vee g$ is the join of f and g. In the dual valuation ring endowed with the join-multiplication, the roles of u and z are reversed, i.e., z is the unit of the ring and u is the integral.

Generalized Boolean Duality

The dual role of the meet and join multiplications extends Boolean duality to arbitrary valuation rings. This duality is realized by the *complementation* endomorphism $\tau:V(L,A)\rightarrowtail V(L,A)$, which can be defined on the valuation ring by

$$\tau(f) = \varepsilon(f)(u+z) - f$$

Equation 11.3. Complementation Endomorphism on V(L,A)

for any f in V(L,A) (even if the original lattice L was not complemented). If x is a lattice element, then we have $\tau(x) = u+z-x$ so

$\tau(u) = z$ and $\tau(z) = u$. Moreover, if x does have a complement $\neg x$ in L, then $\tau(\neg x) = \varepsilon(\neg x)(u+z) - \neg x = x \vee \neg x + x \wedge \neg x - \neg x = x$. Complementation is also equal to its own inverse in the sense that $\tau(\tau(f)) = f$ for any f in V(L,A).

Let $(V(L,A),\wedge)$ denote the valuation ring with the usual meet-multiplication, and let $(V(L,A),\vee)$ be the ring with the join-multiplication. Then complementation

$$\tau:(V(L,A),\wedge) \rightarrowtail (V(L,A),\vee)$$

is an anti-isomorphism of augmented algebras that interchanges the two multiplicative structures

$$\tau(f \cdot g) = \tau(f) \vee \tau(g)$$

and which commutes with the augmentation, i.e., $\varepsilon(\tau(f)) = \varepsilon(f)$.

A function $\varphi:V(L,A) \rightarrowtail V(L,A)$ is *linear* if $\varphi(ax+by) = a\varphi(x)+b\varphi(y)$ for all a,b in the ring A. A function $\varphi:V(L,A) \times V(L,A) \rightarrowtail V(L,A)$ is *bilinear* if $\varphi(ax+by,w) = a\varphi(x,w)+b\varphi(y,w)$ and similarly for the second argument for all a,b in A. The bilinearity of meet-multiplication is just the distributivity law. But the join and complementation are not bilinear or linear as operations on a Boolean ring (considered as a $\mathbf{Z}_2$-module). The valuation ring construction linearizes all these operations. Both multiplications are bilinear and the complementation is linear on arbitrary valuation rings V(L,A).

Part of the "trick" that allows the duality represented by the complementation anti-isomorphism is the fact that z is not the zero of the ring V(L,A). A valuation ν is *normalized* if $\nu(z) = 0$. Given a valuation ring V(L,A), the ring obtained by setting z equal to 0, i.e., V(L,A)/(z), will be called the *normalized valuation ring*. If "normalized valuation" is substituted for "valuation," then Theorem 1 will describe the universality property enjoyed by normalized valuation rings.

When L is a Boolean algebra B and $A = 2(= \mathbf{Z}_2)$, then $(V(B,2),\wedge)/(z)$ is simply B construed in the usual manner as a Boolean ring:

addition	= exclusive or (= nonequivalence)
multiplication	= meet
unity (1)	= u
zero (0)	= z.

This choice of the meet-multiplication breaks the symmetry on V(B,2) and ignores the other multiplication. But as Herbrand pointed out, a Boolean algebra can also be interpreted as a Boolean ring in another way with a join-multiplication:

addition	= equivalence
multiplication	= join
unity (1)	= z
zero (0)	= u

[see Church 1956, 103–4 for a history of these two interpretations of a Boolean algebra as a Boolean ring]. The usual Boolean ring-theoretic treatment of Boolean algebras made no particular sense out of this alternative definition; it was just an odd footnote. This other Boolean ring can be obtained as $(V(B,2),\vee)/(u)$, the quotient of the valuation ring with the join-multiplication by setting the maximal element u equal to zero.

The (prequotient) valuation ring V(B,2) maintains the symmetry by carrying both ring structures. The two interpretations of B as a Boolean ring can be obtained as the two symmetry-breaking quotients that set either z or u equal to 0. By choosing one of the quotients, one loses not only the other multiplication but also the augmentation and the complementation anti-isomorphism.

The Boolean duality principle for Boolean algebras is usually formulated in an ad hoc nonalgebraic manner by showing that any theorem remains valid under the interchange of the meet and join, and the interchange of the minimal element z and the maximal element u. On the (prequotient) valuation ring V(B,2), this Boolean duality principle is realized algebraically by the complementation ring anti-isomorphism, which interchanges the meet and join multiplications as well as the minimal and maximal elements.

This formulation of Boolean duality generalizes with the Boolean algebra B replaced by any distributive lattice L and with 2 $(=\mathbf{Z}_2)$ replaced by any commutative ring A. Any equation in V(L,A) can be dualized by applying the complementation anti-isomorphism τ. Thus "Boolean" duality generalizes far beyond the two-valued case where the ring of coefficients is $\mathbf{Z}_2$. For instance, the valuation ring $V(B,\mathbf{Z}_n)$ might prove useful for an algebraic treatment of multivalued logic. This generalization of Boolean duality to arbitrary valuation rings was due to Ladnor Geissinger, whose papers [1973] should be consulted for further analysis.

Valuation Rings on Free Boolean Algebras

Let B(P) be the free Boolean algebra on the set P [nota bene: not the power set Boolean algebra of P]. The conventional algebraic treatment of propositional logic is based on the free Boolean algebra B(P) where P is the set of propositional variables. This treatment can be generalized to V(B(P),A) where A is any commutative ring. Instead of constructing B(P) and then V(B(P),A), we will give a direct characterization of the valuation rings V(B,A) for free Boolean algebras B as special types of polynomial rings.

Let P be a set and let z be an element not in P. For any commutative ring A (always with unity 1), let $A[P \cup \{z\}]$ be the polynomial ring generated by the elements of P and the element z as indeterminates. Let I be the ideal generated by the elements $p^2 - p$ and $pz - z$ for all p in P and the element $z^2 - z$. Let $A^*[P] = A[P \cup \{z\}]/I$ be the quotient so that in $A^*[P]$, the elements of P and z are all idempotent (i.e., $p^2 = p$ and $z^2 = z$) and z absorbs the elements of P (i.e., $pz = z$). Polynomial rings $A^*[P]$ generated in this way from a set P and a ring A will be called *augmented idempotent polynomial rings*.

Since z absorbs the generators of $A^*[P]$, the product fz for any f in $A^*[P]$ has the form $\varepsilon(f)z$ for some scalar $\varepsilon(f)$ in the ring A. Indeed, this defines $\varepsilon: A^*[P] \rightarrow A$, which is the *augmentation* ring homomorphism. The join-multiplication is defined on $A^*[P]$ by $f \vee g = \varepsilon(f)g + \varepsilon(g)f - fg$, and the complementation homomorphism is defined by $\tau(f) = \varepsilon(f)(1+z) - f$ for any f and g in $A^*[P]$.

Our main characterization theorem is that the augmented idempotent polynomial rings are precisely the valuation rings on free Boolean algebras [see appendix for the proof].

CHARACTERIZATION THEOREM: $A^*[P] \cong V(B(P),A)$ for any set P and ring A.

The *idempotent polynomial rings* $A[P]/(p^2 - p)$ are constructed without the extra element z and by dividing by the ideal generated by the element $p^2 - p$ for p in P.

COROLLARY 1: The idempotent polynomial rings are the normalized valuation rings of free Boolean algebras, i.e.,

$$A[P]/(p^2 - p) \cong V(B(P),A)/(z)$$

[for a direct proof, see Ellerman and Rota 1978].

COROLLARY 2: The free Boolean algebras construed as Boolean rings (meet-multiplication) are the idempotent polynomial rings over $\mathbf{Z}_2$, i.e.,

$$\mathbf{Z}_2[P]/(p^2-p) \cong V(B(P),\mathbf{Z}_2)/(z) \cong B(P).$$

These normalized valuation rings on free Boolean algebras (i.e., the "unaugmented" idempotent polynomial rings) do not have the augmentation homomorphism, the complementation isomorphism, or the join-multiplication. Hence we will continue the development using the augmented idempotent polynomial rings.

Duality in Augmented Polynomial Rings

Each element of A*[P] is an equivalence class of polynomials. Since all the indeterminates are idempotent and z absorbs the other indeterminates, each class can be represented by a polynomial f in the *standard form*, which is a sum of first degree monomials $ax_1 \cdots x_n$ involving only x's in P, a constant term $a_u 1$ and a *co-constant* term $a_z z$ for a, a_u and a_z in A:

$$f = \Sigma\{ax_1 \cdots x_n\} + a_z z + a_u 1.$$

Equation 11.4. Standard Form Polynomial in Augmented Idempotent Polynomial Rings

The "Boolean duality principle" on augmented idempotent polynomial rings expresses the fact that complementation is an anti-isomorphism that interchanges the two multiplications, and interchanges 1 and z. Any polynomial transforms into a dual polynomial, and any polynomial equation transforms into a dual polynomial equation. The dual of a polynomial in standard form can be computed.

$$\tau(f) = \tau(\Sigma\{ax_1\cdots x_n\} + a_z z + a_u 1)$$

$$= \Sigma\{a\tau(x_1\cdots x_n)\} + a_u z + a_z 1$$

$$= \Sigma\{a[1+z - x_1\cdots x_n]\} + a_u z + a_z 1$$

$$= -\Sigma\{ax_1\cdots x_n\} + (\Sigma a + a_u)z + (\Sigma a + a_z)1$$

$$= \Sigma\{-ax_1\cdots x_n\} + (\varepsilon(f) - a_z)z + (\varepsilon(f) - a_u)1$$

Equation 11.5. Dual of a Polynomial in Standard Form

If the augmentation of a polynomial in A*[P] is zero, then the dual of the polynomial is simply the negative of the polynomial. The polynomial $1+z$ is self-dual. The dual of the dual polynomial is the original polynomial.

Each equation in the polynomial algebra has a dual equation. For instance, the fact that z is absorbing on P under the usual multiplication is expressed by the equation $z(1-p)=0$ for any p in P. Applying the complementation to both sides yields $\tau(z(1-p))=\tau(0)$, which simplifies to:

$$1\vee(p-1)=\tau(z)\vee\tau(1-p)=\tau(z(1-p))=\tau(0)=0, \text{ or}$$
$$1\vee(p-1)=0.$$

That dual equation expresses the fact that 1 is absorbing on P for the join-multiplication. The dual of $x\vee\tau(x)=1$ is $x\tau(x)=z$.

Equations involving both multiplications can also be dualized. For instance, the simple case of the inclusion-exclusion principle

$$x\vee y = x + y - xy$$

dualizes to

$$(1+z-x)(1+z-y)=(1+z-x)+(1+z-y)-(1+z-x)\vee(1+z-y)$$

for x and y in P. To use the overcount-undercount interpretation, consider two subsets X and Y in a finite universe U. Interpret x as the cardinality #(X) of X, $1+z$ as the cardinality #(U) of the universe U, $1+z-x$ as the cardinality #(¬X) of the complement of X, $x\vee y$ as the cardinality #(X∪Y) of the union of X and Y, and so forth. The overcount-undercount principle says that the number of elements in either X or Y can be calculated as the number of elements of X plus the number of elements of Y minus the number of elements that are both X and Y:

$$\#(X \cup Y) = \#(X) + \#(Y) - \#(X \cap Y).$$

Equation 11.6. Overcount-Undercount Principle

The dual principle says that the number of elements that are both non-X and non-Y can be calculated by adding the elements of non-X and non-Y and then subtracting the number of elements that are either non-X or non-Y:

$$\#(\neg X \cap \neg Y) = \#(\neg X) + \#(\neg Y) - \#(\neg X \cup \neg Y).$$

Equation 11.7. Dual to Overcount-Undercount Principle

The dual applies the overcount-undercount principle to the complements. Because of our focus on propositional logic, we will use idempotent variables, but polynomial duality could be investigated on general augmented polynomial rings.

Generalized Propositional Logic

Valuation rings of free Boolean algebras allow propositional logic to be generalized in the context of an arbitrary ring of coefficients. The characterization of the valuation rings of free Boolean algebras as the augmented idempotent polynomial rings allows generalized propositional logic to be treated using a simple "plus-and-times" algebra of polynomials.

A polynomial f in A*[P] is said to be a "provable" polynomial if it equals its augmentation (times unity) in A*[P], and f is a "refutable" polynomial if it equals its augmentation times z in A*[P][see Halmos 1963, pp. 45-46 to motivate these definitions in the case $A = Z_2$]:

f is *provable* if $f = \varepsilon(f)1$ in A*[P], and

f is *refutable* if $f = \varepsilon(f)z$ in A*[P].

Equation 11.8. Definition of Provable and Refutable Polynomials

For instance, $x + \tau(x) - x\tau(x)$ is provable and $x\tau(x)$ is refutable for any x in P. The complementation interchanges provable and refutable polynomials.

Every map $w{:}P \cup \{z\} \rightarrow A$ such that w(p) and w(z) are idempotent and w(z) absorbs w(p) for all p in P will extend to an A-algebra homomorphism $w^*{:}A^*[P] \rightarrow A$ (and all such homomorphisms induce such a map on the generators). A polynomial is said to be a "tautology" if it is always mapped to its augmentation (times unity, which is the image of the unity in the polynomial ring), and f is said to be a "contradiction" if it is always mapped to its augmentation times the image of z, i.e., for all A-algebra homomorphisms $w^*{:}A^*[P] \rightarrow A$,

$$\text{if } w^*(f) = \varepsilon(f)1 \ [= \varepsilon(f)w^*(1)], \text{ f is a } \textit{tautology}, \text{ and}$$

$$\text{if } w^*(f) = \varepsilon(f)w^*(z), \text{ f is a } \textit{contradiction.}$$

Equation 11.9. Definition of Tautologous and Contradictory Polynomials

This generalizes the usual "truth table" definitions of tautologies and contradictions. The complementation interchanges tautologies and contradictions. Clearly a theorem is a tautology and a refutable polynomial is a contradiction. The converse is the generalization of the completeness theorem.

GENERALIZED COMPLETENESS THEOREM: If a polynomial f in A*[P] is a tautology, then f is provable.

Proof: Since by assumption $w^*(f - \varepsilon(f)) = 0$ for all homomorphisms w^*, it suffices to prove the theorem in the form: if $w^*(f) = 0$ in A for all w^*, then $f = 0$ in A*[P]. This can be shown using elementary reasoning about polynomials. Let f be represented in standard form:

$$f = \Sigma\{ax_1 \ldots x_n\} + a_z z + a_u 1.$$

By taking different choices of a $w{:}P \cup \{z\} \rightarrow A$ mapping the x_i's in P and the z to 1's and 0's, the coefficients in A can all be shown to be 0 (but if $w(z) = 1$ then $w(x) = 1$ for all x in P).

If $w(x) = w(z) = 1$ for all x in P, then $w^*(f) = \Sigma a + a_z + a_u = \varepsilon(f) = 0$.
If $w(x) = w(z) = 0$ for all x in P, then $w^*(f) = a_u = 0$ so $a_u = 0$.

If $w(x)=1$ for all x in P and $w(z)=0$, then $w^*(f)=\Sigma a=0$ so by the above, $a_z=0$.

For each single x_i in P, set $w(x_i)=1$ and the other $w(x)=0$ and $w(z)=0$, so the coefficient of each x_i must be 0.

For each pair x_i and x_j in P, set $w(x_i)=w(x_j)=1$ and the other $w(x)=0$ and $w(z)=0$, so the coefficient of x_ix_j must be 0.

By continuing the reasoning for each triple of x's and so forth, all the coefficients of f are shown to be 0.

The classical completeness theorem for propositional logic is the special case $A=Z_2$.

References

Church, A. 1956. *Introduction to Mathematical Logic*. Princeton: Princeton University Press.

Ellerman, David and Gian-Carlo Rota. 1978. "A Measure Theoretic Approach to Logical Quantification." *Rend. Sem. Mat. Univ. Padova* 59: 227–46.

Geissinger, L. 1973. "Valuations on Distributive Lattices I." *Arch. Math.* 24: 230—39.

———. 1973. "Valuations on Distributive Lattices II." *Arch. Math.* 24: 337–45.

———. 1973. "Valuations on Distributive Lattices III. *Arch. Math.* 24: 475–81.

Halmos, Paul. 1963. *Lectures on Boolean Algebras*. Princeton: Van Nostrand Company.

Rota, Gian-Carlo. 1971. "On the Combinatorics of the Euler Characteristic." In *Studies in Pure Mathematics*. ed. L. Minsky, 221–33. Academic Press: London.

———. 1973. "The Valuation Ring of a Distributive Lattice." In *Proc. Univ. of Houston Lattice Theory Conference*, 575–628. Houston.

Appendix: Proof of Characterization Theorem

CHARACTERIZATION THEOREM: The valuation rings over free Boolean algebras are the augmented idempotent polynomial rings, i.e., $V(B(P),A)\cong A^*[P]$ for any set P and commutative ring (with unity) A.

Proof: Let $B_0=\{f\in A^*[P]: f^2=f \text{ and } \varepsilon(f)=1\}$ be the set of idempotents of $A^*[P]$ with unitary augmentation. B_0 becomes a Boolean algebra with the operations defined by $f \vee g = f + g - fg$, $f \wedge g = fg$, and $\neg f = 1 + z - f$. Since the generators P are included in B_0, there exists, by the universality property of the free Boolean algebra B(P), a unique Boolean algebra homomorphism $v: B(P) \rightarrow B_0 \subseteq A^*[P]$ that commutes with the insertion of P. Since ν is a Boolean algebra homomorphism, we have

$$\nu(z) = z,\ \nu(x \wedge y) = \nu(x) \wedge \nu(y) = \nu(x) \cdot \nu(y), \text{ and}$$
$$\nu(x \vee y) = \nu(x) \vee \nu(y) = \nu(x) + \nu(y) - \nu(x \wedge y)$$

for any x and y in B(P). Hence ν is a multiplicative valuation on B(P) with values in the A-algebra A*[P], so by Theorem 1 (for multiplicative valuations), there exists a unique A-algebra homomorphism ν^* such that the following diagram commutes.

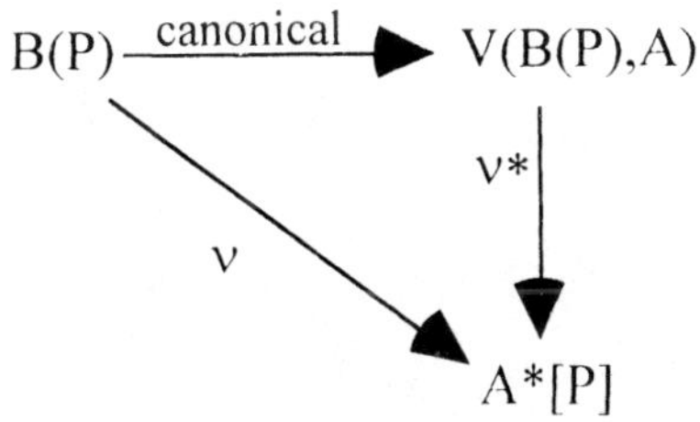

Figure 11.3. Existence of A-Algebra Homomorphism $\nu^*: V(B(P),A) \rightarrow A^*[P]$

Let $w: P \cup \{z\} \rightarrow V(B(P),A)$ be the insertion of the elements of $P \cup \{z\}$ into the A-algebra V(B(P),A). Then by the universality property of the polynomial ring $A[P \cup \{z\}]$, there exists a unique A-algebra homomorphism w′ such that the left-hand triangle in the following diagram commutes.

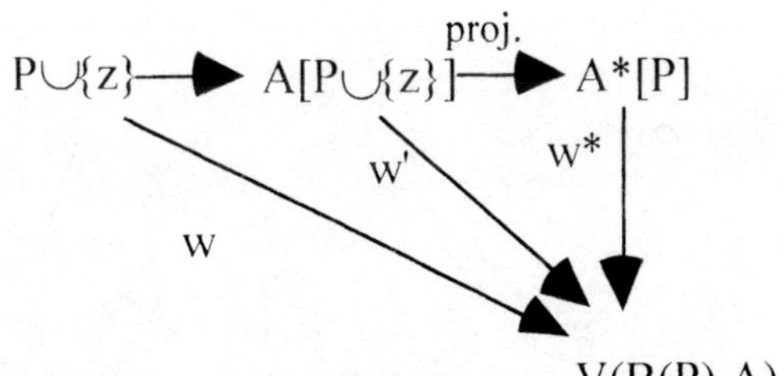

Figure 11.4. Existence of A-Algebra Homomorphism $w^*: A^*[P] \rightarrow V(B(P),A)$

Then for any p in P, we have $w'(p^2-p)=w'(p)^2-w'(p)=p-p=0$, $w'(pz-z) = w'(p)z-z=z-z=0$, and $w'(z^2-z)=0$ so I is contained in the kernel of w′. Hence there exists a unique A-algebra homomorphism w* such that w′ = w*· proj., i.e., the right-hand triangle commutes.

Now consider the following diagram.

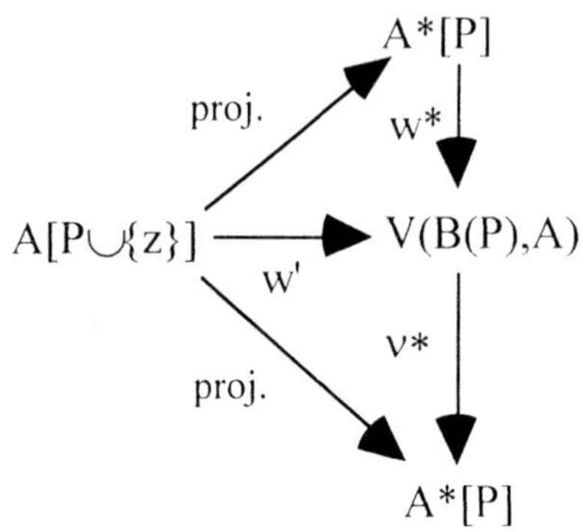

Figure 11.5. ν*w* is the Identity on A*[P]

We have just seen that the upper triangle commutes. To see that the lower triangle commutes, note that ν*w′ and proj. are both A-algebra homomorphisms A[P∪{z}→A[P∪{z}]/I = A*[P] which commute with the insertion of P∪{z}. By the universality property of A[P∪{z}], there is only one such map so ν*w′ = proj. Since w′ = w*· proj., we have that proj. = ν*w*· proj., i.e., the outer triangle commutes. By the universality property of quotient rings, the identity is the unique A-algebra homomorphism A*[P]→A*[P] that commutes with the projections, so ν*w* is the identity on A*[P].

It remains to consider the following diagram.

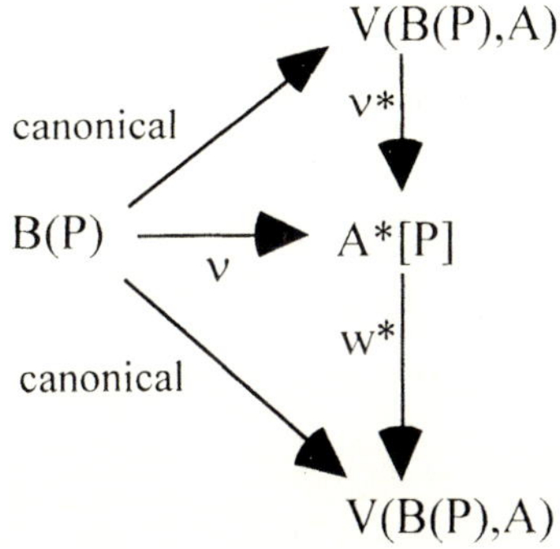

Figure 11.6. w^*v^* is the Identity on V(B(P),A)

We have seen that the upper triangle commutes. To see that the lower triangle commutes, note that when the A-algebra homomorphism w^* is restricted to B_0, then it is a Boolean algebra homomorphism into the Boolean algebra of idempotents of V(B(P),A). Hence w^*v and the canonical map are both Boolean algebra homomorphisms $B(P) \rightarrowtail$ V(B(P),A), which agree on the insertion of P. By the universality property of the free Boolean algebra B(P), there is only one such map so $w^*v =$ canonical, i.e., the lower triangle commutes and thus the outer triangle commutes as well. By the universality property of V(B(P),A) (Theorem 1), the identity is the unique A-algebra homomorphism $V(B(P),A) \rightarrowtail V(B(P),A)$, which commutes with the canonical map as a multiplicative valuation, so w^*v^* is the identity on V(B(P),A). Hence we have the isomorphism: $A^*[P] \cong V(B(P),A)$.

Chapter 12

Parallel Addition, Series-Parallel Duality, and Financial Mathematics

Introduction

In economic theory, "duality" means "convex duality," which includes duality in linear and non-linear programming as special cases. Series-parallel duality has been studied largely in electrical circuit theory and, to some extent, in combinatorial theory. Series-parallel duality also occurs in economics and finance, and it is closely related to convex duality.

When resistors with resistance a and b are placed in series, their compound resistance is the usual sum (hereafter the *series sum*) of the resistances a + b. If the resistances are placed in parallel, their compound resistance is the *parallel sum* of the resistances, which is denoted by the full colon:

$$a\!:\!b = \left(a^{-1} + b^{-1}\right) = \frac{1}{\frac{1}{a} + \frac{1}{b}} = \frac{ab}{a+b}.$$

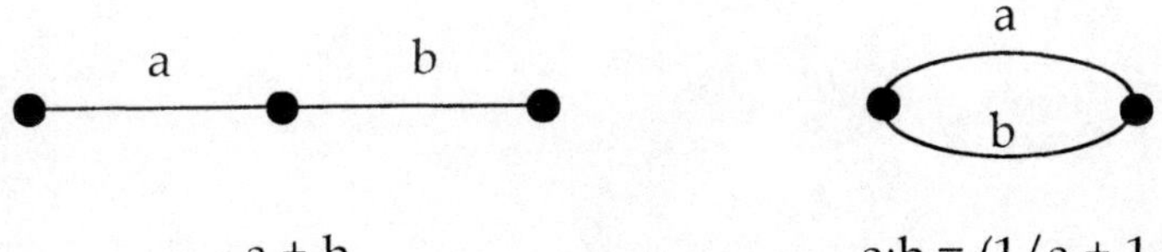

a + b $a\!:\!b = (1/a + 1/b)^{-1}$

Figure 12.1. Series and Parallel Sums

The parallel sum is associative x:(y:z)) = (x:y):z, commutative x:y = y:x, and distributive x(y:z) = xy:xz. On the positive reals, there is no identity element for either sum but the "closed circuit" 0 and the "open circuit" ∞ can be added to form the extended positive reals. Those elements are the identity elements for the two sums, $x+0 = x{:}\infty$.

For fractions, the series sum is the usual addition expressed by the annoyingly asymmetrical rule: "Find the common denominator and then add the numerators." The parallel sum of fractions restores symmetry since it is defined in the dual fashion: "Find the common numerator and then (series) add the denominators."

$$\frac{a}{b}:\frac{a}{d}=\frac{a}{b+d}$$

The parallel sum of fractions can also be obtained by finding the common denominator and taking the *parallel* sum of numerators.

$$\frac{a}{b}:\frac{c}{b}=\frac{a{:}c}{b}$$

The usual series sum of fractions can be obtained by finding the common *numerator* and then taking the *parallel* sum of the denominators.

$$\frac{a}{b}+\frac{a}{d}=\frac{a}{b{:}d}$$

The rules for series and parallel sums of fractions can be summarized in the following four equations.

$$\frac{a}{1}+\frac{b}{1}=\frac{a+b}{1} \qquad \frac{a}{1}:\frac{b}{1}=\frac{a{:}b}{1}$$

$$\frac{1}{a}:\frac{1}{b}=\frac{1}{a+b} \qquad \frac{1}{a}+\frac{1}{b}=\frac{1}{a{:}b}$$

Series Chauvinism

From the viewpoint of pure mathematics, the parallel sum is "just as good" as the series sum. It is only for empirical and perhaps even some accidental reasons that so much mathematics is developed using the series sum instead of the equally good parallel sum. There is a whole "parallel mathematics" which can be developed with the parallel sum replacing the series sum. Since the parallel sum can be defined in terms of the series sum (or vice versa), "parallel mathematics" is essentially a new way of looking at certain known parts of mathematics.

Exclusive promotion of the series sum is "series chauvinism" or "serialism." Before venturing further into the parallel universe, we might suggest some exercises to help the reader combat the heritage of series chauvinism. Anytime the series sum seems to occur naturally in mathematics with the parallel sum nowhere in sight, it is an illusion. The parallel sum lurks in a "parallel" role that has been unfairly neglected.

For instance, a series chauvinist might point out that the series sum appears naturally in the rule for working with exponents $x^a x^b = x^{a+b}$ while the parallel sum does not. But this is only an illusion due to our mathematically arbitrary symmetry-breaking choice to take exponents to represent powers rather than roots. Let a pre-superscript stand for a root (just as a post-superscript stands for a power) so ${}^2x$ would be the square root of x. Then the rule for working with *these* exponents is ${}^a x\, {}^b x = {}^{a:b}x$ so the parallel sum does have a role symmetrical to the series sum in the rules for working with exponents.

Parallel Sums in High School Math

In high school algebra, parallel sums occur in the computation of completion times when activities are run in parallel. If pump A can fill a reservoir in a hours and pump B can fill the same reservoir in b hours, then running the two pumps simultaneously will fill the reservoir in a:b hours.

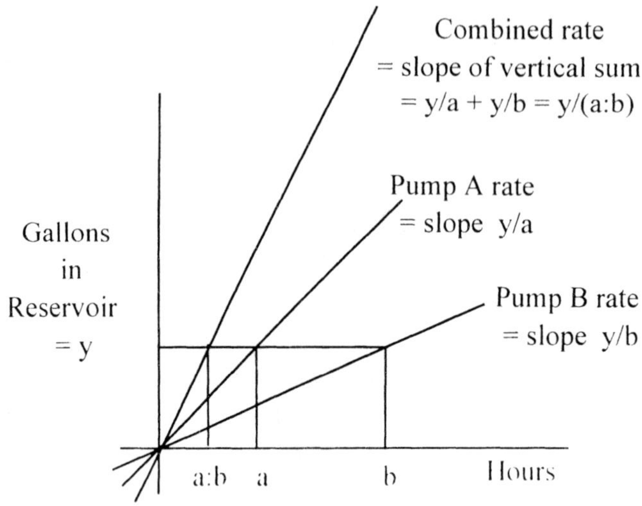

Figure 12.2. Vertical Sum of Lines

In the previous example, the slope of the vertical sum of two positively sloped straight lines was the series sum of the slopes. The "dual" of vertical sum is the horizontal sum. The slope of the horizontal sum of two positively sloped straight lines is the parallel sum of the slopes. Inverting the previous case yields an example.

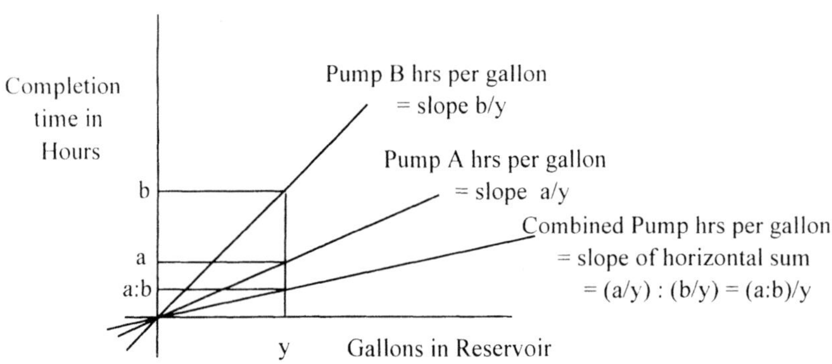

Figure 12.3. Horizontal Sum of Lines

Series-Parallel Duality and Reciprocity

The duality between the series and parallel additions on the positive reals R^+ can be studied by considering the bijective reciprocity map

$$\rho{:}R^+ \rightarrow R^+ \text{ defined by } \rho(x) = 1/x.$$

The reciprocity map preserves the unit $\rho(1) = 1$, preserves multiplication $\rho(xy) = \rho(x)\rho(y)$, and *interchanges* the two additions:

$$\rho(x+y) = \rho(x){:}\rho(y) \text{ and } \rho(x{:}y) = \rho(x)+\rho(y).$$

The reciprocity map captures series-parallel duality on the positive reals just as an analogous anti-isomorphism (which interchanges two dual multiplications and preserves addition) on Rota's valuation rings captures Boolean duality [see previous chapter].

Much of the previous work on series-parallel duality has used methods drawn from graph theory and combinatorics [e.g., MacMahon 1881, Riordan and Shannon 1942, Duffin 1965, and Brylawski 1971]. MacMahon called a series connection a "chain" and a parallel connection a "yoke" (as in ox yoke). A *series-parallel network* is constructed solely from chains and yokes (series and parallel connections). By interchanging the series and parallel connections, each series-parallel network yields a *dual* or *conjugate* series-parallel network. To obtain the dual of an expression such as $a+((b+c){:}d)$, apply the reciprocity map but, for the atomic variables, replace $1/a$ by a and so forth in the final expression. Thus the dual expression would be $a{:}((b{:}c)+d)$ (see next page).

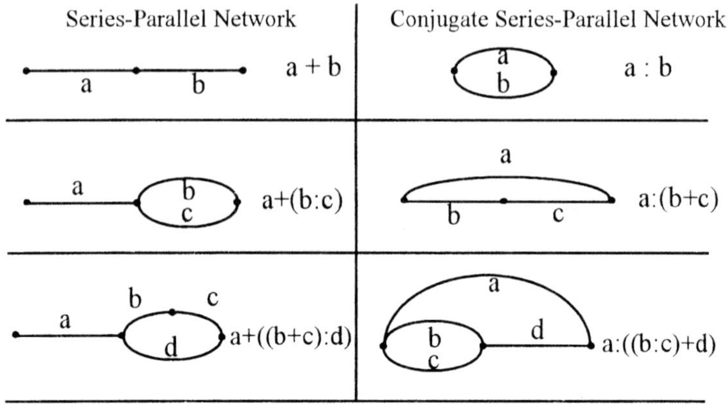

Figure 12.4. Conjugate Series-Parallel Networks

If each variable a, b, ... equals one, then the reciprocity map carries each expression for the compound resistance into the conjugate expression. Hence if all the "atomic" resistances are one ohm, a = b = c = d = 1, and the compound resistance of a series-parallel network is R, then the compound resistance of the conjugate network is 1/R [MacMahon 1881, 1892]. With any positive reals as resistances, MacMahon's chain-yoke reciprocity theorem continues to hold if each atomic resistance is also inverted in the conjugate network.

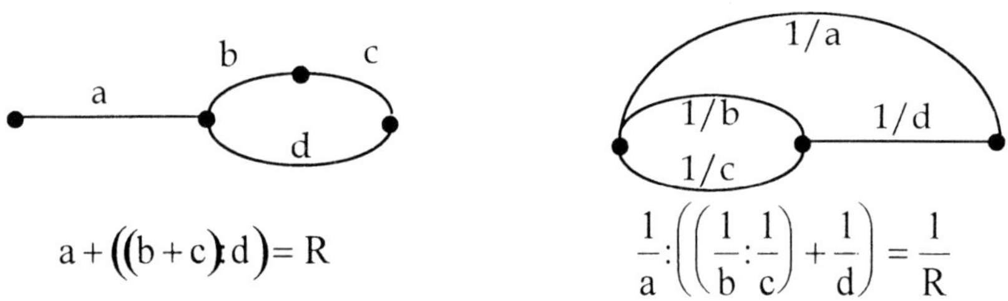

Figure 12.5. MacMahon Chain-Yoke Reciprocity Theorem

The theorem amounts to the observation that the reciprocity map interchanges the two sums while preserving multiplication and unity.

Dual Equations on the Positive Reals

Any equation on the positive reals concerning the two sums and multiplication can be dualized by applying the reciprocity map to obtain another equation. The series sum and parallel sum are interchanged. For example, the equation

$$\frac{1}{3}\left(5+\frac{2}{5}+\frac{3}{5}\right)=2$$

dualizes to the equation

$$3\left(\frac{1}{5}:\frac{5}{2}:\frac{5}{3}\right)=\frac{1}{2}.$$

The following equation

$$1=(1+x):\left(1+\frac{1}{x}\right)$$

holds for any positive real x. Add any x to one and add its reciprocal to one. The results are two numbers larger than one and their parallel sum is exactly one. Dualizing yields the equation

$$1=\left(1:\frac{1}{x}\right)+(1:x).$$

for all positive reals x. Taking the parallel sum of any x and its reciprocal with one yields two numbers smaller than one which sum to one.

For any set of positive reals $x_1,\ldots,x_n$, the parallel summation can be expressed using the capital P:

$$\mathop{\mathrm{P}}_{i=1}^{n} x_i=\left(\sum_{i=1}^{n} x_i^{-1}\right)^{-1}.$$

Equation 12.1. Parallel Summation

The binomial theorem

$$(a+b)^n = \sum_{k=0}^{n} \binom{n}{k} a^k b^{n-k}$$

dualizes to the parallel sum binomial theorem (where "1/a" is replaced by "a" and similarly for "b"):

$$(a{:}b)^n = \mathrm{P}_{k=0}^{n} \binom{n}{k}^{-1} a^k b^{n-k}.$$

Equation 12.2. Parallel Sum Binomial Theorem

Taking a = 1 + x and b = 1 + 1/x (and using a previous equation on the left-hand side), we have a nonobvious identity

$$1 = \mathrm{P}_{k=0}^{n} \binom{n}{k}^{-1} (1+x)^k \left(1+\frac{1}{x}\right)^{n-k}$$

for any $x > 0$.

Series and Parallel Geometric Series

The following formula (and its dual) for partial sums of geometric series (starting at i = 1) are useful in financial mathematics (where x is any positive real).

$$\sum_{i=1}^{n} (1{:}x)^i = \sum_{i=0}^{n-1} (1{:}x)^{-i}{:}x = x(1-(1{:}x)^n)$$

Equation 12.3. Partial Sums of Geometric Series

Dualizing yields a formula for partial sums of parallel-sum geometric series.

$$\mathrm{P}_{i=1}^{n} (1+x)^i = \mathrm{P}_{i=0}^{n-1} (1+x)^{-i} + x = \frac{x}{1-(1+x)^{-n}}$$

Equation 12.4. Partial Sums of Dual Geometric Series

Dualization can also be applied to infinite series. Taking the limit as $n \rightarrow \infty$ in the above partial sum formulas yields for any positive reals x the dual summation formulas for series and parallel sum geometric series that begin at the index i = 1.

$$\sum_{i=1}^{\infty} (1{:}x)^i = x = \underset{i=1}{\overset{\infty}{\mathrm{P}}} (1+x)^i$$

The parallel sum series in the above equation can be used to represent a repeating decimal as a fraction. An example will illustrate the procedure so let z = .367367367...where the "367" repeats. Then since 1/a + 1/b = 1/(a:b), we have:

$$z = .367367\ldots = \sum_{i=1}^{\infty} \frac{367}{(1000)^i} = \frac{367}{\underset{i=1}{\overset{\infty}{\mathrm{P}}} (1000)^i}.$$

Taking y = x + 1 for x > 0 in the previous geometric series equation yields

$$\underset{i=1}{\overset{\infty}{\mathrm{P}}} y^i = y - 1$$

for y > 1 which is applied to yield

$$z = .367367\ldots = \frac{367}{\underset{i=1}{\overset{\infty}{\mathrm{P}}} (1000)^i} = \frac{367}{1000-1} = \frac{367}{999}.$$

For any positive real x, the dual summation formulas for the geometric series with indices beginning at i = 0 can be obtained by serial or parallel adding $1 = (1{:}x)^0 = (1+x)^0$ to each side.

$$\sum_{i=0}^{\infty} (1{:}x)^i = (1+x)$$

Equation 12.5. Geometric Series for any Positive Real x

$$\mathop{\mathrm{P}}_{i=0}^{\infty} (1+x)^{i} = (1:x).$$

Equation 12.6. Dual Geometric Series for any Positive Real x

The Harmonic Mean

The *harmonic mean* of n positive reals is n times their parallel sum. Suppose an investor spends \$100 a month for two months buying shares in a certain security. The shares cost \$5 each the first month and \$10 each the second month. What is the average price per share purchased? At first glance, one might average the \$5 and \$10 prices to obtain an average price of \$7.50—but that would neglect the fact that twice as many shares were purchased at the lower price. Hence one must compute the weighted average taking into account the number of each purchased at each price, and that yields the harmonic mean of the two prices.

$$\frac{(20\times\$5)+(10\times\$10)}{30} = 2(\$5{:}\$10) = \$6\frac{2}{3}.$$

This investment rule is called "dollar cost averaging." A financial advisory letter explained a benefit of the method.

> First, dollar cost averaging helps guarantee that the average *cost* per share of the shares you buy will always be lower than their average *price*. That's because when you always spend the same dollar amount each time you buy, naturally you'll buy more shares when the fund's price is lower and fewer shares when its price is higher. [Scudder Funds 1988]

Let $p_1, p_2, \ldots, p_n$ be the price per share in each of n time periods. The average cost of the shares is the harmonic mean of the share prices, $n(p_1 : p_2 : \ldots : p_n)$, and the average price is just the usual arithmetical mean of the prices, $(p_1 + p_2 + \ldots + p_n)/n$.

The inequality that the average cost of the shares is less than or equal to the average of the share prices follows from

$$(A : B) + (C : D) \leq (A+C) : (B+D)$$

Equation 12.7. Lehman's Series-Parallel Inequality

for positive A, B, C, and D [1962; see Duffin 1975].

This application of the series-parallel inequality can be seen by considering the prices as resistances in the following diagram (note how each of the n rows and each of the n columns contains all n resistances or prices).

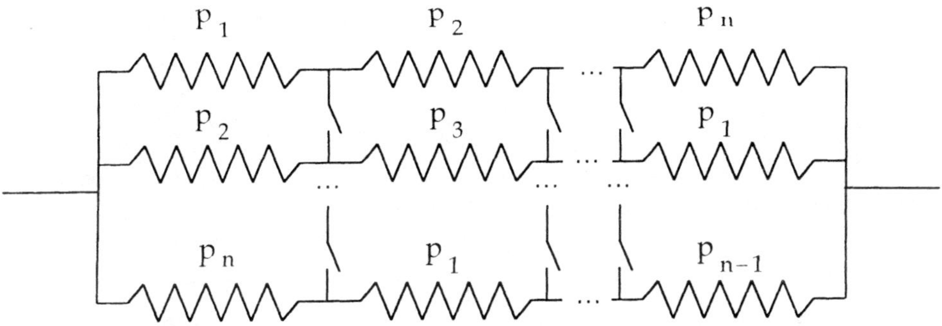

Figure 12.6. Intuitive Proof of Lehman's Inequality

When all the switches are open, the compound resistance is the parallel sum (n times) of the series sum of the prices, which is just the arithmetical mean of the prices. When the switches are closed, the compound resistance is the series sum (n times) of the parallel sum of the prices, which is the harmonic mean of the prices. Since the resistance is smaller or the same with the switches closed, we have for any positive $p_1, p_2, \ldots, p_n$,

$$\text{Harmonic Mean} = n \mathop{\mathbf{P}}_{i=1}^{n} p_i \leq \frac{\sum_{i=1}^{n} p_i}{n} = \text{Arithmetical Mean}$$

Geometric Interpretation of Parallel Sum

The harmonic mean of two numbers is twice their parallel sum, just as the usual series or arithmetical mean is half their series sum. The geometric interpretation of the harmonic mean will lead us into geometric applications of the parallel sum. Draw a line FG through the point E where the diagonals cross in the trapezoid ABDC.

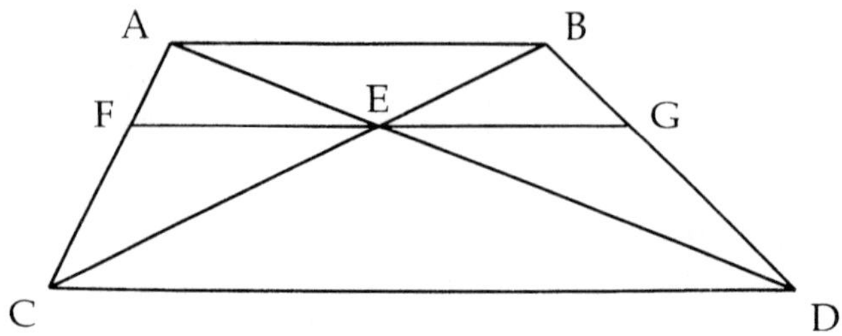

Figure 12.7. Geometry of Parallel Sum

Then FG is the harmonic mean of parallel sides AB and CD, i.e., FG = 2(AB:CD). Since E bisects FG, the distance FE is the parallel sum of AB and CD, i.e., FE = AB:CD.

The basic geometrical fact can be restated by viewing AC as being horizontal (see following diagram). Given two parallel line segments AB and CD, draw BC and AD, which cross at E. The distance of E to the horizontal line AC in the direction parallel to AB and CD is the parallel sum AB:CD.

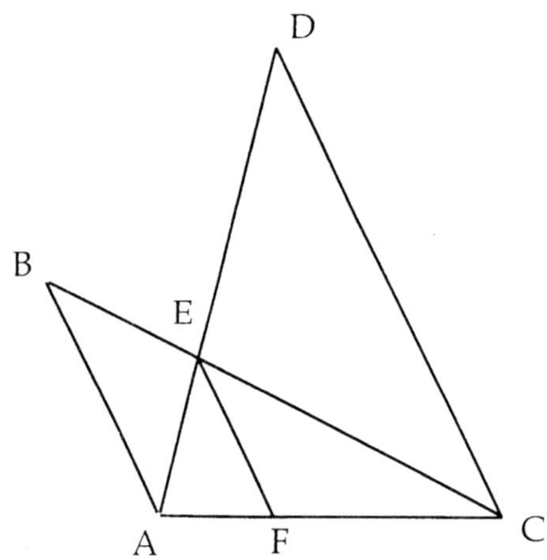

Figure 12.8. EF = AB:CD

It is particularly interesting to note that the distance AC is arbitrary. If CD is shifted out parallel to C′D′ and the new diagonals AD′ and BC′ are drawn (as if rubber bands connected B with C and A with D), then the distance E′F′ is again the parallel sum of AB and CD (=C′D′).

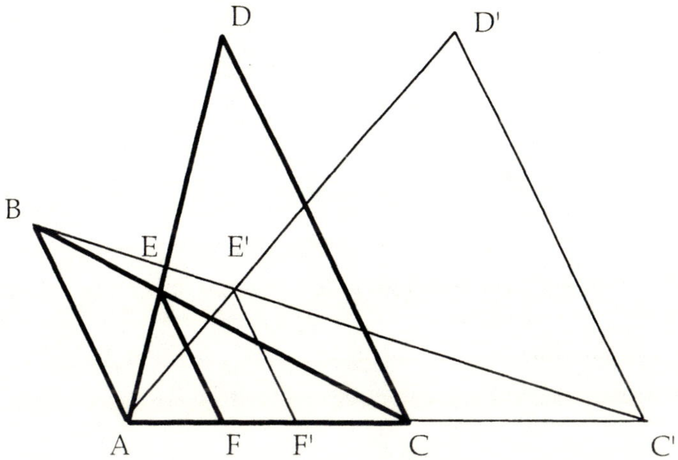

Figure 12.9. EF = E′F′ = AB:CD where CD = C′D′

The Gaussian equation for thin lenses presents the focal length f = FE as the parallel sum of the distance d of the object (the arrow A′A) from the lens plane BEC and the distance d′ of the image (the arrow D′D) from the lens plane.

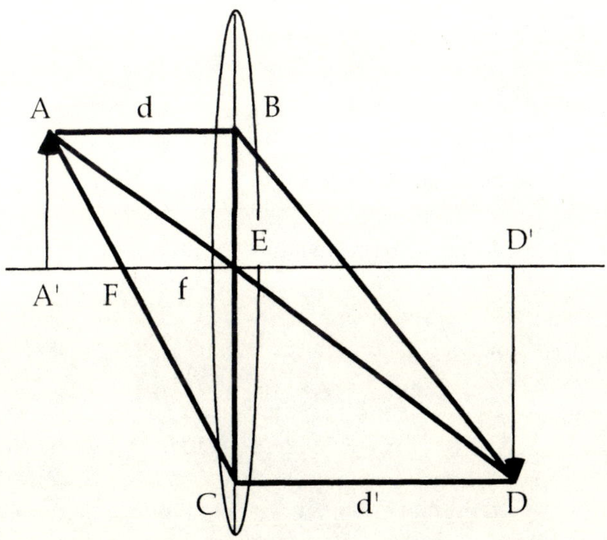

Figure 12.10. Gaussian Thin Lense Diagram

The thickened lines in the diagram show that f = d : d′ or, as the formula is usually written:

$$\frac{1}{d} + \frac{1}{d'} = \frac{1}{f}.$$

Equation 12.8. Gaussian Thin Lense Equation

Solutions of Linear Equations: Geometric Interpretation

Solutions to linear equations can always be presented as the parallel sum of quantities with a clear geometrical interpretation. Consider the case of two linear equations.

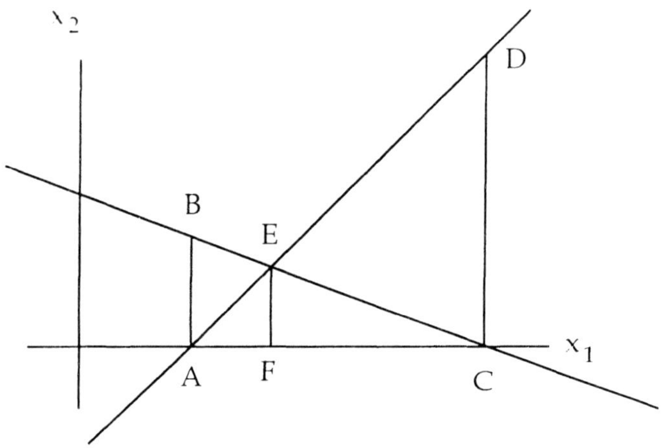

Figure 12.11. Linear Equations and Parallel Sum EF = AB:CD

For instance, the x_2 solution EF is the parallel sum of AB and CD, which are the "pillars" that rise up to each line from where the other line hits the x_1 floor.

This procedure generalizes to any nonsingular system of n linear equations. Suppose we wish to find the solution value of x_j. Each of the linear equations defines a hyperplane in n-space. For each i = 1,...,n, the n-1 hyperplanes taken by excluding the ith hyperplane intersect to form a line which, in turn, intersects the x_j = 0 floor at some point called the "base of the ith pillar." The perpendicular distance from that base point on the $x_j = 0$ floor up to the ith hyperplane is the height c_i of the "i^{th} pillar" (on the $x_j = 0$ floor). If the perpendicular line through the base point does not intersect the ith hyperplane, then the height c_i of the ith pillar can be taken as ∞ ("∞" is "open circuit" element that is the identity for the parallel sum, $\infty : x = x$, and absorbs under the series sum, $\infty + x = \infty$). The parallel sum of the pillars is the solution value of x_j:

$$c_1 : c_2 : \ldots : c_n = x_j \text{ solution.}$$

For $i = 1,\ldots,n$, the base of the ith pillar is the solution of the system of equations if the ith equation is replaced by $x_j = 0$. Now replace $x_j = 0$ with the ith equation but ignore the effect x_j has in the other equations, i.e., temporarily set the coefficient of x_j in the other equations equal to zero. Then the x_j solution of those modified equations is the ith pillar c_i. Thus each pillar measures the effect of each equation on determining x_j if the role of x_j in the other equations is ignored. The parallel sum of these isolated effects is the x_j solution.

The proof of this result uses Cramer's Rule. Consider each column of a square matrix $A = [a_{ij}]$ as a (reversible) linear activity that uses n inputs supplied in given amounts (the b_i constants). The jth activity is given by a column vector $(a_{1j},\ldots,a_{nj})^T$ (where the "T" superscript indicates transpose). Each unit of the jth activity uses up a_{ij} units of the ith input. With given input supplies $b = (b_1,\ldots,b_n)^T$, the levels of the n activities $x = (x_1,\ldots,x_n)^T$ are determined by the matrix equation $Ax = b$.

To isolate the effect of x_j on using the ith input, replace the jth activity by the column $(0,\ldots,0,a_{ij},0,\ldots,0)^T$ so the jth activity only uses the ith input. The x_j solution of the resulting equations is the ith pillar c_i. Hence by Cramer's Rule, the ith pillar is (if the denominator is zero, take $c_i = \infty$):

$$c_i = \frac{\begin{vmatrix} a_{11} \ldots b_1 \ldots a_{1n} \\ \ldots \ldots \ldots \ldots \\ a_{n1} \ldots b_n \ldots a_{nn} \end{vmatrix}}{\begin{vmatrix} a_{11} \ldots & 0 & \ldots a_{1n} \\ \ldots \ldots & a_{ij} & \ldots \ldots \\ a_{n1} \ldots & 0 & \ldots a_{nn} \end{vmatrix}}.$$

The parallel sum of these pillars c_i for i = 1,...,n will give the correct value of x_j.

The parallel sum of fractions with a common numerator is that numerator divided by the (series) sum of the denominators. The (series) sum of the denominators in the above calculation of c_i for i = 1,...,n is the cofactor expansion of |A| by the jth column. Hence the result follows by Cramer's Rule:

$$x_j = \mathop{\mathrm{P}}_{i=1}^{n} c_i = \frac{\begin{vmatrix} a_{11} \dots b_1 \dots a_{1n} \\ \dots \dots\dots\dots \dots \\ a_{n1} \dots b_n \dots a_{nn} \end{vmatrix}}{|A|}.$$

Equation 12.9. Solution as Parallel Sum of "Pillars"

Duality in Financial Arithmetic

Parallel Sums in Financial Arithmetic

The parallel sum has a natural interpretation in finance so that each equation and formula in financial arithmetic can be paired with a dual equation or formula. The parallel sum "smoothes" balloon payments to yield the constant amortization payment to pay off a loan. If r is the interest rate per period, then $PV(1+r)^n$ is the one-shot balloon payment at time n that would pay off a loan with the principal value of PV. The similar balloon payments that could be paid at times t = 1, 2,..., n, any one of which would pay off the loan, are

$$PV(1+r)^1, PV(1+r)^2, \dots, PV(1+r)^n.$$

But what is the equal amortization payment PMT that would pay off the same loan when paid at each of the times t = 1, 2, ..., n? It is simply the parallel sum of the one-shot balloon payments:

$$\begin{aligned} PMT &= PV(1+r)^1 : PV(1+r)^2 : \dots : PV(1+r)^n \\ &= \mathop{\mathrm{P}}_{i=1}^{n} PV(1+r)^i. \end{aligned}$$

Equation 12.10. Amortization Payment is Parallel Sum of Balloon Payments

How does the total amount of money paid with equal loan payments compare with the one-time balloon payments? The sum of all the amortization payments nPMT is the harmonic mean of the balloon payments.

This use of the parallel sum is not restricted to financial arithmetic. For example, suppose a forest of initial size PV (in harvestable board-feet) grows at the rate r_i in the ith period. Then

$$P_m = PV\prod_{i=1}^{m}(1+r_i)$$

would be the *one-shot harvest* that could be obtained at the end of the mth period. For instance, P_3, P_{17}, and P_{23} are the amounts that could be harvested if the whole forest was harvested at the end of the 3rd, 17th, or the 23rd period. But what is the smooth or equal harvest PMT so that if PMT was harvested at the end of the 3rd, 17th, and the 23rd periods, then the forest would just be completely harvested at the end of that last period? That smooth harvest amount is just the parallel sum of the one-time harvests:

$$PMT = P_3 : P_{17} : P_{23}.$$

The total harvest under the equal harvest method is the harmonic mean of the three one-shot harvests.

Returning to financial arithmetic, the discounted present value at time zero of n one dollar payments at the end of periods 1, 2,..., n is a(n,r), the *present value of an annuity of one*.

$$a(n,r) = \frac{1}{(1+r)^1} + \frac{1}{(1+r)^2} + \cdots + \frac{1}{(1+r)^n}.$$

Equation 12.11. Present Value of an Annuity of One

Dualizing yields:

$$\frac{1}{a(n,r)} = (1+r)^1 : (1+r)^2 : \cdots : (1+r)^n.$$

Equation 12.12. Installment to Amortize One

For the principal value of one dollar at time zero, the one-shot payments at times 1,2,..., n that would each pay off the principal are the compounded principals $(1'r)^1$, $(1+r)^2$,..., $(1+r)^n$. The parallel sum $(1+4)^1$: $(1+r)^2$ paid at times 1 and 2 would pay off the \$1 principal. Similarly, the parallel sum of the first three one-shot payments paid at times 1, 2, and 3 would pay off the \$1 principal, and so forth.

Suppose the constant interest rate is 20 percent per period.Then the discounted present value of two amortization payments of 1 at the end of the first and second period is the principal value of the loan paid off by those payments, i.e., 55/36:

$$a(2,.20) = \frac{55}{36} = \frac{1}{(1.2)^1} + \frac{1}{(1.2)^2}.$$

The equation dualizes to:

$$\frac{1}{a(2,.20)} = \frac{36}{55} = (1.2)^1 : (1.2)^2.$$

The amounts $(1.2)^1$ and $(1.2)^2$ are the compounded principal values of a \$1 loan so they are the one-shot or balloon payments that would pay off a loan of principal value \$1 if paid, respectively, at the end of the first or the second period. Their parallel sum, 36/55, is the equal amortization payment that would pay off that loan of \$1 if paid at the end of both the first and second periods.

These facts can be arranged in the following dual format.

Primal Fact:	Dual Fact:
The series sum of the discounted amortization payments for a loan is the principal of the loan.	The parallel sum of the compounded principals of a loan is the amortization payment for the loan.

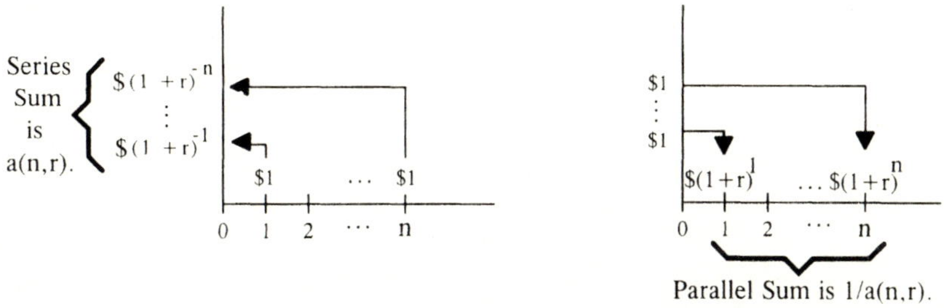

Figure 12.12. Illustrations of Primal and Dual Identities

The example illustrates some of the substitutions involved in dualizing the interpretation.

series sum	⇔	parallel sum
discounting	⇔	compounding
principals	⇔	payments

Future Values and Sinking Fund Deposits

Another staple of financial arithmetic is the computation of sinking fund deposits. The compounded future value at time n of n one-dollar deposits at times 1,2...,n is s(n,r), the *accumulation of one per period.*

$$s(n,r) = (1+r)^{n-1} + (1+r)^{n-2} + \cdots + (1+r)^{1} + 1$$
$$= a(n,r)(1+r)^{n}.$$

Equation 12.13. Accumulation of One per Period

The discounted values $1/(1+r)^{n-1}, \ldots, 1/(1+r)$, 1 of a one-dollar fund are the one-shot deposits at times $1, \ldots, n-1$, n that would each by itself yield a one-dollar future value for the sinking fund at time n. The parallel sum of these one-shot deposits is the (equal) sinking fund deposit at times $1, \ldots, n-1$, n that would yield a one-dollar fund at time n:

$$\frac{1}{s(n,r)} = \frac{1}{(1+r)^{n-1}} : \cdots \frac{1}{(1+r)^{1}} : 1.$$

Equation 12.14. Sinking Fund Factor

The sum of the smooth sinking fund deposits is the harmonic mean of the one-shot deposits.

The dual interpretations might be stated as follows.

The series sum of the n compounded one-dollar deposits is the sinking fund that is accumulated by the one-dollar deposits.	The parallel sum of the n discounted one-dollar funds is the deposit that accumulates to a one-dollar sinking fund.

Infinite Streams of Payments

The formulas for amortization payments can be extended to an infinite time horizon. This involves a financial interpretation for the dual geometric series with indices beginning at i = 1:

$$\sum_{i=1}^{\infty}(1:x)^{i} = x = \mathbf{P}_{i=1}^{\infty}(1+x)^{i}.$$

Taking $x = 1/r$ so that $1:x = 1:1/r = 1/(1+r)$ in the series summation yields the fact that the discounted present value of the constant stream of one-dollar payments at times 1,2,... is reciprocal of the interest rate $x = 1/r$.

$$\sum_{i=1}^{\infty}(1+r)^{-i} = \frac{1}{(1+r)^{1}} + \frac{1}{(1+r)^{2}} + \cdots = \frac{1}{r}.$$

Equation 12.15. Perpetuity Capitalization Formula

Taking $x = r$ in the parallel summation yields the fact that the parallel sum of compounded values of one dollar is the interest rate r, the constant payment at $t = 1,2,\ldots$ that pays off a principal value of one dollar. Thus the dual to the annuity capitalization formula is the fact that the constant income stream of r is the equivalent of the capital of \$1.

The series sum of the stream of discounted \$1 amortization payments (which is the principal amortized by a \$1 amortization payment) is the reciprocal of the interest rate, $(1+r)^{-1}+(1+r)^{-2}+\cdots=r^{-1}$.	The parallel sum of the stream of compounded \$1 principals (which is the payment that amortizes a \$1 principal) is the interest rate, $(1+r)^{1}:(1+r)^{2}:\cdots=r$.

Adding Groups of Payments

The first use of the parallel sum was based on the fact that given a series of balloon payments at different times that each would pay off the same principal, then their parallel sum was the smooth payment that would pay off the principal if paid at all of those times. This fact can be generalized. For each balloon payment substitute a stream of equal payments. For example, suppose that PMT_1 paid at each of a set of times will pay off the principal of PV, and suppose that PMT_2 paid at each of another set of times will pay off the same principal PV. Then the parallel sum $PMT_1{:}PMT_2$ paid at the combined set of times will pay off the principal PV.

This more general use of the parallel sum can be demonstrated by dualizing the identities in financial arithmetic obtained by considering two groups of payments, n payments at the times $t = 1,2,\ldots,n$ and then m payments at $n+1$, $n+2,\ldots$, $n+m$. One-dollar payments at times $1,\ldots,n$ have the present value $a(n,r)$. One-dollar payments at times $n+1,\ldots$, $n+m$ have the value $a(m,r)$ at time n and the value $(1+r)^{-n}a(m,r)$ at time zero. The present value of the combined stream of payments is $a(n+m,r)$ so:

$$a(n+m,r)=a(n,r)+\frac{a(m,r)}{(1+r)^{n}}.$$

Dualizing, $1/a(n,r)$ is the amortization payment at times $1,\ldots,n$ that pays off a \$1 principal while $(1+r)^n/a(m,r)$ is the payment at time n + 1,..., n + m that pays off the same principal of $1 at time zero. Thus the parallel sum of the payments is the payment at the combined times 1,..., n, n + 1,..., n + m that pays off the $1 principal. But 1/a(n + m,r) is the amortization payment at those times for a $1 principal so we have the dual identity:

$$\frac{1}{a(n+m,r)} = \frac{1}{a(n,r)} : \frac{(1+r)^n}{a(m,r)}.$$

Multiplying the series-sum identity through by $(1+r)^{n+m}$ and using $s(k,r) = (1+r)^k a(k,r)$ yields the corresponding identity for sinking fund deposits:

$$s(n+m,r) = (1+r)^m s(n,r) + s(m,r)$$

which dualizes to:

$$\frac{1}{s(n+m,r)} = \frac{(1+r)^{-m}}{s(n,r)} : \frac{1}{s(m,r)}.$$

The deposit $(1+r)^{-m}/s(n,r)$ at times 1,...,n accumulates to a future fund value of $1 at time n + m as does the deposit 1/s(m,r) at times n + 1,.., n + m. Hence their parallel sum deposited at the combined times accumulates to $1 at time n + m, but 1/s(n + m,r) deposited at the same times accumulates to the same fund value so it is the same deposit.

The present value of an annuity of one can be expressed by the formula $a(n,r) = [1-(1+r)^{-n}]/r$ which can be rearranged as $1/r = (1+r)^{-n}/r + a(n,r)$. This formula can be obtained by considering two groups of payments, the payments at times 1,...,n and the infinite stream of payments thereafter.

The time zero present value of an infinite stream of one-dollar payments, i.e., the reciprocal of the interest rate, is the series sum of the value of the infinite stream at time n discounted to time zero and the present value of the \$1 payments at t = 1,...,n: $\frac{1}{r} = \frac{(1+r)^{-n}}{r} + a(n,r).$	The payment that in an infinite stream amortizes a \$1-principal at time zero, i.e., the interest rate, is the parallel sum of the payment that amortizes the time n compounded \$1-principal and the payment at t = 1,...,n that amortizes the \$1 principal: $r = r(1+r)^{n} : \frac{1}{a(n,r)}.$

The payment $a(n,r)^{-1}$ at $t = 1,\ldots,n$ amortizes a \$1 principal as does the payment $r(1+r)^n$ at $t = n+1,\ldots$ so the parallel sum of the two payments will amortize the \$1 principal if paid at the combined times $t = 1,\ldots,n,n+1,\ldots$. However, the amortization payment of r at the same times will amortize the same \$1 principal, so the two payments are equal.

Duality can be applied as well to identities involving a continuously compounded interest rate r. For instance, the present value of a continuous payment stream of one dollar per period from time 0 to time T is:

$$\int_0^T e^{-rt}dt = \frac{1-e^{-rT}}{r}$$

while the value of the same stream from time T onward is:

$$\int_T^\infty e^{-rt}dt = \frac{e^{-rT}}{r}.$$

The series sum of the two present values is 1/r, the present value of the same stream from time 0 onwards.

$$\frac{1-e^{-rT}}{r} + \frac{e^{-rT}}{r} = \frac{1}{r}.$$

Dualizing, the continuous payment stream from time 0 to time T that pays off a principal of one dollar is $r/[1-e^{-rT}]$ and the continuous stream from time T onward that pays off the same principal is r/e^{-rT}. Hence the parallel sum of these streams is r, the stream from time 0 onward that pays off the one-dollar principal.

$$\frac{r}{1-e^{-rT}}:\frac{r}{e^{-rT}}=r.$$

Principal Values as Parallel Sums

In previous formulas using the parallel sum in financial arithmetic, the parallel sum of two or more amortization payments, each of which when paid at some series of times pays off the same principal, yields the amortization payment that will pay off the same principal when paid at the combined series of times. In the dual formulas, principal values were obtained as series sums. It is also possible to obtain amortization payments as series sums so that the dual formulas will then yield principal values as parallel sums.

The amortization payment at times $t = 1,\ldots,n$ that will pay off the principal of 1 at time 0 is expressed as a series sum by the following interesting formula:

$$\frac{1}{a(n,r)}=\frac{1}{s(n,r)}+r.$$

Equation 12.16. Amortization Payment = Sinking Fund Factor plus Interest

The formula can be easily interpreted. Suppose that at the times $1,\ldots,n$ the interest r on a principal of 1 was paid. In addition, the sinking fund deposit of $1/s(n,r)$ was made at the times $1,\ldots,n$. Those sinking fund deposits accumulate to the fund of 1 at time n so the full principal of 1 could be paid all at once at time n along with the last interest payment. Thus the constant stream of payments $r + 1/s(n,r)$ at the times $1,\ldots,n$ will pay off the principal of 1 at time 0. The constant payment $1/a(n,r)$ at those times will pay off the same principal so the two payments must be equal.

Since the above formula expresses an amortization payment as a series sum, the dual equation will express a principal value as a parallel sum:

$$a(n,r) = s(n,r){:}\frac{1}{r}.$$

The present value of the series of payments of 1 at the times 1,...,n is equal to the parallel sum of the sinking fund s(n,r) accumulated at time n from the same payments and the principal l/r at time 0 would generate the series of 1's as just the interest on that principal. This duality can be expressed in the familiar way.

$\frac{1}{a(n,r)} = \frac{1}{s(n,r)} + r.$	$a(n,r) = s(n,r){:}\frac{1}{r}.$
The amortization payment at t = 1,...n for the principal value of 1 at time 0 in the series sum of the sinking fund deposit at t = 1,...,n to accumulate the sinking fund amount of 1 at time n and the interest on the principal of 1.	The principal value at time 0 of the amortization payments of 1 at t = 1,...,n is the parallel sum of the sinking fund at time n accumulated by the sinking fund deposits of 1 at t = 1,...,n and the principal with the interest of 1.

Summary of Duality in Financial Arithmetic

Each equation involving the series sum, the parallel sum, and multiplication can be dualized by interchanging the series and parallel sum, taking the reciprocal of each constant or variable term, and leaving multiplication unchanged. Equations in financial arithmetic expressing principal values as a series sum dualize to equations expressing amortization payments as parallel sums. An equation expressing the amount of a sinking fund as a series sum dualizes to an equation expressing a sinking fund deposit as a parallel sum. In the last section, we saw an equation expressing an amortization payment as a series sum, which dualized to an equation expressing a principal value as a parallel sum.

In addition to precise mathematical procedures for dualizing equations, it is also possible to establish the duality at a conceptual level so that verbal statements of an equation can be immediately dualized into the verbal statement for the dual equation. This conceptual duality can be summarized in the following table.

Concept in Financial Arithmetic	*Example*	*Dual Example*	*Dual Concept*
Series Sum	$x+y$	$1/x : 1/y$	Parallel Sum
Discounting	$(1+r)^n$	$1/(1+r)^n$	Compounding
Principal Value	$a(n,r)$	$1/a(n,r)$	Amortization Payment
Sinking Fund Amount	$s(n,r)$	$1/s(n,r)$	Sinking Fund Payment
Interest on Principal of 1	r	$1/r$	Principal with Interest of 1

Appendix: Series-Parallel Algebras

Commutative Series-Parallel Algebras

A *commutative series-parallel (SP) algebra* is a set containing a unit element 1, having a multiplication (indicated by juxtaposition) and having two additions (indicated by "+" and ":") that satisfy the following axioms:

a. Multiplicative Identity: $x1 = 1x = x$

b. Associativity:
$$(x(yz)) = ((xy)z)$$
$$(x+(y+z)) = ((x+y)+z)$$
$$(x:(y:z)) = ((x:y):z)$$

c. Commutativity:
$$xy = yx$$
$$x+y = y+x$$
$$x:y = y:x$$

d. Distributivity:
$$x(y+z) = (xy)+(xz)$$
$$x(y:z) = (xy):(xz)$$

e. Modular Law: $(x+y)(x:y) = xy$

The standard example of a commutative series-parallel algebra is the positive reals R^+ with parallel addition defined as above. A commutative SP algebra is a commutative bi-semiring where the additions are related by the modular law (5). The series and parallel sum operations are *dual* in the sense that the axioms (1)–(5) remain the same under the interchange of the two sums. This *series-parallel duality principle* is analogous to the Boolean duality principle, which states that any theorem of Boolean algebra remains valid under the interchange of conjunction and disjunction (including the interchange of the null element and unit). Any proof and theorem for commutative series-parallel algebras remains valid under the interchange of series and parallel sums.

The series-parallel duality exhibited in the axioms for commutative series-parallel algebras does not presuppose a reciprocity map ρ. A *series-parallel division algebra* is an SP algebra that is also a multiplicative group (i.e., each element has a multiplicative inverse). In a SP division algebra, the reciprocity map $\rho(x) = x^{-1}$ is an anti-isomorphism between the two additive structures, i.e., it interchanges the two sums and preserves multiplication and the unit. The positive reals R^+ and the positive rationals Q^+ are examples of commutative SP division algebras.

Every commutative group has an extension that is a series-parallel division algebra. Let G be a commutative multiplicative group with the identity 1. A *free bi-semiring* BSR(G) is constructed from G by taking all finite formal products and sums (no additive inverses) using two sum operations: a series sum $x+y$ and a parallel sum $x{:}y$. For any elements x, y, and z thus formed, the universal relations expressed in the first four axioms (above) are imposed in BSG(G). The *series-parallel algebra of G,* denoted SP(G), is formed by taking the quotient of the bi-semiring BSR(G) by the modular law.

The *reciprocity map* ρ: SP(G)$\rightarrowtail$SP(G) is defined first on the elements of G by $\rho(g) = g^{-1}$ and then it is extended to all the elements of SP(G) by preserving multiplication and interchanging series and parallel sums:

$$\begin{aligned} \rho(xy) &= \rho(x)\rho(y) \\ \rho(x+y) &= \rho(x) : \rho(y) \\ \rho(x:y) &= \rho(x) + \rho(y). \end{aligned}$$

By the duality principle, ρ respects the universal relations (1)–(5) defining series-parallel algebras so it is a well-defined self-map on SP(G) which preserves multiplication and interchanges series and parallel sums.

It can then be verified that for any x in SP(G), $\rho(x)x = 1$ so it carries each element to its multiplicative inverse. In particular, this shows that SP(G) is a group itself, i.e., a SP division algebra, which could be called the *series-parallel completion of G.* For example, the series-parallel extension of the trivial group is the positive rationals, i.e.,

$SP(\{1\}) = Q^+$. Intuitively, a series-parallel circuit with resistance equal to any positive rational can be constructed soley from one ohm resistances.

Adding Ideal Elements

The ideal elements 0 and ∞ can be added to the positive reals to form the extended positive reals. In the electrical interpretation, 0 is the "short circuit" of zero resistance and ∞ is the "open circuit" with infinite resistance. The operations in the extended reals are series sum, parallel sum, and multiplication.

Adding a short circuit in parallel to any resistance gives a short circuit so for any x, $x : 0 = 0 : x = 0$. Adding a short circuit in series with any resistance does not change that resistance so for any x: $x + 0 = 0 + x = x$. Adding an open circuit in parallel to any resistance does not change that resistance so for any x, $x : \infty = \infty : x = x$. Adding an open circuit in series with any resistance creates an open circuit, so for any x: $x + \infty = \infty + x = \infty$.

Multiplication is only a partially defined operation on the extended positive reals since the product of 0 and ∞ is undefined. Elsewhere, 0 and ∞ are absorbing:

$$0\,x = x\,0 = 0 \text{ for } x \neq \infty \text{ and } \infty\, x = x\,\infty = \infty \text{ for } x \neq 0.$$

The definition $0\,\infty = 1$ is tempting but it leads to disaster, e.g.,

$$1 = \infty(0) = \infty(0 + 0) = \infty 0 + \infty 0 = 1 + 1 = 2,$$

so the product of 0 and ∞ is left undefined. However, the reciprocity map $\rho(x) = 1/x$ can be directly extended by $\rho(0) = \infty$ and $\rho(\infty) = 0$ (instead of trying to make sense of $\rho(0) = 1/0 = \infty$ or $\rho(\infty) = 1/\infty = 0$). Then $x + \infty = \infty + x = \infty$ dualizes to $x : 0 = 0 : x = 0$ (replacing 1/x by x after applying the reciprocity map) so the duality results apply as well to the extended positive reals.

An *extended commutative series-parallel algebra* has elements 0 (the "closed circuit") and ∞ (the "open circuit") such that 0∞ is undefined and that satisfy the following axioms:

f. $x : 0 = 0 : x = 0$	and	$x + 0 - 0 + x = x$	for any x.
g. $x : \infty = \infty : x = x$	and	$x + \infty = \infty + x = \infty$	for any x.
h. $0x = x0 = 0$ for $x \neq \infty$	and	$\infty\, x = x\,\infty = \infty$	for $x \neq 0$.

The standard example of an extended commutative SP algebra is the extended non-negative reals, i.e., the positive reals R^+ together with 0 and ∞. The above axioms transform into one another under the interchange of the sums and of the ideal elements 0 and ∞. Thus series-parallel duality extends to extended commutative SP algebras in the sense that any axiom and thus any proof and theorem remains valid under the interchange of the sums and of the ideal elements 0 and ∞.

Noncommutative Series-Parallel Algebras

A general not-necessarily-commutative *series-parallel algebra* has two additions, denoted + and :, and multiplication defined on a set S satisfying the following axioms:

a. Multiplicative Identity. $x1 = 1x = x$
b. Associativity: $(x(yz)) = ((xy)z)$
$$(x+(y+z)) = ((x+y)+z)$$
$$(x:(y:z)) = ((x:y):z)$$
c. Commutativity. $x+y = y+x$
$$x:y = y:x$$
d. Right-Distributivity over + $\quad (x+y)z = (xz + yz)$
Left-Distributivity over : $\quad z(x : y) = (zx : zy)$
e. Modular Law. $(1 : x)(1 + x) = x$
f. Two-Sided Inverses. if $xy = 1$ then $yx = 1$.

A general *duality principle* is obtained in any series-parallel algebra by interchanging series addition (+) with parallel addition (:) and reversing the order of multiplications. Swapping the sums and permuting the products transforms any of the above axioms into another axiom so all theorems would be preserved under that transformation.

Any group, not necessarily commutative, generates a series-parallel algebra that is a group, i.e., a series-parallel division algebra, that is its series-parallel completion. On any SP division algebra, duality is realized by the reciprocity map that interchanges the two additions, permutes the order of multiplication, and preserves the unit.

The principal model for a noncommutative SP algebra is the algebra of monotonic increasing real functions on a single real variable. Series and parallel sums are respectively the vertical and horizontal sums of functions. Multiplication is the composition of functions so the reciprocal or inverse of an element is its functional inverse.

Series-Parallel Duality as the "Derivative" of Convex Duality

Series-parallel duality can be related to the form of duality most familiar in economics, namely the duality of convex functions that includes duality in linear and nonlinear programming [see Rockafellar 1970].

General SP duality is to the convex duality of functions as the derivative of a function is to the function. The derivatives of differentiable strictly convex functions of a single variable are monotonic increasing functions. In addition to the usual sum of convex functions, there is a "dual" [Rockafellar 1970, 145] addition for convex functions, namely the "infimal convolution" [Rockafellar 1970, 34]:

$$(f \oplus g)(x) = \inf_y \{f(x-y) + g(y)\}.$$

For instance, if a firm can produce the same type of output in a number of plants, the firm's cost function is the infimal convolution of the plant cost functions. The derivatives of the ordinary and dual (infimal convolution) sums of differentiable strictly convex functions are, respectively, the vertical (series) and horizontal (parallel) sums of the derivatives. The "inverse" or dual of a convex function f(x) is its "convex conjugate":

$$f^*(x) = \sup_y \{xy - f(x)\}.$$

The derivative of the convex conjugate is the inverse of the derivative in the SP algebra of monotonic increasing functions.

The relationship between convex duality and series-parallel duality is summarized in the following table.

Convex Duality	*Derivative →*	*Series-Parallel Duality*	
Primal	*Dual*	*Primal*	*Dual*
Convex Function	Convex Conjugate	Increasing Function	Inverse Function
Sum of Convex Functions	Infimal Convolution	Vertical Sum	Horizontal Sum

For a simple example of SP duality as the derivative of convex duality, consider the strictly convex functions of the form $y = ax^2/2$ for positive constants a that correspond by differentiation to the positively sloped straight lines through the origin. Given two such functions $ax^2/2$ and $bx^2/2$, their series sum is, of course, $(a+b)x^2/2$. Furthermore, their infimal convolution is $(a: b)x^2/2$. The derivatives of these dual sums of convex functions are the vertical (series) and horizontal (parallel) sums of the derivatives in the SP algebra of monotonic increasing functions. The convex conjugate of $ax^2/2$ is $(1/a)x^2/2$ [note that composition is not defined for convex functions—only for their derivatives]. The derivatives are multiplicative inverses in the SP algebra of monotonic increasing functions.

References

Brylawski, T. 1971. "A Combinatorial Model for Series-Parallel Networks." *Trans. Amer. Math. Soc.* Vol. 154 (Feb. 1971), 1–22.

Duffin, R. 1965. "Topology of Series-Parallel Networks." *J. Math. Anal. Appl* 10: 303–18.

———. 1975. "Electrical Network Models." In *Studies in Graph Theory, Part I* (D. R. Fulkerson, ed.), Math. Assn. of America: 94–138.

Lehman, Alfred. 1962. "Problem 60-5-A Resistor Network Inequality." *SIAM Review* 4: 150–55.

MacMahon, Percy A. 1881. "Yoke-Chains and Multipartite Compositions in Connexion with the Analytical Forms called 'Trees'." *Proc. London Math. Soc.* 22: 330–46.

———. 1892. "The Combinations of Resistances." *The Electrician* 28. 601–2.

———. 1978. *Collected Papers: Volume I. Combinatorics.* Edited by George E. Andrews. Cambridge, Mass.: MIT Press.

Riordan, J., and C. Shannon. 1942. "The Number of Two-Terminal Series-Parallel Networks." *J. Math. Phys. of MIT* 21: 83–93.

Rockafellar, R. T. 1970. *Convex Analysis.* Princeton: Princeton University Press.

Scudder Funds 1988. *News from the Scudder Funds.* (Spring). Boston, Mass.

Index

About the Author

David P. Ellerman is an economist, mathematician, business consultant, and writer. He was educated at M.I.T. and at Boston University, where he received two masters degrees in philosophy and in economics and a doctorate in mathematics. Dr. Ellerman has taught over a twenty-year period in five disciplines: economics, mathematics, computer science, operations research, and accounting. He has taught at Tufts University, Boston College School of Management, University of Massachusetts (Boston and Amherst), and Boston University. Currently, he works for the Economic Development Institute (EDI) of the World Bank.

Dr. Ellerman has published over fifty articles in scholarly journals in economics, mathematics, philosophy, and law. He has published three books: *Economics, Accounting, and Property Theory*, *The Democratic Worker-Owned Firm*, and *Property and Contract in Economics: The Case for Economic Democracy*.